THE
SEXUAL
POLITICS OF
EMPIRE

**NATIONAL WOMEN'S STUDIES ASSOCIATION /
UNIVERSITY OF ILLINOIS PRESS FIRST BOOK PRIZE**

A list of books in the series appears at the end of this book.

THE
SEXUAL
POLITICS OF
EMPIRE

POSTCOLONIAL
HOMOPHOBIA
IN HAITI

ERIN L. DURBAN

**UNIVERSITY OF
ILLINOIS PRESS**
Urbana, Chicago, and Springfield

Manufactured in the United States of America
1 2 3 4 5 C P 5 4 3 2 1
∞ This book is printed on acid-free paper.

Publication supported by a grant from the University of Illinois Press
Fund for Anthropology.

Library of Congress Cataloging-in-Publication Data
Names: Durban, Erin, author.
Title: The sexual politics of empire : postcolonial homophobia in
    Haiti / Erin L. Durban.
Description: Urbana : University of Illinois Press, [2022] | Series:
    National Women's Studies Association / University of Illinois
    First Book Prize | Includes bibliographical references and
    index.
Identifiers: LCCN 2022021135 (print) | LCCN 2022021136 (ebook)
    | ISBN 9780252044755 (cloth) | ISBN 9780252086847
    (paperback) | ISBN 9780252053801 (ebook)
Subjects: LCSH: Homophobia—Haiti. | Homophobia—Religious
    aspects—Christianity. | Sexual minorities—Haiti—Social
    conditions. | BISAC: SOCIAL SCIENCE / LGBTQ+ Studies /
    General | RELIGION / Sexuality & Gender Studies
Classification: LCC HQ76.45.H2 D87 2022 (print) | LCC HQ76.45.H2
    (ebook) | DDC 306.76/6097294—dc23/eng/20220518
LC record available at https://lccn.loc.gov/2022021135
LC ebook record available at https://lccn.loc.gov/2022021136

For the *ti masisi*, *ti madivin*, Black femmes, afro-punks,
"Voodoo Divas" (à la Maksaens Denis),
"Voodoo Dolls" (à la Assotto Saint),
and revolutionary lovers in Haiti and its diaspora
who have been envisioning and creating better worlds for all of us
and
For my loves (big and little)
Miranda Joseph and Fenniver Stronghold Durban-Albrecht-Joseph

CONTENTS

Acknowledgments   ix

Dedications   xvii

Introduction   1

1 Perverting Haiti: The Transnational Imperialist Discourse
   of the Black Republic as the Premodern Land
   of "Voodoo/Vaudoux"   23

2 The Missionary Position: U.S. Protestant Missionaries
   and Religious Homophobia   53

2008

3 Evangelical Christian Homophobia
   and the Michèle Pierre-Louis Controversy   87

4 "Zonbi, Zonbi" at the Ghetto Biennale:
   A Queer Act of Intervention
   against Postcolonial Homophobia   105

2010

5 The Sexual Politics of Rescue: The Global LGBTQI
   and Postcolonial Homophobia after the
   2010 Earthquake in Haiti   129

2013

6   The Emergence of a Social Movement
    against Homophobia   159

    Epilogue: The Transnational
    #BlackLivesMatter Movement
    and the Serialization of Black (Queer) Death   187

    Notes   193

    Bibliography   203

    Index   221

ACKNOWLEDGMENTS

José Esteban Muñoz once encouraged me to write the book that my fifteen-year-old self needed but did not exist in the world. This both is and is not that book. The book that I thought that I needed in the sense that Muñoz meant was about the way that the drug wars and the U.S. prison industrial complex had shaped my life as a kid whose first steps were in the prison camp of the Leavenworth Federal Penitentiary. Once, after the 2010 earthquake, when I was overwhelmed by grief, I tried abandoning the project about the sexual politics of empire in Haiti that I had been working on in various forms for six years to start new research about racial capitalism and affective attachments to prisons because it seemed—somehow, inexplicably—less excruciatingly painful and therefore possible. Friends and mentors overwhelmingly encouraged me to work through that pain and continue the project that would become the book in your hands now.

My retrospective desire for a book with a sophisticated analysis of the U.S. prison industrial complex by and for prison kids was premised on what I thought of as "personal" as a teenager. When I was fifteen years old, my dad lived in a halfway house after recently being released from his second of what became three prison terms, and I wanted more than anything to live with him. If I had heard of Haiti by that time (doubtful), I could not point to it on a map. I had no clue that my grandparents took a memorable mid-century cruise that included a Haitian destination and that my dad and uncle had resided in the capital in the 1970s. The basket that carried me home from the hospital when I was born was woven by Haitian hands, a remnant of my dad's time in the country working with his brother Kevin to initiate an export

Eugene, Marie Maude Evans, FACSDIS, Abigayl Fletcher, the Florida International University Haitian Summer Institute, FOSAJ, Susan "Sue" Frame (and parents!), the Ghetto Biennale curators and artists, Jean-Élie Gilles, Leah Gordon, Gran Lakou, the Haitian Studies Association, Leonie Hermantin, George Hoagland, Paul Humphrey, Jakmel Ekspresyon, Ryan Joyce, Kouraj, Lakou, Ebby Angel Louis, Ivy McClelland, Claudine Michel, Lenelle Moïse, POZ, Marc Prou, Jean Lesly René, Mark Schuller, Kenia Selamy, Lynn Selby, SEROvie, Katherine Smith, Talitha Stam, Roberto Strongman, Patrick Sylvain, Joel Théodat, the Transnational Hispaniola Collective, Reginald Turnier, Omise'eke Natasha Tinsley, the UMass Boston Haitian Creole Language and Culture Summer Institute, Laura Wagner, and Mabelle Williams. This project would not have been possible without the various Haitian and U.S. interlocutors who—for confidentiality—are not named here but to whom I am nonetheless immensely grateful. I especially want to honor those who have crossed over: Flores "Flo" McGarrell, Mildred Gerestant, and Charlot Jeudy. Mèsi anpil!

This book has benefitted tremendously from audiences at presentations I gave at the Thinking Transnational Feminisms Summer Institute, the University of Cincinnati, Duke University, the Ohio State University, Emory University, Ball State University, the University of Colorado–Boulder, Illinois State University, the University of Minnesota, the University of Arizona, Wesleyan University, the Counter Accounting Workshop, and Transnational Hispaniola II. Participating in the Tepoztlán Institute for the Transnational History of the Americas was an intellectually transformative experience for me, and I feel lucky that I also met people who have become my closest friends and colleagues. I am also grateful for the enduring relationships that I have built through the National Women's Studies Association, the Haitian Studies Association, the Caribbean Studies Association, the American Anthropological Association, and the American Studies Association. Thank you to the ASA Ralph Henry Gabriel Dissertation Prize Committee (Alyosha Goldstein, Lisa Hajjar, and Karen Shimakawa) for their positive and encouraging feedback about my work.

The dissertation that transformed into this book received financial support from the American Association for University Women, the University of Arizona Social and Behavioral Sciences Research Institute, the Confluencenter for Creative Inquiry, a Foreign Language and Area Studies Summer Language Grant, the Women's Studies Advisory Council, and the National Women's Studies Association Lesbian Caucus. I also received a Mary Lily Research Grant from the Sallie Bingham Center for Women's History and

Culture at Duke University (thank you, Kelly Wooten!). I acknowledge the many other archivists who supported this project at the Schomburg Center for Research in Black Culture, the New York Public Library ACT UP Archives, the Yale Beinecke Rare Book and Manuscript Library (though they also told me to use my breast pump in their multi-stall bathroom), the Marine Corps Research Center Archives, and the University of Florida George A. Smathers Libraries.

I have been fortunate to have financial support for completing this book from sources beyond my various departments, including from the University of Minnesota Provost's Office, the College of Liberal Arts, Global Studies, the McKnight Land-Grant Professorship, and the University of Illinois Press in the form of an advance for being awarded the National Women's Studies Association/UIP First Book Prize. I am thankful that Dawn Durante at the University of Illinois Press was enthusiastic about my project and encouraged me to apply for that prize. It was a dream to work with a talented and supportive editor who enacts feminist practices in academic publishing and is as easy to get along with as an old friend. Thanks to Dominique Moore, Ellie Hinton, Tad Ringo, and the entire UIP team for getting the book across the finish line during the COVID-19 pandemic. I also thank the NWSA/UIP First Book Prize committee—Judith A. Howard, Erica Lorraine Williams, and Jocelyn Fenton Stitt—for their initial insightful guidance, as well as the two anonymous reviewers who provided substantial comments.

I started in the University of Minnesota Department of Anthropology in 2017 in no small part due to the efforts of then-incoming chair Karen-Sue Taussig. The department has provided invaluable material resources and other support for this project, including mentoring, intellectual companionship, staff time and expertise (thank you, Zarlasht Niaz and Christina Wiencke!), putting my work forward for grants and awards—most substantially the McKnight Land-Grant Professorship—and encouragement to explore new fields and ways of doing scholarship as an interdisciplinary scholar. Course releases, a short leave, and research funds benefitted the book by—among other things—allowing me to hire research assistants for help with citation management, fact checking, and copyediting (thank you, Nithya Rajan, Sailer, Jen Hughes, and Nicolette Gullickson!). Department research funds additionally facilitated the convening of a book manuscript review workshop. I appreciate that Dána-Ain Davis, Janet Jakobsen, and Mark Schuller braved traveling to the Twin Cities for the workshop in late spring 2018. They—along with Jean Langford, Beaudelaine Pierre, and Miranda Joseph from UMN—provided crucial feedback about the draft chapter-by-chapter over two days. I was nervous to have such intense, intimate engagement of my work, even though I was the one who had sought out the opportunity. The process was better than I imagined it would be, and I am deeply appreciative of the reviewers' close reading of the manuscript, thoughtful comments, and encouragement to consider the content and structure of the book in new ways.

Many people have shaped this project and moved my writing forward, more than can ever be named here. Sometimes it has been through direct engagement: inquiring about my writing, reading drafts, convening panels, asking questions, opening conversations, creating opportunities to write together, responding to presentations, inviting me to participate in reading groups or scholarly collaborations, and more. Other times the influence has come from offering exactly the right insights or encouragement at exactly the right time, keeping me going through a stressful and lonely process, providing childcare, inviting me and my family to meals and holidays, putting together meal trains, celebrating small accomplishments along the way, and creating a welcoming home in Illinois and then Minnesota, where people have gone above and beyond at every turn.

At the top of my list to acknowledge are the faculty on my mentoring committee at the University of Minnesota: Jean Langford, Karen Ho, Kat Hayes, Jigna Desai, David Valentine, and Kate Derickson. Likewise, Stuart McLean has been a tremendous colleague who never fails to attend my presentations or events that I organize. This list needs to include my initial lifesaving National Center for Faculty Diversity and Development support group (Daniel, Sari, and T.J.), as well as my post Faculty Support Program writing and support group with friends (Aisha, Mingwei, and Anahi). Generous colleagues from many different places in my life have made my academic life better, brighter, and more meaningful: UMN Geography (George, Kate, and Bruce); UMN American Studies (Elliot, Bianet, Jennifer, Kevin, Martin, and Terrion); UMN Gender, Women & Sexuality Studies (Aren, Diyah, Jigna, and Zenzele); the UMN Center for Race, Indigeneity, Disability, Gender, and Sexuality Studies (RIDGS); the Association for Feminist Anthropology; the Association for Queer Anthropology; the UIUC Queer Studies Reading Group (thank you, Silas!); and many other reading groups—including the pandemic Critical Disability Studies Reading Group convened by Sumi Colligan.

Without the support of crip mentors and a network of disabled scholars, this book would have never been finished. The Critical Disability Studies Collective kept me afloat as I adjusted to working in crip spacetime, and for that I especially want to thank Angela, Jessica, J Row, and Jigna for their generosity, friendship, and ongoing efforts to create a more humane academy. I am also grateful to the people outside the academy whose work has made my work possible: Chris, Emi, Erin, Eve, Jessie, Ka, Maddy, Sara, Sarah, and my team of health-care providers at Mayo and UMN.

In addition to the mentors, colleagues, and friends already named, I would especially like to thank my friends Carly and Anahi, Lorena, Jakeet, Tracey and David, George and Rachel, George and Rebecca, Josie and David, Jean and Sharon, Rob and Travis, Adela and Jamie, Zeynep and Can, Shannon, Alexis, and my other University Grove neighbors.

Finally, I want to thank my family—now including the Joseph/Katzoff branches—for their support. I am grateful to have shared Haiti with many family members, including my sister Jennifer, niece Aurelia, and kid Fen. Fen gestated and then has lived with this book her entire life, and she has both been a welcome distraction from having it consume my life and a much-needed encouragement to finish it. I am extremely lucky that my partner Miranda Joseph accompanied me on the last and hardest part of the journey of writing this book, at a time when so much of our energy went to figuring out how to live with my chronic illnesses. Her intimate encounters with book writing helped me better understand the feelings, rhythms, and oddities of the process, and helped me adapt them in our life together. Miranda—more than anyone—advocated for me to protect my writing time and put in a tremendous amount of her own time and other resources to see this through to the end. Thank you, my love.

DEDICATIONS (PART I)

I carry you with me.

Whereas the acknowledgments make apparent certain kinds of intellectual genealogies and debts accrued though this project's undertaking, I also offer "dedications" to honor and invoke some of the same-sex-desiring and gender-creative Haitian people—friends, accomplices, ancestors, familiar strangers—who have traveled alongside me.[1] This book is an incomplete record of our lives together.

I carry you with me,
Even when our paths have crossed only briefly.

The chef: a Queens, New York–based, Haitian Gays and Lesbians Alliance organizer who returned to Haiti after the 2010 earthquake and opened a successful restaurant in Pétion-Ville. While running her business—a gathering place for middle- and upper-class socialites—she and her partner also raise a son together.

The disciple: an earnest and shy "homosexual" who grew up in a Roman Catholic orphanage and works for the church, primarily cleaning and performing odd jobs. The nuns told him that he must never act on his sexual desires for another man, a command he had dutifully obeyed through the time I met him in his fifties. He found me through a friend of a friend who he had met by calling the wrong cell phone number.

The translator: a tattoo-covered, chain-smoking femme from Flatbush who the police charged with shoplifting and thereby set in motion the procedures for deportation even though she had lived almost her entire life in the United States. She earns money translating for Americans working at NGOs in Port-au-Prince.

The mechanic: a self-described "masculine woman" who moved with her younger sister from the countryside to the southern coastal city of Jacmel for work opportunities. She studied the men fixing things in their street-side workshops, and eventually earned a spot apprenticing for a mechanic. Covered in grease with her hair pulled back under her signature trucker's hat (or beanie in the winter), she is often mistaken for a man by women passing by the shop, who she takes as a challenge and delight to seduce.

I carry you with me,
Even when your (at least "twice-told") stories have been relayed by others.[2]

The milk queen: "When I was a kid, a very effeminate man came to my house each week with his cow to provide milk for my family. He would make my parents laugh and laugh with his jokes and mannerisms. My dad would laugh *hahaha!*, my mom would laugh *hahaha!*, and I would look at them like, *wow!* This queen was from the countryside, barefoot and everything, and I do not know where he could have learned something like that."

The persistent patient: "A man would come into the clinic where I worked as a nurse in the 1980s, and he wanted our help to become a woman. He asked us for help, but we said we were not set up for those kinds of things. He came again and again, even though there was nothing we could do for him."

The matriarch: "My grandma was tough as nails and did not take shit from anyone. She lived in the countryside with her husband and his other wives, and after he died from tuberculosis, one of her lovers—a much-younger woman—came to live with the rest of our family. No questions asked, nothing. People respected my grandma, and so they received her [lover] into our family. The two of them ran everything and did everything on the land. My dad grew up in this world of women, part of Haiti but outside of the macho men patriarchal bullshit that you get other places."

I carry you with me.

DEDICATIONS (PART II)

I carry you with me.

I carry you with me:
Those whose stories and lives changed me.
Those who insisted I do the work.
Those who trusted me to do it well.

The following same-sex-desiring and gender-creative Haitians profoundly shaped the path of my research and life over the decade I worked on the project described in this book. They have a special place among my intimates: people with whom I have shared not just work-in-common or the occasional meal, but toothbrush space and bonds that extend into our families of birth and choice. Our relationships with each other have changed dramatically over the years, as inevitably we all have changed. The portraits I offer below focus on the circumstances of our initial connection.

Avadra[3] was one of the first people I met in Haiti, when I stayed at the beach home not too far from Jacmel that he shared with his boyfriend Franck and my friend Flo, who I met through the UMass Boston Haitian Creole Language and Culture Summer Institute. He and Franck generously offered that my partner and I could sleep in their bed, in a messy artists' room filled with passionate notes, inspirational objects, and dirty clothes. Avadra was the first one to insist that I learn about same-sex-desiring people's daily lives and struggles in Haiti, over "morning" coffee (on gay standard time—really the early afternoon) on the back porch that overlooked the Caribbean. He took it as his mission to introduce me, my partner at the time, and my teenage stepson to as many same-sex-desiring and gender-creative Jacmelians as possible during our brief initial visit. I followed along as he strutted through town to show me his favorite places in the area—the public and private beaches, the waterfalls at Bassin Bleu, the vendors with the best *pwason* (fish), *pikliz* (spicy coleslaw), and *griot* (marinated fried pork), and so on. My initial impression of him as earnest and dorky (mostly because he wore glasses and had a kind of scraggly beard) changed as we spent more time together once my research project got off the ground and as he started styling himself differently. I learned quickly that his comportment and newly grown dreads (sometimes covered in a backward baseball hat), jeans, alternately super colorful or black clothes, and silver and black bracelets marked him as a "bad boy" who was part of a countercultural artist fringe. Yet he had a way with even the well-coiffed people who cast silent judgment or implored him to cut his hair or "clean up," sweet-talking them and reminding them about their relations with him (because for a city, Jacmel has the feel of a small town where everyone is only once-removed from everyone else). That skill has served him well as an artist, organizer, and lover.

When I first met **Mirabo**, he came across as shy and unassuming with a tendency toward politeness and formality. He is bald with a tall and slender build under khaki pants and button-down shirts, and his movements glide like a dancer's. Unlike most of the artists I hung out with when I moved to Jacmel, Mirabo seemed most comfortable receding into the background of busy social scenes by engaging in care work—especially cooking—for his friends. He is perhaps the most understated of those artists in his day-to-day life relaxing at home, riding the tap-tap, buying food at the market, or walking through the streets of Jacmel; however, Mirabo is totally transformed through performance—his body bursts with kinetic energy, taking on stature and a mesmerizing authority. Whether singing or dancing (or even calling out directions during rehearsals), it was impossible for me or anyone else around not to be transfixed by Mirabo. In this state he can be demanding, not only of the audience's attention, but of perfection—from himself, dance students, and other performers. It is therefore quite intimidating to take his classes, as I learned when he placed me in line with his younger pupils at a girls' school in Jacmel. He is completely devoted to the performing arts, he would say, as an expression of Haitian culture.

Busy lives in downtown Port-au-Prince, in the bustling neighborhood along the Grand Rue that is home to the sculptors of Atis Rezistans. She grew up not too far away from where she is raising her three children, two daughters and a son. (Busy told me that she had wanted a son because she felt she could relate more to a boy because of her own masculinity, finding her daughters' feminine interests and pursuits alien even as she endeavors to support them.) I met her during the inaugural Ghetto Biennale in 2009 when Haitian and international artists congregated in her neighborhood for several weeks of artistic projects and performances. Busy and her friends partied at the Hotel Oloffson with our transnational queer and trans* film crew for *Kathy Goes to Haiti* (a project that Flo had invited me to participate in), and she approached me one night in our suite filled with people in all kinds of altered states to find out why I was not interested in hooking up with anyone at the event. Feeling ashamed of being perceived as prudish among sexually and socially adventurous queer artists, I responded that I was in a monogamous relationship, which seemed the easiest answer at the time. This expression of fidelity (a word that I have a difficult time even typing) strangely opened up a kind of quick intimacy between us, first as friends and then in a relationship more like sisters. That is to say that in the years since, Busy, who is at least ten years my senior, has constantly kept tabs on what I am doing and looked out for me in a thousand ways that I have often resisted (only to be trumped)—from walking me home to regularly proffering advice.

Jean-Élie, or "Professor Gilles," is someone whose reputation precedes him. The Jacmelians I interacted with regarded him as an educated advocate of Haitian arts and culture, though I had also heard a thing or two about the elaborate dinner parties he sometimes hosts at his two-story family home in central Jacmel. We finally crossed paths one day at the Hotel Florita bar a block away from the FOSAJ arts center, where I could get more reliable wi-fi and cold lime juice. He was far more dressed-up than the other patrons. He dresses this way most days because he goes from meeting to meeting to support arts and education in the region. Jean-Élie invited a group of us to his house, where he offered us a tour of his incredible collection of Haitian, U.S., and European music, books, art, and historical artifacts. He had received his doctorate in French literature at the University of Washington and showed us an article hanging on the kitchen wall about his time as a student in the United States. It was late in the tour when Zaka (my friend and roommate at FOSAJ) mentioned Jean-Élie's self-published novel featuring a same-sex-desiring protagonist, which Jean-Élie then offered me a copy of as a gift. He also asked if I had seen a particular artistic film about same-sex sexuality in Haiti, which I had by then, though I had not recognized Jean-Élie from his appearance in it. He promised to have me back for a live classical music concert where he would sing with piano accompaniment, and although that plan has yet to pan out, since then we have spent lots of time together discussing religion, history, literature, politics, art, and sex. Because, like the playful spirits of the dead on whose day of celebration Jean-Élie was born, he enjoys earthly pleasures and mischievousness.

Kelly used to travel by car from the capital city of Port-au-Prince to Jacmel on weekends to see her boyfriend (at the time, Avadra), attend religious ceremonies, and spend time on the beach with friends. She would also hang out at FOSAJ, an artists' space where I lived when I started my research. Kelly would brush past the artists and local youths lounging in the warehouse and hole up in the office on the second floor. She would hold court on the large hammock under the windows with me, Flo (the U.S. director of FOSAJ who was also transgender), and Zaka (the assistant director and a student at the Ciné Institute) perched alongside her or on a desk or chair while we all snacked on whatever treat Flo furnished for the occasion. During one of these visits, Kelly invited me to the "gay" (her word) organization where she worked in Port-au-Prince to meet people outside of Jacmel. I traveled over the mountains in a jam-packed minivan before dawn to reach the capital before it was too crowded with traffic to meet Kelly at the organization. I almost did not recognize her when she met the public taxi I had taken from the station: her vacation wear of sandals, bandana, tank top, and shorts thrown over a bikini was replaced with preppie work drag. Even though her work was volunteered, she took it quite seriously, and it was clear from the beginning of my time at the organization that the participants held her in high regard.

Like Kelly, **Daniel** worked for an organization by and for "men who have sex with men" (MSM) in Port-au-Prince, and I met him because the two are long-time friends. She had described him to me as "probably really transgender" by way of explaining their affinity, and I was therefore surprised to meet someone at the organization's office nearly as tall as us, with all-boy accoutrements (minus the ear studs): closely cropped hair, a colorful T-shirt, and khaki pants. But Daniel's nelly queen came through in the introduction, most noticeable in the lilt of his voice as he welcomed me while kissing cheeks and in the flirtatious winning smile that followed. Of all the people I came to know in Haiti,

Daniel initially reminded me the most of myself. We are the same age and both learned organizing and outreach skills as peer educators for HIV-prevention organizations that also doubled as crucial social spaces for same-sex-desiring and gender-creative people. This institutional familiarity—and likely our mutual adoration of Beyoncé—facilitated our friendship in spite of our social, political, and personality differences. By my estimation, he is one of the best public-health organizers I have met, both because of his passion for the work and his truly remarkable ability to compassionately engage with people who most others—including me—consider to be endlessly tiring or irritating. That is to say that Daniel's work embodied the philosophy that "no one is disposable" in a way that I have rarely seen.

I had no idea that **Franck** was famous when I stayed at the house where he lived with Avadra and Flo. He is the son of a well-known classical musician and is a multimedia artist with an international reputation. The most he mentioned about having any kind of cultural capital or class mobility—over one of our home-cooked candlelit dinners one night when the electricity failed—was that he had gone to school in France but much preferred living in Haiti. During those first couple of weeks, Franck struck me as humble (especially for an artist) and hardworking, often foregoing social events to work on projects and visit the boys and young men with whom he had developed relationships at a nearby orphanage. The kids from the orphanage followed Franck around Jacmel. It was clear that they were captivated by his style: shaved head with "tribal" tattoos, a notable piercing peeking above his glasses to the side of one eyebrow, a goatee, and punk jewelry. At least one or two always flanked our little group as we ran errands, ate meals, and listened to the run-up to the 2008 U.S. presidential election: "O-ba-ma! McCain ka-ka!" Franck's interactions with them—and with my teenage stepson, who was newly into graffiti, longboarding, and getting high—made me think that he would make a great parent, something Franck expressed wanting and was soon to be in the works. Before we had the time to really develop a friendship, though, he went through a traumatic event that resulted in living outside the country for several years. So unlike the others listed here in the dedications, I would not describe Franck as a friend or companion, though our lives have continued to be intimately intertwined in delightfully unexpected ways.

I carry you with me.
I carry you with me.

THE
SEXUAL
POLITICS OF
EMPIRE

INTRODUCTION

One of the aftershocks of the 2010 earthquake in Haiti was a flare-up of homophobic violence. As same-sex-desiring and gender-creative Haitians were
pulled by their friends and neighbors from underneath the rubble of buildings, some were confronted by doctors who refused them medical treatment
because they were (or were perceived to be) HIV-positive, radio sermons
proclaiming that Haitian homosexuals were responsible for the disaster, and
individuals shouting "death to gays!" Evangelical Christian discourse claimed
that the earthquake was caused by the societal tolerance of homosexuality,
the widespread practice of the Afro-syncretic religion of *Vodou*, the preponderance of other sins, and the Roman Catholic Church's willingness to turn a
blind eye toward behaviors that God does not favor. The last of these was supposedly signaled by the destruction of Catholic churches in the earthquake.

The idea that there were controllable causes for the earthquake and ways
of preventing another disaster was as seductive within Haiti as outside it.
Evangelical churches in Haiti filled beyond capacity with converts, who were
willing to take action to prevent Haiti from facing the fate of Sodom and
Gomorrah. Missionaries from the United States flocked to Haiti to conduct
relief work and hopefully save souls along the way. They were supported
by transnational Christian networks that channeled tremendous financial
resources into the country for these purposes. Taken together, these influences created sweeping social change in a relatively short time. Such change
had, and continues to have, negative ramifications for same-sex-desiring and
gender-creative Haitians.

Meanwhile, U.S.-based lesbian, gay, bisexual, transgender, queer, and intersex (LGBTQI) human rights organizations offered emergency assistance to

the few organizations in Haiti working with same-sex-desiring and gender-creative people, with which they had established connections only as recently as 2008 and 2009. While these resources were miniscule compared to the funds that these human rights organizations distribute worldwide—and certainly paled in comparison to the large-scale resources flowing into Haiti from the U.S. Christian right—U.S.-based LGBTQI organizations nonetheless had a major impact on the lives of same-sex-desiring and gender-creative people in Haiti. Their resources transnationally carried a form of identity politics that introduced specific configurations of U.S. social categories—"LGBT community"—and aspirational politics, such as state recognition and national belonging. The relationships forged through this process became the basis for a social movement consisting of public health, advocacy, arts, and activist organizations that emerged in full force at the historic gathering of three hundred people for the Congrès National de la Population LGBT (National Conference of the LGBT Population) on the 2012 International Day Against Homophobia.

These two transnational movements that have been gaining influence in Haiti since the earthquake—evangelical Christianity and global LGBTQ human rights—are, by all appearances, at odds with each other. The first of these, after all, equates same-sex sexuality with social problems, sin, satanism, and widespread devastation. Global LGBTQI human rights, on the other hand, promotes rights for gender and sexual minorities and, more generally, freedom of sexual expression. Its mission—as stated most prominently by one of the key players in Haiti after the earthquake, the International Gay and Lesbian Human Rights Commission (IGLHRC, now Outright Action International)—is to counteract the violent effects of the former, whose tendrils can be acutely felt in places like Uganda, where U.S. missionaries led a successful campaign with Ugandan ministers to criminalize same-sex sexuality.

While I certainly have more sympathy for LGBTQI human rights, I contend that there is much more to the seeming opposition between promoting homophobia or promoting homo-protectionism, to use queer theorist Cricket Keating's term to refer to advocacy efforts for state protections of same-sex-desiring and gender-creative people (2013, 246). The ways these two movements are understood by many of the Haitians with whom they have traction is one place to begin deconstructing this opposition. Same-sex-desiring and gender-creative Haitians claim that homophobia is a foreign import, and I document throughout this book how different forms of homophobia in Haiti are products of French colonial and U.S. imperialist intervention. Haitian Protestants claim that homosexuality—and more recently rights for homosexuals (or LGBT, LGBTQ, LGBTQI, or LGBTI rights)—are foreign imports. They associate homosexuality and homosexual rights with contemporary imperialist ills, such as humanitarian work and the ongoing UN Stabilization Mission in Haiti (MINUSTAH). Let me begin by showing the extent to which both of these claims are correct.

As historians of sexuality point out, while what we think of as same-sex desire and sexuality in different configurations have existed in all times and places, the concept of sexual dimorphism (male/female) and the speciation of first "the homosexual" and then "the heterosexual" have a European origin. Queer Indigenous and queer postcolonial scholars have illuminated how this particular framework of sex and sexuality—homosexuality/heterosexuality—traveled with European colonialism throughout the world and continues to follow transnational flows of U.S. imperialism. These are the routes through which this framework arrived on the shores of what is now Haiti. Since Spanish colonizers perpetrated genocide of the Indigenous peoples on the island that Haiti shares with the Dominican Republic, there is no way to know for certain what ways of thinking about bodies and intimacy were superseded by this violent process of racial capitalism. However, queer anthropologists and queer postcolonial scholars have traced how the process of replacing this population with people from nations in what is now Africa through the transatlantic slave trade introduced specific forms of gendered/sexed/raced/classed relationality to the Americas.

Masisi, the Kreyòl term that references male same-sex desire and sexuality as well as male effeminacy, is possibly one such form of relationality. One theory of the origins of *masisi*, articulated by Caribbeanist Roberto Strongman, is that use of the term in the context of Haiti's Afro-syncretic religion of Vodou closely resembles the use of the Fon term *mamisis* to describe male devotees of the spirit Mami Wata, who Strongman refers to as the African counterpart of Haitian Lasirenn (the mermaid). He quotes anthropologist Judy Rosenthal's ethnography of Vodou in Togo and Benin: "Mami Wata is about fertility, femaleness, and beauty. Mostly women become *Mamisis*; men who become *Mamisis* are particularly good-looking and often dress and plait their hair like women" (Strongman 2008, 25). Another theory is that the term *masisi* came about in the context of Saint Domingue, the French colony that would become Haiti. Haitian scholar Jean-Élie Gilles recounted to me an article he read in the French magazine *Historia* that proposes alternate origins:

> This word dates from seventeenth-century France, when Le Marquis de Cinq Mars was one of the "mignon" [lover, confidant, and friend] of the king of

> France. . . . When the King of France wanted to take Le Marquis de Cinq Mars,
> he used to say: "Mars, *ici!*" (Mars, come here). . . . The buccaneers who came to
> Haiti and who didn't have any women with them at the beginning made love
> with their male companions. . . . When they began to have slaves in the colony
> . . . the homosexual masters used to say to the . . . black slaves "Allons faire 'Mars
> *ici!*'" (Let's go do "Mars ici!") to imitate the king and Marquis de Cinq Mars.

However, the most common theory told to me by Haitians is that the term
dates to the period of the U.S. occupation, as a variation on "sissy." But another
possibility is that *masisi*—in true creole fashion—is a mélange of *mamisis*,
"Mars, *ici!*," and sissy. In later chapters I discuss at length the ways that *masisi*, *madivin*, and other terms marking Haitian same-sex desire and gender
creativity functioned during the time of my fieldwork. Suffice it to say for
now that homosexuality/heterosexuality—and the terms imported from
the United States that privilege same-sex desire, such as "men who have sex
with men" (MSM), "gay," "LGBT," and "LGBTI"—exist in tension with these
other categories.

Next is the related claim that rights for homosexuals is a political strategy
that comes from outside of Haiti. Again, there is some truth to this claim. The
biggest concern of Haitian evangelicals is that homosexual activists are going
to petition for same-sex marriage, against which evangelicals staged large
public demonstrations in 2013. While several same-sex-desiring Haitians
told me that they would like state recognition of their primary relationship
in this way, there are many more who consider it an "American thing" or a
"French thing." Haitian feminist sociologist Carolle Charles contends from
extensive research that many women in Haiti are not married, although
"the ideology of marriage is still strong" (1994, 48). Charles notes that long-
term monogamous marriages are more common among the upper classes, a
finding in my research in a more contemporary queer context as well. Polyamory (multiple simultaneous sexual partnerings) was much more prevalent
among my informants than monogamy, which was most common among
women—not men—of the upper classes. Same-sex-desiring women were
also more likely to be heterosexually married than men. In Haiti, moreover,
the institution of marriage is closely connected with colonial and imperialist
legacies. The French Code Noir legislated marriages and extramarital relationships to discourage interracial mixing; this contributed to the prevalence
of *plasaj* (nonlegal unions), which became a site of Protestant missionary
reform beginning in the mid-twentieth century—as I explain in chapter 2,
"The Missionary Position." All that being said, it was never a serious political
strategy for same-sex-desiring Haitians to obtain the right to marry.

The rights the global LGBTQI brought to Haiti sometimes, but not always, meshed with the visions of those same-sex-desiring and gender-creative Haitians who had already been organizing for social change. One of the strategies that the IGLHRC proposed and tried to facilitate through its collaborations with Haitian organizations was the creation of a law in Haiti that protects the LGBT community, one that would essentially function like a hate crimes law. Suspending for a moment radical critiques of such laws in the United States that may or may not be relevant in Haiti, there was never serious consideration given to this question: *what does it mean to ask the state for protections under conditions of foreign occupation?* Practically, it meant that the global LGBTQI's partnering organizations would petition the United Nations and other intergovernmental organizations to apply pressure on the Haitian state to enact legislation, and along the way it meant that Haitian organizations would collaborate with UN agencies in Haiti—including MINUSTAH "peacekeeping" officials of the occupying force—to conduct their work. Beyond seeking to remedy homophobia in Haiti through the influence of the occupiers, a strategy that correctly acknowledged who deals the cards, so to speak, but that does not serve same-sex-desiring and gender-creative Haitians in the long run, the global LGBTQI has neglected to address the conditions of foreign militarization in Haiti and the effects of U.S. imperialism writ large. Little attention has been paid to the history of U.S. interventions—military and otherwise—or to the United Nations occupation under MINUSTAH as phenomena that have detrimental impacts on the lives of same-sex-desiring and gender-creative Haitians.

Which brings me to the association of homosexuality with MINUSTAH, as well as leaders in the Haitian state who are perceived to be puppets for U.S. interests. These associations have been particularly prevalent in graffiti art in Port-au-Prince, a popular form of political discourse in Haiti. In an image of a mural circulated by the activist organization Kouraj (fig. 1), *masisi* is prominently displayed around an anti-UN symbol along with the words *kolera* (cholera), *kidnapè* (kidnappers), *asasen* (assassins), *vòlò* (robbers), and *kadejakè* (rapists). Nearby, a demon wearing a MINUSTAH soldier helmet stirs blood into a glass of what had presumably been clean water, a difficult-to-access life-giving resource for many Haitians. This depiction drawing associations between masisi and MINUSTAH is likely a reference to the documented male UN soldiers' rape of Haitian young men, rather than the global LGBTQI and Haitian LGBT organizations' collaborations with the United Nations.[1] However, it problematically associates rapes and pedophilia with male same-sex sexuality in general rather than violent and exploitative power relations exercised through sexuality. (By this logic, the widespread prevalence of UN soldiers raping Haitian women would be attributed to male heterosexuality, rather than rapists or imperialist sexual violence.) In this instance, anti-MINUSTAH sentiment was recoded as homophobia.

A strange effect is produced between the transnational circulations of these two social movements, evangelical Christianity and global LGBTQI human rights. While within the context of Haiti these movements each accuse the other of being connected to foreign intervention, their U.S. counterparts—evangelicals supported by neoconservatives on the one hand and global LGBTQI organizations like IGLHRC on the other—hide or at least downplay the fact that *Haiti has been a laboratory for U.S. empire for the last century* in order to make a case for their solution to Haiti's problems through future interventions. As I argue throughout the book, their cases for foreign intervention are articulated through two transnational imperialist discourses about Haiti.

The first is that the Black Republic is the dark and dangerous *premodern* land of Voodoo (English)/*Vaudoux* (French). To be clear, the "voodoo/vaudoux" of this discourse is a white Euro-U.S. imaginary—or really, a nightmarish fantasy of Haitian Vodou.[2] This discourse has two related iterations. The explicitly religious version represents the flourishing of "voodoo" as a devil-worshipping superstitious cult from Africa that encourages all kinds

Figure 1. Anti–United Nations mural in Port-au-Prince, 2011. (AP Photo, Ramon Espinosa)

of perverse behavior, including same-sex sexuality. This discourse came into prominence before the U.S. occupation of Haiti (1915–34) as a way to malign the Black republic—render it abnormal and freakish. Yet the U.S. occupation gave it new force along with a seemingly secular version of the same discourse that constructs Haiti as progress resistant, a place riddled with cultural deficits related to its religious ones. In this version, Haiti requires external supervision because these deficits—the practice of "voodoo," immediate gratification, bad childrearing practices, rampant sexual immorality (including polygamy and homosexuality)—lead to political instability and lack of "proper" development. As I document, the extensive circulation of fantastic, imagined stories about Haiti during the occupation sparked interest in widespread U.S. Protestant missionary work in Haiti that resulted in significant changes in sexual politics. This imperialist discourse has not lost its explanatory power for problems in the Black republic and remains the dominant one about Haiti to this day.

The second imperialist discourse about Haiti is that it is *modern* with a corrupt/failed state that exists only in its repressive capacities, including the enactment of homophobia and other violences. This discourse emerged after the 2010 earthquake in the context of the global LGBTQI's work with same-sex-desiring and gender-creative Haitians, and it brings Haiti within the realm of other postcolonial spaces—particularly in Africa, the Middle East, and the Caribbean—that are defined through their problems with exceptional homophobia.[3]

According to the reasoning of global LGBTQI human rights organizations, the state homophobia in Haiti is related to a socially conservative Catholic culture that comes from European colonialism. These organizations ignore or sideline other kinds of homophobia in Haiti connected to U.S. imperialism in the postcolonial period—most prominently evangelical Christian religious homophobia. Rather than purposeful omissions, this mistake points to limits in the way that global LGBTQI human rights organizations identify problems for same-sex-desiring and gender-creative people in places where they do not have established offices or long-term relationships. They work in partnerships with organizations that are already highly connected to U.S. and United Nations resources and/or by conducting long-distance research or brief site visits/research trips through those partnering organizations. Also, global LGBTQI human rights organizations are particularly interested in the state as a site of intervention, either because the state maintains laws against same-sex sexuality or lacks laws punishing those who discriminate against and oppress gender and sexual minorities.[4]

While not necessarily discounting the effects of European colonialism in shaping current conditions, each of these narratives ultimately constructs postcolonial Haiti as an autonomous nation riddled with problems of its own creation, thereby disavowing the effects of U.S. imperialism and ongoing foreign militarization. As with other imperialist discourses about Haiti, the underlying problems are attributed to its Black/African rather than its white/European roots: in other words, Haiti's particular postcolonial problems are a product of race or "culture" rather than anti-Black racism and imperialism. This is the postcolonial effect—blaming "independent" nations for colonial legacies and the effects of subsequent imperialist interventions and influences—in sexual terms. The dominant discourse claims that Haiti is *too queer*; the emergent one is that it is *too homophobic*. These conflicting discourses come together in their promotion of U.S. exceptionalism—that the United States and its allies have the *right* solutions for Haiti's postcolonial predicament.

Against the claims that the Black republic is premodern or modern-but-failing, this book shows that transnational Haiti is a postcolonial nation-state targeted by military, political, economic, cultural, and religious interventions that are currently being played out by two transnational social movements—Christian evangelicals and global LGBTQI human rights—whose "culture wars" are fought in the register of homophobia and homo-protectionism. These movements and the interplay of their discursive production—what I call postcolonial homophobia—influences the ways that same-sex-desiring and gender-creative subjects come to understand, constitute, define, and organize themselves in postcolonial Haiti. By highlighting their struggles and achievements throughout this book, my hope is that people will not just understand same-sex-desiring and gender-creative life in Haiti in a different way than what the dominant narratives have told us, but that the account I/we offer will provide another opening to rethink the Black republic in relation to the supposedly benevolent U.S. empire.

POSTCOLONIAL HOMOPHOBIA

After the transnational turn in queer studies in the late 1990s and early 2000s, scholars in this interdisciplinary field theorized homophobia only to the extent that it functioned as a manifestation of queer liberalism. As articulated in the introduction to the *Social Text* special issue "What's Queer about Queer Studies Now?," the transnational turn has been animated by questions, such as these: "What does queer studies have to say about empire, globalization, neoliberalism, sovereignty and terrorism? What does queer studies tell us about immigration, citizenship, prisons, welfare, mourning, and human rights? What is the relationship between *Lawrence v. Texas*, the exalted 2003 Supreme Court decision decriminalizing gay sex, and the contemporaneous USA PATRIOT ACT [that extended national surveillance and security apparatuses with the justification of fighting terrorism]?" (Eng, Halberstam, and Muñoz 2005, 2). This scholarship primarily addresses homophobia in terms of the efforts of the Gay International (Massad 2002), here referred to as "the global LGBTQI" to reflect the particular configuration of terms used during the years of my fieldwork: lesbian, gay, bisexual, transgender, queer, intersex. These are U.S.- and European-based organizations and foundations with the mission to end discrimination and oppression of gender and sexual minorities wherever it occurs, a missionary impulse that queer postcolonial theorist Joseph A. Massad contends has an underlying Orientalist logic. To be more specific, not only do these organizations circulate Euro-U.S. identity politics throughout the world, their framework for addressing homophobia produces postcolonial spaces like the Middle East as backward/traditional and the United States as exceptionally liberated/liberating. Jasbir K. Puar (2007) usefully shows that the global LGBTQI's campaigns against homophobia as merely sexual repression fuels racist, anti-immigrant, and Islamophobic discourses of U.S. exceptionalism.

In the last decade, there has been a return to what queer theorist Eve Kosofsky Sedgwick (1990) calls antihomophobic theorizing that contends specifically with different homophobic social structures and state projects (or "political homophobia") in the context of postcolonial spaces. These are respectively the foci of two anthologies: *Homophobias: Lust and Loathing across Time and Space* (2009), edited by anthropologist David A. B. Murray, and *Global Homophobia: States, Movements, and the Politics of Oppression* (2013), edited by political scientists Meredith L. Weiss and Michael J. Bosia. These scholars note the difficulty of shaking the liberal underpinnings of the term "homophobia" but nevertheless continue to use the recognizable term to document and theorize the forms of violence attendant to normative gender and sexuality that they contend have been globalized to a greater extent than LGBTQI rights and politics.

This strand of scholarship on the globalization of homophobia has two notable components. First, the literature tends to focus on homophobia as a European colonial legacy, particularly of British imperialism, that transmitted laws against sodomy around the globe. The vast majority of this scholarship, then, focuses on places where same-sex sexual practices are in some way criminalized, especially countries in Africa and the West Indies. Second, it deals with the political homophobia of anticolonial nationalisms that have emerged in the postcolonial period, making the case that they "invoke colonialist precepts of gender and sexuality at the same time that they disavow the violences of colonialism" (Currier 2012, 6).

This is true of feminist sociologist Ashley Currier's "Political Homophobia in Postcolonial Namibia," which draws historical "continuity in the content of colonial, apartheid, and postcolonial homophobias"(2010, 114). She uses postcolonial homophobia to refer to Namibian—and more broadly African— nationalisms that "differed from predecessor ideologies [in the colonial and apartheid periods] in that African nationalist leaders deployed [homophobia] to emasculate white, western men and nations" (114). Currier maintains that political homophobia is wielded as a tool of phallic agency by anticolonial nationalists in the postcolonial period to "enhance . . . the leaders' masculinist position and legacy as liberators" (110) from white colonial rule, in ways that had deleterious effects on a nascent LGBT movement.

Weaving together elements of these two strands of scholarship, in this book I expand the definition of postcolonial homophobia beyond the homophobic strategies of anticolonial nationalisms in Africa and other postcolonial spaces as outlined by Currier and other scholars and by keeping in mind the critique of queer liberalisms. I theorize postcolonial homophobia as the compounded effects of historical and contemporary Western imperialist biopolitical interventions to regulate/manage/control/govern/liberate gender and sexuality.

These interventions, I show, have harmful consequences for all postcolonial subjects, albeit to greater and lesser extents, related in no small part to their contribution to the general effects of imperialism—economic sanctions, militarization, other forms of structural violence, and circumscribing autonomy and self-determination. These forms of power are not merely repressive, however, but are productive in the Foucauldian sense. As Judith Butler asks, "given that there is no sexuality outside of power, how can regulation itself be considered a productive or generative constraint on sexuality?" (1993, 95). Such vectors of imperialist power create new social relations and influence how same-sex-desiring and gender-creative subjects come to understand, constitute, define, and organize themselves in postcolonial contexts.

The case of Haiti is helpful for understanding the broad impact of postcolonial homophobia. Unlike many case studies in scholarship on the globalization of homophobia, Haiti is a place where laws against same-sex sexuality and laws that prohibit changing one's sex designation on official documents have not defined state homophobia. Focusing on Haiti gets us beyond thinking about homophobias as legacies of only European imperialisms, French colonialism in the Haitian case, prompting us to take into account the effects of neo-imperialism. Here I join those scholars who implicitly or explicitly focus on homophobia in relation to U.S. imperialism. These include M. Jacqui Alexander's theorization of heteropatriarchal recolonization of the Bahamas for the purposes of tourist consumption (1997), David A. B. Murray's discussion of homophobia in Barbados as Euro-U.S. imperial debris (2012), and Kapya J. Kaoma's scholarship on U.S. evangelical Christianity, or "moral imperialism," in relationship to the criminalization of same-sex sexuality in Uganda (2013). Haiti, which has been shaped by U.S. empire for nearly a century, offers an opportunity to understand the *new* (homo)sexual politics that have been emerging in these former European colonies.

This project is particularly important because the charged sexual politics around homophobia constraining Haiti traverse the Caribbean, which *Time* magazine infamously declared to be "the most homophobic place on earth"(Padgett 2006). These discourses about the Caribbean being *too homophobic* produced an understandable wariness or aversion to focusing on homophobia in critical queer Caribbean scholarship, as reflected in Lyndon K. Gill's important question in *Erotic Islands*: "To what extent does overemphasizing exclusions prematurely blind us to various kinds of queer *embeddedness* seldom remarked upon in scholarly literature racing to demonstrate and document systematic homophobia in the region?" (2018, 1). Gill is among the scholars who have dedicated themselves to bringing "careful attention to these remarkably Caribbean queer worlds" (2018, 219).[5] Yet, as I learned through participating in queer worlds in Haiti, homophobic violence shapes people's daily lives (as do other forms of power) and therefore needs to be directly addressed—especially in relation to empire. So, along with other Caribbeanist scholars, I press into the trouble of "Caribbean homophobia" in order to shape other kinds of narratives.[6] This work necessarily takes to heart Rosamond S. King's words: "The challenge for those of us who study nonheteronormative sexualities in the Caribbean is determining how to acknowledge real—and yes, sometimes violent—homophobia without endorsing the idea that the Caribbean is uniquely and exceptionally homophobic" (2014, 83).

INTERDISCIPLINARY INQUIRY

While I intend for the framework of postcolonial homophobia to enact reparative work in transnational queer studies, the interdisciplinary inquiry at the heart of this book is "unruly," that is to say, it "participates in and contributes to wide-ranging debates that traverse multiple fields and disciplines" (Luibhéid 2008, 169). This unruly undertaking borrows elements from disciplines in the arts, humanities, social sciences, and law without belonging to any of them. These elements will make certain parts of this book as familiar to some readers as they are strange to others, and the project—really the multiple projects of the book—exceeds disciplinarity entirely. This unruly interdisciplinarity is characteristic of activist scholarship that produces knowledge about and for progressive social movements (Sudbury and Okazawa-Rey 2015). The interdisciplines where I found my footing as a scholar—critical ethnic studies, Latin American studies, feminist studies, and queer studies—are the institutional academic arms of intersectional social movements that grew me as an activist. For me, these interdisciplines are defined less by certain objects of inquiry—for example, "women" or "gender"—than their investments in analyzing oppression to create change in and beyond the academy. My formal training emphasized the interrelations of historical, social, political, economic, and cultural processes as ways into understanding individual/collective experiences and their transformation, which has been necessary and advantageous to this project about postcolonial homophobia.

In the process of describing postcolonial homophobia in Haiti, this book relies on knowledge from and contributes to inquiries, debates, archive building, and scholarly activist undertakings in multiple fields and interdisciplines. It is in conversation with (often already overlapping) literatures about gender and sexuality in the Caribbean; the "coloniality of religion" and religious gender and sexual politics in religious studies; racialized conceptions of "the human," racial capitalism, diaspora, and Black resistance in Black studies; the performance of collective memory, representations of violence and trauma, and performance as a mode of resistance in performance studies; European colonial legacies, U.S. military interventions, and increases in Protestant influence in Caribbean and Latin American studies. It offers an ethnography of U.S. empire that joins with others (e.g., McGranahan and Collins 2018) that document settler colonialism and the wide-ranging impacts of U.S. imperialism highlighted in American studies. The critical engagements with identity, community, (non)normativity, racialized sexuality, AIDS activism, and nonprofitization/institutionalization are indicative of a queer studies project, and this one takes up these questions within the field of transnational queer studies. This field—and transnational sexuality studies broadly—is interconnected with transnational feminisms. Both are shaped by postcolonial theory and concerned with the gender and sexual dimensions of colonialism/

imperialism and anticolonial/anti-imperialist/decolonial efforts, cultural nationalism, progressive social movements, humanitarian projects of rescue, nongovernmental organizations, and human rights.

Within Haitian studies, the book is situated alongside many others with these overlapping concerns. It is also one of a small handful of monographs in what my colleagues Dasha A. Chapman, Mario LaMothe, and I called queer Haitian studies (2017). Dasha and Mario invited me to edit a special issue of *Women and Performance: A Journal of Feminist Theory* with them, following up on a symposium that Dasha organized and we participated in at Duke University titled "Nou Mache Ansanm (We Walk Together): Performance, Gender, and Sexuality in Haiti" in fall 2015. We crafted a call for papers for the special issue with the new title, "Nou Mache Ansanm (We Walk Together): Queer Haitian Performance and Affiliation," and organized conference panels at the Haitian Studies Association, the Caribbean Studies Association, and the National Women's Studies Association to coincide with the first published compilation of academic work in the field we called queer Haitian studies. That issue includes a review of the literature in the "small place" of queer Haitian studies—particularly drawing on U.S. queer of color critique (always already engaged with the transnational—e.g., Ferguson 2015), feminist scholarship in Haitian studies, and scholarship on gender and sexuality in the Caribbean and African diaspora—that we each contribute to with our work.[7] In this field that so-often highlights Afro-centric radical, revolutionary, subversive, and resistant performances of gender and sexuality, this project provides some balance—or at least sketches out a bigger picture—by focusing on structures of violence, normativities, complicities, and necropolitics.

The core of this book is informed by a multi-sited ethnographic research project about the life constraints and possibilities for same-sex-desiring and gender-creative Haitians, which spanned from 2008 to 2016. The idea of multi-sited ethnography marks a decolonial turn *away* from "sites" as conceived of in traditional anthropological fieldwork models by Bronisław Malinowski geared toward the holistic documentation of native cultures and their internal logics in a particular place and *toward* "chains, paths, threads, conjunctions, juxtapositions, or locations in which the ethnographer establishes some form of literal, physical presence, with an explicit, posited logic of association or connection among sites" (Marcus 1995, 105). "Queer Haiti" formed the logic of association in this instance, which I understood broadly to concern Haitian same-sex desire and gender creativity, gender and sexual identity formations and social norms in Haiti and its diaspora, and a myriad of political projects articulated through/with Haitian gender and sexuality.

"Queer" originally meant (too) many things simultaneously. The expansiveness of the term, the way that it did not "fix" gender and sexuality while marking a sense of coalition in recognized Otherness, indicated my distance from heteronormative life. It marks my formal training in queer theory and interdisciplinary queer studies, which is to say what I have read and who I am in conversation with academically. I have hopes for the radical possibilities of "queer" that you will see throughout the book as well as an understanding of its annihilating potential when it is fixed in identitarian form and read onto others from the position of the Western academy. This is something that Dasha, Mario, and I tried to highlight in our special issue, but while the "queer Haiti" (or by then #queerHaiti) framework was incredibly generative for our collective project, it alienated some antihomophobic academics with whom we had hoped to be in conversation who preferred broader frameworks like "gender and sexuality."

"Queer" became troublesome for another reason. Whereas this term was mostly unknown in Haiti during the early years of my fieldwork, by the time I was writing this book, activists and human rights advocates had explicitly rejected "queer" as a term that had relevant application there. In chapter 5, I trace the emergence of an LGBT community in Haiti, and during my last summer of fieldwork in 2016 the preferred configuration of terms in English was "LGBTI community." The "I" of intersex had lagged behind LGBT, but it caught up nonetheless. The "Q" was conspicuously absent. "Queer" with its Anglo pronunciation does not lend itself to easy creolization. However, activists and advocates told me that "queer" was a *blan* (white/foreign) idea imported to Haiti, though the particular problem with this term remained elusive when so many others—like gay, lesbian, and LGBT—were likewise imported. Yet the problem with "queer" seems less specific to the geopolitics of Haiti, as global LGBTQI organizations have started to drop the "Q" as well.

Ultimately "queer Haiti" was a provisional way of knowing—an enactment of a particular anthropological imaginary like "transgender" for David Valentine (2007)—that I traveled with and passed through, though it did important work along the way. It connected me to a range of same-sex-desiring and gender-creative Haitians who affiliate with one or more of the following terms: gay, *masisi*, *makomè* or *makomer*, men who have sex with men (MSM), lesbian, *lèsbyèn*, *madoda*, *madivin*, *yon fi ki prefere fi* (a girl who prefers girls), bisexual, *biseks* or *biseksyèl*, *miks*, *entènasyonal* (international), homosexual, *homosexuelle*, *omoseksyèl*, transgender, *trani*, trans, LGBT, LGBTI, pomosexual, and even queer. "Queer Haiti" immersed me in organizations with which these Haitians were connected and the social worlds between and extending out from them, namely an arts center in Jacmel and several organizations based in Port-au-Prince: a national HIV/AIDS outreach organization for MSM, a service organization for LGBTI Haitians, an activist organization comprised of same-sex-desiring and gender-creative Haitians, and a feminist organization led by same-sex-desiring women, trans women, and women who are sex workers. These loosely comprise my field sites.

The connecting thread of "queer Haiti" did much more than take me, and often my family members, to these "sites." I found myself in other spaces of congregation for same-sex-desiring and gender-creative Haitians in Jacmel, Port-au-Prince, and the surrounding metropolitan areas: dance classes, private parties, restaurants, nightclubs, cultural events (e.g., art openings, performances, and academic lectures), beaches, Catholic mass, and Vodou ceremonies. "Queer Haiti" linked me with members of new groups and organizations, as often as it linked me with people who never went to any meetings and support groups or otherwise received direct services from organizations.

It also led me on paths through a variety of other places in Haiti, the Dominican Republic, the United States, Canada, and France. One of the notable aspects of these travels—besides the amount of time I have spent in cars, buses, and airplanes—is that the destinations have almost always been cities: brief excursions to Paris, Montréal, and Santo Domingo; longer stays in New York, Boston, Dorchester, Mattapan, and Little Haiti in Miami; and then, of course, extended work in Jacmel and Port-au-Prince. This geography would initially suggest that this project had the same metronormative (Halberstam 2005; Thomsen 2021) impulses as U.S.-based queer studies in general, constructing cities as the site of same-sex-desiring and gender-creative life and possibilities. However, I would more likely characterize these spaces as hubs of gathering that are intimately connected to rural Haiti—where same-sex-desiring and gender-creative Haitians live, grow up, have family connections, and make pilgrimages for personal and spiritual purposes. Thus I have passed a lot of time *andeyò* (in the countryside) during many years of fieldwork.

From the span of these years and the list of places that I traveled, those trained in anthropology will recognize that I had a fieldwork experience that has been theorized as patchwork ethnography (Günel, Varma, and Watanabe 2020) shaped by familial, financial, and health constraints. Unlike those people who spend a full year or two years in one place, I was constantly moving. I spent the most time in Haiti between 2008 and 2011, interspersed with trips to prominent places in the diaspora for language training, research, academic events, and advocacy work. Then my trips to Jacmel and Port-au-Prince were limited to twice a year during academic breaks and lasted between two weeks and six weeks. My last extended stay in Haiti for this project was in summer 2016, and after that time I conducted additional interviews and took research trips to New York to interview staff and volunteers of U.S.-based organizations working with same-sex-desiring and gender-creative Haitians. I have remained in contact with people in Haiti and the diaspora throughout the years via phone, video calls, and email, though Facebook and WhatsApp were our substantial modes of communication.

My fieldwork practices included participant observation, focus groups in organizational contexts, and one-on-one semi-structured formal interviews with more than seventy same-sex-desiring and gender-creative Haitians, as well as many more Haitians and blan who are in relation to and support same-sex-desiring and gender-creative people in Haiti and the diaspora. These people significantly included a high percentage of women, unusual in that the overwhelming majority of research about same-sex sexuality in Haitian contexts is about men. I am quite certain that bringing my family made it possible to develop connections with women in the field, and that it enabled this research project overall. As Haitian women indicated, in order to establish any sense of trust it was important for them to know who my *moun* (people/family) were and how we interacted with each other.

The insights of this book also came from other kinds of methods. I complemented data from the field with creative work by same-sex-desiring and gender-creative Haitians, as well as documents about sexuality and gender gleaned from newsletters, newspapers, magazines, social media sites, organizations and foundations' public records, and scholarly work in anthropology, history, and public health. This archive has grown over the years with materials given to me by people who were aware of my research interests, such as an article on "revenge lesbianism" in an issue of the fashion magazine *Rebelle Haiti* and a limited-circulation art film about homophobia in Haiti by Maksaens Denis called *Voodoo Divas*. Many gifts came from Jean-Élie Gilles, who wrote the first novel about male same-sex sexuality in Haiti, *Sur les pas de Diogène* (1995). But sometimes these gifts would come from strangers. Early on in my fieldwork I was riding in a tap-tap through Delmas talking about my work with a man who expressed interest in my research, and he asked me to follow him to his house to share something that would help me, which turned out to be a pirated copy of *Des hommes et dieux/Of Men and Gods* (Lescot and Magloire 2002), an ethnographic documentary about masisi in Haitian Vodou.[8] Remarkably, unsolicited, other strangers presented me with their own pirated copies at other times; I was heartened that the documentary had a life outside of the academy and that people I did not know were excited to share it with me. I also came across relevant materials by happenstance, as when I was buying books at Librari Mapou in Little Haiti and noticed an article on the front page of *Haïti en Marche* titled "Haïti ou la 'dépravation sexuelle.'"

In order to find historical information to contextualize the contemporary lives and struggles of same-sex-desiring and gender-creative Haitians, I conducted research in eight archival collections related to U.S. involvement in Haiti, including the U.S. Department of State records about the occupation of Haiti from 1915 to 1934, the personal papers of occupying marines, the papers of anthropologists who wrote about same-sex sexuality in Haiti during or immediately after the 1915–34 occupation, and the records of the AIDS Coalition to Unleash Power (ACT UP) Haiti Working Group. Many other texts from the late nineteenth and twentieth centuries I found online or through interlibrary loan. These are primarily texts that made Haiti "almost an invention of the United States," as J. Michael Dash (1988, 2) puts it in his reformulation of Edward Said's concept of Orientalism (1979), rendering the postcolonial nation through an imperialist imaginary. These include published or recorded work by lawmakers, diplomats, missionaries, adventurers, journalists, artists, U.S. Marines, and anthropologists.

My analysis of these texts has been most influenced by the queer theory tradition of reading against the grain, particularly within the fields of queer of color critique and queer postcolonial studies that analyze racialized gender and sexuality. Following Emma Pérez's methodology to unravel colonialist ideology in the U.S.-Mexican borderlands, I started with the question: "For whom and by whom has [gender and] sexuality been defined?" (2003, 125). This Foucauldian-inspired question goes beyond "finding" or "recovering" Haitian subjects that we might consider to be something akin to homosexual or transgender in the archives, to tracing the outlines of normative regimes of gender and sexuality under different kinds of empire. This project, then, is inherently about power and the production of imperialist relationships through racialized gender and sexuality.

ORGANIZATION OF THE BOOK

Unlike interdisciplinary academic books with chapters organized around questions, theories, themes, or problems, this book proceeds loosely following chronological convention. The first two chapters provide transnational histories of European colonialism and U.S. imperialism in Haiti from

Columbus to the early twenty-first century so as to contextualize contemporary gender and sexual politics. The remaining chapters focus on events during the years of my fieldwork in relation to the episodic "flare-ups" of homophobic violence: the controversy over the soon-to-be prime minister's sexuality in 2008, the 2010 earthquake for which evangelical Christians blamed "homosexual" Haitians by making Haiti fall out of favor with God, the summer 2013 marches against same-sex marriage in major metropolitan cities, and the cancellation of an LGBTI film festival in 2016. Readers might therefore perceive that the book is about a series of sequential and interrelated "events," and while that is partially true, the intention of the chapter organization is rather to impart a sense of displacements, disruptions, continuities, dispersals, and accretions over time.

Chapter 1 tells the transnational history of colonialism and imperialism in Haiti through a queer postcolonial lens with attention to racialized sexuality. It is the story of enslaved Black people who overthrew their white colonizers and formed an independent state—perhaps the largest undertaking of what queer theorist Michael Warner calls "more thorough resistance to regimes of the normal" (1993, xxvi)—as well as a story about its demise. I argue that this revolutionary project was undermined by the transnational Euro-U.S. discourse of Haiti as the dark and dangerous land of "voodoo/vaudoux," which perverted the revolutionary project of the Black republic and provided justification for its recolonization in the twentieth century in terms of racialized sexuality.

To make this argument, I concentrate on five periods—European colonialism (1492–1791), the Haitian Revolution (1791–1804), independence (1804–1915), the first U.S. occupation (1915–34), and the early years of the AIDS epidemic (1980s and 1990s)—configured in relation to the figure of the Haitian *zonbi*. There are two reasons behind telling the history of transnational Haiti in relation to the zonbi. The zombie is one of the best examples of how U.S. representations of Haiti in the twentieth century have produced its perversity in ways loosely connected to imaginaries of voodoo. The zonbi, which blurs the binary between life and death, is similarly situated to the homosexual in nationalist and Christian religious discourses as being "perverse" and "unnatural." These two loathsome figures were linked in U.S. representations of the Black republic in the late and post-occupation period in a way that justified the military intervention and obscured its violences. For these reasons, as I discuss in chapter 4, the zonbi was reclaimed by same-sex-desiring and gender-creative Haitians to perform anti-imperialist queer critique about homophobia.

The second chapter, "The Missionary Position: U.S. Protestant Missionaries and Religious Homophobia," elaborates postcolonial homophobia by tracing the long-term effects of the circulation of the transnational imperialist discourse of Haiti as the perverse premodern land of voodoo laid out in the previous chapter. Specifically, the widespread circulation of such representations of the Black republic during and after the U.S. occupation generated interest in U.S. missionary work in Haiti. U.S. missionaries proliferated in Haiti during the mid-twentieth century, evangelizing the natives and engaging in development work, to uplift a place—by their logic—riddled with superstition and an accompanying array of cultural deficits.

In the process, evangelical Christianity introduced a kind of religious homophobia to Haiti that has dramatically shifted sexual politics and negatively impacted the material conditions of same-sex-desiring and gender-creative Haitians, which I describe in-depth from my fieldwork. Unlike Vodou, which honors many kinds of social relations that are nonnormative by Euro-U.S. standards, Catholicism and Protestantism consider same-sex sexuality to be a sin and thus have attendant forms of religious homophobia that are more and less negotiable for same-sex-desiring and gender-creative Haitians. The treatment of homosexuality in these two forms of Christianity in many ways parallel each religion's treatment of Vodou. In Catholicism, the practice of same-sex sexuality and Vodou (not necessarily together) operate as an open secret. In evangelical Christianity in particular, the practices are supposed to be exposed and rejected based on religious conceptions of grace; this plays out through economies of annunciation and denunciation with regard to homosexuality—a quality that brought evangelical Christian sexual politics front and center in national debates about the future of Haiti.

Chapter 3 delves into a controversy in Haiti and the diaspora about a nominee to the position of prime minister in 2008. Michèle Duvivier Pierre-Louis was publicly accused of being a lesbian and, therefore, of being morally unfit to be the head of state. Because these kinds of accusations had not been wielded against men, including "known homosexuals," Haitian feminist organizers considered the tarnishing of Pierre-Louis's reputation to be a way of keeping women out of leadership. To add a layer to this analysis about heteropatriarchal politics in Haiti, I elaborate how the Pierre-Louis controversy is a case study in postcolonial homophobia. The transnational imperialist voodoo discourse and the resulting rise in Protestantism shaped the controversy that took place in the register of evangelical Christian homophobia through its emphasis on annunciation and denunciation. The incitement to discourse about homosexuality in Haiti and the diaspora surrounding the controversy coincided with a flare-up of homophobic violence, a violent backlash against Haitians known or perceived to be same-sex desiring. The verbal and physical assaults were a precursor to the homophobic aftershocks to the earthquake just a year later. Unexpectedly, however, this flare-up of homophobic violence—coupled with the way that Pierre-Louis responded to the accusations in a national radio address by refusing to either confirm or deny that she is a lesbian—fomented public and organized queer resistance in Haiti.

Chapter 4 highlights a queer anti-imperialist performance organized in the wake of the Pierre-Louis controversy and performed by the Haitian performance troupe Lakou at the 2009 Ghetto Biennale in Port-au-Prince. In the performance of "Zonbi, Zonbi," Lakou rehearsed and held space for the history of slavery in the colonial period, the Haitian Revolution, and subsequent U.S. interventions in the postcolonial period. "Zonbi, Zonbi" articulated queer politics in the register of Vodou as a medium of anti-imperialist resistance, following in Haitian tradition. I argue that Lakou's activist memory-history project reworked the transnational imperialist discourse of Haiti as a premodern land of "Voodoo" through the figure of the zonbi. Lakou's performance illuminates these histories and argues that the liberation of same-sex-desiring and gender-creative people from postcolonial homophobia is bound up in the liberation of all Haitians from imperialist domination.

The fifth chapter, "The Sexual Politics of Rescue: The Global LGBTQI and Postcolonial Homophobia after the 2010 Earthquake in Haiti," marks the emergence of the transnational imperialist discourse of Haiti as inherently homophobic. I show that this emergence is tied to the influence of global LGBTQI rights organizations who conducted relief work after the 2010 earthquake. Transnational identity politics produced responses to the disaster that constituted LGBT Haitians as a population in need of rescue from otherwise unlivable conditions. I explain that the central role the global LGBTQI takes in post-earthquake knowledge production about nonnormative gender and sexuality in Haiti results in reaffirming the characterization of the Haitian state as ineffective at best and violent at worst, thereby inviting future rescue missions by U.S. Americans and other foreigners to save LGBT people.

Chapter 6 analyzes an emergent social movement by and for LGBT Haitians that coalesced around a shared commitment to challenging homophobia. I mark this emergence at the International Day Against Homophobia (IDAHO) events in 2012, when a variety of organizations—focused on health, advocacy, and activism—collaborated on a three-hundred-person conference against *omofobi* (homophobia) in Haiti. These organizations had different frameworks for theorizing homophobia and enacting antihomophobic politics that was emphasized by large Christian demonstrations against same-sex marriage in 2013. In the chapter, I focus on the relationship between two collaborating organizations—Fondasyon SEROvie and Kouraj—to trace debates about homophobia in Haiti connected to the influences of evangelical Christianity on the global LGBTQI.

Even though the events in this book end in 2013, the epilogue connects to the transnational Black Lives Matter movement to highlight and contextualize the fatal implications of postcolonial homophobia in the years since the inauguration of a social movement by and for same-sex-desiring and gender-creative Haitians and the public demonstrations against same-sex marriage. In the wake of these events and other reverberations of the interplay between evangelical Christianity and global LGBTQI human rights, same-sex-desiring and gender-creative Haitians have lost their lives. With the exception of the violent murder of the Kouraj president in 2019, most of these deaths have been attributed to individual circumstances and barely registered beyond the intimate circles of Haitians in the country and in the diaspora. Following the work of Black Lives Matter activists and scholars who theorize the serialization of Black death, and especially the work of Black feminists, I end by rethinking the material conditions of postcolonial homophobia that have made these lives expendable in the hope that we can all, from our different positions, work toward more vital and sustainable futures for same-sex-desiring and gender-creative Haitians.

1

PERVERTING HAITI

The Transnational Imperialist Discourse of the Black Republic
as the Premodern Land of "Voodoo/Vaudoux"

I begin with a queer transnational history of Haiti. It is a version of the story of enslaved Black people who overthrew their white colonizers and formed an independent nation-state—perhaps the largest undertaking of queer politics according to social theorist Michael Warner's definition as "more thorough resistance to regimes of the normal" (1993, xxvi). It is also a story about how Euro-U.S. imperialisms have discredited and undermined this Black revolutionary project, though its promise cannot be extinguished. These well-documented histories are not recounted in every detail here; rather my purpose is to provide context for an analysis of sexual politics in postcolonial Haiti from 2008 to 2016.

The chapter unfolds chronologically, though it is not a conventional historiography. I follow the lead of queer Chicana historian Emma Pérez in "Queering the Borderlands: The Challenges of Excavating the Invisible and Unheard." Pérez's decolonizing method is not necessarily a recovery of the fleeting histories of same-sex desire in the archives, but rather asking the question about how normativity is produced by empire: "For whom and by whom has sexuality been defined [in colonialist and imperialist contexts]?" (2003, 125). To answer that question, I highlight five periods of transnational Haitian history that profoundly shape contemporary queer sexual politics: European colonialism (1492–1791), the Haitian Revolution (1791–1804), the Black republic (1804–1915), the first U.S. occupation (1915–34), and the early years of the AIDS epidemic (1980s and 1990s). Readers familiar with Haitian history will notice gaps, such as the Duvalier dictatorship and late twentieth-century U.S. interventions. My history is not comprehensive; Haitian and/

or Haitian studies scholars have already compiled great volumes that those interested should consult.[1] However, in the tradition of Haitian spiralism, subsequent chapters layer and deepen historical knowledge, to ultimately "unravel (imperialist) ideology" (Pérez 2003, 123).

Toward that end and of importance to this book's trajectory toward an analysis of postcolonial homophobia, this chapter traces the emergence of the transnational Euro-U.S. imperialist discourse of Haiti as the premodern dark and dangerous land of "voodoo" (English), alternately spelled "vaudoux" (French)—I keep spellings in their original contexts. The voodoo/vaudoux of this discourse bears phantasmic resemblance to the beliefs, principles, and practices of the Afro-syncretic religion of Vodou in Haiti.[2] Nightmarish tales of demonic possession, physical torture, ingestion of human and nonhuman animal body parts, kidnapping, murder, mind control, fates and fortunes redirected by black magic, and evildoing pervade Euro-U.S. representations of the Black republic vis-à-vis voodoo/vaudoux. Racialized (hyper)sexuality is key to the imperialist imagination of this supposed devil-worshipping cult; thus the representations feature orgies or group sex, uncontrollable desires, profligate sexuality, public nudity or sex, and pathological seduction.[3]

The circulation of the transnational Euro-U.S. imperialist discourse of voodoo/vaudoux worked to justify Haiti's recolonization by the United States in the twentieth century by perverting the Black republic—rendering it abnormal, freakish, and queer. U.S. representations of Haiti's Black perversions during the time of the early twentieth century occupation newly featured same-sex desires and sexuality in voodoo/vaudoux, layering onto well-established imperialist anti-Black representations of moral corruption through racialized sexuality. This biopolitical shift in the production of Haitians as a population appeared in popular, academic, and medical texts and is essential to understanding postcolonial homophobia. The representation of (potential) same-sex sexuality as an integral part of Haiti's perversity affirmed the supposed necessity of foreign management and laid down the path for a new U.S. missionary enterprise detailed in the next chapter.

Beginning in the late and post-occupation period, U.S. imperialist discourses situated the figure of the homosexual in a similar way to the figure of the zombie (which blurs the Western binary between life and death) and its maker (the predatory architect of unnatural violence). Zombies have predominated in United States imaginations of Haiti's freakishness vis-à-vis voodoo/vaudoux and become one of the primary modes through which to express white imperialist anxieties about racialized sexuality. Because of this fact, anti-imperialist histories and critiques understandably tend to distance themselves from such representations by steering clear of mentioning zombies except to describe their place in the pantheon of racist depictions of Haiti that produce its Otherness. However, in doing so, they engage in a version of respectability politics that eerily aligns with the violent desire of evangelical missionaries—among others—to eradicate same-sex sexuality and/or Vodou.

Another anti-imperialist approach deploys the figure of the zonbi allegorically to cultivate knowledge of the past-presents of colonialism and imperialism; following that tradition in Haitian literature and cultural work, I configure the transnational history of Haiti in relation to the zonbi. Introducing the zonbi here, I prefigure the queer Haitian anti-imperialist performance, "Zonbi, Zonbi," by a dance troupe called Lakou (see chapter 4). "Queer," as I use it here, indexes not only same-sex desire and gender creativity but also an expansive nonnormativity in line with Warner's "more thorough resistance to regimes of the normal" (1983, xxvi) as well as Cathy Cohen's (1997) radical coalitional politics to transform dominant systems and uproot oppression. The "Zonbi, Zonbi" performance creatively enacted queer politics specifically to illuminate the production of Haiti as perverse in Western imperialist discourses of voodoo/vaudoux and to illuminate its devastating impacts through postcolonial homophobia as well as to "funk the erotic" (Stallings 2015) under conditions of anti-Black imperialism by disidentifying with reviled and denigrated figures (Muñoz 1999).

For clarification, as with the differences between the Haitian religion of Vodou and the imagined voodoo/vaudoux produced in Euro-U.S. discourses about Haiti, the zonbi and the zombie reflect different conceptions of "the living dead" and produce different kinds of effects through their representation. Thanks to decades of cult classics like *Night of the Living Dead* (1968), blockbuster hits like *28 Days Later* (2002) and *World War Z* (2013), and popular television series like *The Walking Dead* (2010), it can be difficult to imagine a zombie as anything other than a blood-thirsty and/or bio-contaminate animated corpse. The Haitian zonbi, the progenitor to these lumbering monsters of the silver and digital screens, is closely akin to the slave—imagined as a soulless human form from which one can extract labor. As Maya Deren explains, the locus of terror with the zonbi is not necessarily an encounter with one as it is with the zombie, but rather—given not-too-distant histories of slavery and compelled labor—being turned into one (1953, 42). Both figure in meditations on the conditions of modern capitalism, but the zonbi makes apparent the always-racialized dynamics of modern capitalism.

Depending on who you ask, the material zonbi that made its way into U.S. representations of zombies are rare or nonexistent monstrosities created by dark magic. Religious studies scholar Elizabeth McAlister offers a concise description of zonbi that goes beyond the idea of a reanimated corpse:

The notion of using the recently dead to work operates on at least three levels in Haitian culture. First, and most commonly, ritual experts extract the *zonbi* magically and use them for mystical work. . . . Second, there is some evidence for a less frequent (and criminal) practice of poisoning people to induce a lowered metabolic rate so that they appear dead, and then reviving them after they are buried in order to force them into physical labor. The material reality of this practice is contested and has been documented at length in a controversial Harvard study. Third, *zonbi* operate in Haitian culture in the realm of symbol and metaphor. The meaning of the *zonbi* centers around one person imposing his or her will onto another and forcing them to perform work. Thus the *zonbi* have become an allegory for the condition of slavery and servitude that has characterized the history and present-day life of the majority of Haitians. This trope is referenced commonly in conversations and jokes on the streets as well as in literature by Haitian intellectuals. (McAlister 2002, 103)

The first zonbi in this description is the least known outside of Haiti, so McAlister elaborates in reference to this zonbi of the spirit: "In [Vodou] religious practice, *zonbi* is also a spiritual category with a practical dimension. *Zonbi* are spirits of the recently dead who are captured and thence owned by a 'master' and obligated to work. *Zonbi* are used to perform various sorts of work, from general protection to the improving of specific talents like drumming and dancing, or carpentry and tailoring" (McAlister 2002, 102). The zonbi in this spiritual work resembles the others in that they are technically captive, but there are distinct differences that McAlister notes, including the imperative to respectfully care for the spirits until their ceremonial release. These zonbi are moreover willing participants in spiritual work because, as practitioners of Vodou in their lifetime, they have certain obligations to their spiritual community (McAlister 2002, 109). Each of these conceptualizations of the zonbi—as spirit, as flesh, as symbol—has a place in this chapter, if only briefly.

COLONIALISM AND SLAVERY

> Born out of the experience of slavery, the sea passage from Africa to the New World, and revolution on the soil of Saint-Domingue, the zombie tells the story of colonization.
>
> —Colin Dayan, *Haiti, History, and the Gods* (1995)

In what is now known as the Americas, the figure of the zonbi is first and foremost a referent to the history of racial capitalism (Robinson 1983, Melamed 2011), particularly the intertwined institutions of colonialism and slavery or what Karl Marx referred to as so-called primitive accumulation. While genealogies of the zonbi begin with enslavement of Indigenous peoples of Africa, the history of slavery in the Americas precedes the Middle Passage. This history begins with the European-perpetrated genocide of Indigenous peoples in the Western Hemisphere that rarely appears in accounts of the zonbi. The transatlantic slave trade, after all, was initiated by Christopher Columbus who "discovered" the island homes of Taíno nations that included Ayiti, "the land of high mountains," on his first voyage of theft and conquest in 1492. He dubbed this land Isla Española—present-day Haiti and the Dominican Republic, now Hispaniola—the northern coast of which was featured in his first sketch of the "New World." Columbus's journal and letters reveal his intent to subdue any "natives" on behalf of the Spanish Crown, and in a message to a patron he promised that "their Highnesses may see that I shall give them as much gold as they need . . . and slaves, as many as they shall order to be shipped." Pope Alexander VI provided Columbus, as governor of these new territories, the dispensation to carry out this task in 1493 with his issuance of *Inter caetera*, a papal bull that became the basis for dispossessing Indigenous peoples of their dominium, and eventually their freedom, based on their non-Christianity (Williams 1990, 78–88). During his subsequent voyages, he initiated the forcible extraction of the manual labor of Indigenous people—particularly for mineral processing—and transported several hundred of these enslaved "Indians" to Spain. The enslavement of non-Christians was a contested moral issue at the time, and Queen Isabella removed Columbus from his governorship for these practices inconsistent with strands of Catholic ideology that prescribed paternalistic guardianship intended to evangelize infidels and that, therefore, put the Spanish colonial enterprise at risk should later popes find them distasteful. The practices did not change in the new colonies, however, and the papal bull was reinterpreted to justify the encomienda system that perpetuated the violences of relocation and slavery of Indigenous people by granting these "rights" to the colonizers. "The *encomienda* thus embodied the ironic thesis that in administering the pope's Petrine responsibility to save the Indians, the Spanish Crown had to enslave them" (Williams 1990, 84). Hence racialized slavery became an integral part of settler colonialism—and imperial religious doctrine—in the early Americas.

As a concept, the zonbi has distinct connections to the European importation of captive Africans beginning in the early 1500s to complement, and eventually replace, an Indigenous work force on Hispaniola that was diminishing from disease, *marronage*, and overwork. In 1510 King Ferdinand authorized the use of non-Indigenous enslaved labor on the island and started to grant permits to individuals who intended to import Africans. A royal license was granted eight years later to one of the king's acquaintances to import four thousand enslaved Black people to the territories of the Spanish Empire, which laid the groundwork for one of the largest forced movements of people in history: the transatlantic slave trade. The institution of slavery flourished on Hispaniola during the sixteenth and seventeenth centuries, particularly on the eastern part of the island. The Kingdom of France eventually spread its imperial reach to the western third of the island, and Louis XIII authorized the importation of captive African people to this region in 1633. The territory was formally ceded by Spain in the 1697 Treaty of Ryswick and became colonial Saint Domingue. The institution of slavery boomed under the French colonial authority in the eighteenth century with the growth of export agriculture, particularly sugar production. Because of the brutally compelled labor of Black people shipped to the New World, Saint Domingue came to produce greater wealth than any other colony in the Western Hemisphere.

Zonbi play an important role in the mythology of the transatlantic slave trade that brought nearly 700,000 West Africans to Saint Domingue throughout the 1700s. In the historical *Dahomey, An Ancient West African Kingdom*, based on fieldwork by U.S. anthropologist Melville Jean Herskovits and his wife, Frances Herskovits, in the natal homeland of captive Africans shipped to Saint Domingue, a zonbi is described as a being "whose death was not real but resulted from the machinations of sorcerers who made them appear as dead, and then, when buried, removed them from their grave and sold them into servitude in some far-away land" (Herskovits and Herskovits 1938, 243). A contemporary version of this story appears in the title chapter of African American studies scholar Saidiya Hartman's *Lose Your Mother: A Journey along the Atlantic Slave Route* about her pilgrimage to Ghana as a descendent of enslaved people.

> In every slave society, slave owners attempted to eradicate the slave's memory, that is, to erase all evidence of an existence before slavery. This was [as] true in Africa as it was in the Americas. A slave without a past had no life to avenge. No time was wasted yearning for home, no recollections of a distant country slowed her down as she tilled the soil, no image of her mother came to mind when she looked at the face of her child. The pain of all she lost did not rattle in her chest and make it feel tight. The absentminded posed no menace. Yet more than guns, shackles, and whips were required to obliterate the past. Lordship and bondage required sorcery too. Everyone told me a different story about how the slaves began to forget their past. Words like "zombie,"

"sorcerer," "witch," "succubus," and "vampire" were whispered to explain it. In these stories, which circulated throughout West Africa, the particulars varied, but all of them ended the same—the slave loses mother. Never did the captive choose to forget; she was always tricked or bewitched or coerced into forgetting. Amnesia, like an accident or a stroke of bad fortune, was never an act of volition. (Hartman 2008a, 155)

For the ancestors of those who were not forcibly transported across the Atlantic Ocean, the supernatural held the explanatory power for how other people's ancestors from their homelands in West Africa were rendered saleable objects—a magical entity forcibly stripped them of their consciousness, and therefore humanness, and turned them into "strangers," "walking corpses," and the "living dead" (Hartman 2008a, 157). How else to understand such a great betrayal? It is possible that the word *zonbi* came into use to describe the slave trade as it developed in this region with the expansion of European conquest in the Americas, or even in previous eras of the African slave trade.

In a sense, the zonbi was smuggled with/as human cargo through the Middle Passage into the Americas. People who survived the long and merciless passage in the cramped and filthy holds of slave ships bound for Saint Domingue—ships with beautiful names like *Etoile* (star), *Thérèse*, and even the godly *Saint Hilaire* that belied the abject horrors within—carried with them their cultural knowledges, spiritual practices, and languages that described everything from loving same-sex intimacies (Wekker 2006, Tinsley 2008) to forms of human monstrosity. By most accounts, the etymology of the Kreyòl word *zonbi* is West African. Although there are debates as to which nation or kingdom the word comes from, *zonbi* might be connected to the Ki-Kongo *zumbi* (fetish) or *nzambi* (god or spirit of the dead) (McAlister 2014, 415; Davis 1988, 57).

However, *zonbi* reflects an amalgam of cultural influences unique to Haiti, like the syncretic religion of Vodou and the language of Kreyòl, and relates to the embodied experience of enslavement in the New World. The French-educated ethnologist Alfred Métraux asserted that the Haitian figure of the zonbi "is seen in terms which echo the harsh existence of a slave in the old colony of Santo Domingo" (1959, 282). The majority of enslaved persons labored on sugar cane plantations, as Saint Domingue produced more than three-fourths of the world's refined sugar. The sugar plantation, a complex social system that anthropologist Sidney Mintz referred to as "a synthesis of field and factory quite unlike anything known in mainland Europe of the time," is one of the best examples of the colonial system produced by modern capitalism (1985, 47). Tasks on the plantation were as physically demanding as they were dangerous, and work consumed people in Saint Domingue. As historian Laurent Dubois documents, "Slaves died in stunning numbers in the colony; each year between 5 and 10 percent of the slave population [estimated to be between half a million and 700,000 in 1790] succumbed to overwork and disease. Death outpaced births, and only a constant stream of imports sustained the laboring population" (2012, 21).

Yet there were fates worse than death, and enslavement has been qualified as a kind of living death. In his influential book *Slavery and Social Death: A Comparative Study* (1982), sociologist Orlando Patterson describes slavery as "one of the most extreme forms of the relationships of domination, approaching the limits of total power from the viewpoint of the master, and of total powerlessness from the slave" (1). Patterson describes the slave in places like Saint Domingue as "marginal, neither human nor inhuman, neither man nor beast, neither dead nor alive, the enemy within who was neither member nor true alien" (48). The Édit du Roi, Touchant la Police des îles de l'Amérique Française (Royal Edict: The Touch of Police in the Islands of French America), known popularly as the Code Noir, provided a juridical framework for slavery in the French colonial empire, prescribing social death for slaves through complete deference to their masters and legally dictating constraints on intimacy and kinship among slaves, between slaves and free Blacks, and between slaves and white colonists. The Code Noir outlined punishments for offenses committed by slaves against these dictates, although individual colonialists determined their own punishments as well as relationships for the slaves in their charge. Greatly outnumbered by slaves in Saint Domingue, the white colonialists sought to maintain control by generating a climate of terror—including spectacles of punishment reserved for daring resistors—and a regime of domination intended to strip slaves of any remnants of personhood. The slave's existence marked losses greater than lack of legal recognition of personhood—loss of homeland, loss of family, loss of hope for return or a different future, and loss of humanity. This is why the zonbi, a living dead being who labors without consciousness or soul and who seemingly cannot experience natal alienation, is what theologian Laënnec Hurbon called "the perfect realization of the slave condition, the very ideal sought by the master in his slave" (1995a, 192).

THE HAITIAN REVOLUTION (1791–1804)

However, the master's power over the slave—as with the zonbi—is never absolute. Enslaved people from nations of what is now the continent of Africa engaged in coordinated resistance against European colonizers on the island of Hispaniola for as long as they had been forcibly transported to labor there and until their bodies gave out. Slaves mobilized through *grand marronage*—illegally evacuating themselves from plantation life at risk of recapture and torture. The original Black inhabitants of the western third of the island were maroons who sought refuge in the mountainous region that did not lend itself to the creation of plantations. By the eighteenth century, maroon settlements in the mountains included generations of people who had never been enslaved. Newly escaped maroons could thus connect with extensive social networks that enabled nonenslaved Black people to live on the outskirts of plantations and in the swelling towns and cities of Saint Domingue. The networks forged by maroons included enslaved people who would travel between plantations for business. These fugitive settlements and extended networks wreaked havoc on plantations through raids and played a pivotal role in the demise of French colonialism on the island.

A legendary maroon who assumed great stature for his resistance is François Makandal, born in Guinea (Africa) and known as a skilled herbalist. Makandal infamously used poisons and instructed others in his craft to terrorize the white colonizers who had inflicted violence at an unprecedented scale. Colonial authorities eventually captured him, forcing Makandal to wear the public charge of "Seducer, Profaner, and Poisoner" on a sign when they executed him (Dubois 2004, 51). While historians debate the extent that Makandal and his contemporaries orchestrated widespread resistance with poison or whether the specter of poisoning was largely imagined by white colonialists to explain sudden deaths by illness and disease and to punish captive Black people and maroons (Weaver 2006, Mobley 2015), Makandal's legacy undoubtedly looms large and inspired those with the mission "to rid the colony of its white inhabitants and to create an African kingdom in Saint Domingue" (Bellegarde-Smith 2006, 101–2). Some believed that Makandal's power enabled him to survive the execution to fulfill this mission (Bellegarde 1953, 59, quoted in Bellegarde-Smith 2006, 102), but, at the very least, those inspired by this mission carried forward his legacy with talismans bearing his name pressed against their bodies for strength and protection.[4] In this way, and like the zonbi in Vodou ritual practices, Makandal's invincible spirit worked on behalf of his people and reminded the white colonizers of the ever-present threat of death and insurrection. Yet, as historian Michel-Rolph Trouillot famously points out, the mass mobilization of captive and free Africans and their descendants against French colonialism was "unthinkable even as it happened" (1995, 73).

The revolution has since become the most chronicled period in Haitian history, with detailed debates that nevertheless acknowledge the world-changing import of what transpired. One event popularly presented to me as the one that initiated the revolution, a Vodou ceremony at Bwa Kayiman (officially Bois Caïman), is minimized or entirely omitted from many historical accounts because of how white Euro–U.S. Americans have weaponized "voodoo" against Haiti—which has continued into the twenty-first century as I detail in chapter 2—along with other historiographic reasons explained by Kate Ramsey in *The Spirits and the Law: Vodou and Power in Haiti* (2011, 42–44). In the spirit of rehearsing Haitian popular history that centers Black/ African world-making, queerly approaching the revolution to unravel imperialist ideology, and therefore delving into the tension between voodoo and Vodou, I offer a version of the story of Bwa Kayiman.

The Bwa Kayiman ceremony took place in northern Saint Domingue, reputedly near the plantation Makandal had escaped. In mid-August 1791, a week before the armed revolt set off subsequent events that led to the undoing of French colonialism on the island of Hispaniola, Dutty Boukman (a slave of African descent born in Jamaica) and Cécile Fatiman (often unnamed and believed to be a slave of African and Corsican descent) convened a ceremony with maroons and enslaved people that enabled coordinated resistance across plantations to fulfill Makandal's sacred mission. Fatiman offered a black pig to the *lwa* (spirits) while Boukman enjoined everyone in a pledge for Black liberation in the new world. Black feminist scholar Omise'eke Natasha Tinsley offers a queer provocation to dominant historical interpretations of Bwa Kayiman by foregrounding the *lwa* Ezili Dantò—the Black mother of Haiti, alternately referred to as a lesbian or a woman-loving-woman (see chapter 2)—at the heart of the ceremony: "What remains consistent in the stories of Bwa Kayiman is that the most important presence that night was not human at all. Rather, the Haitian Revolution began with the arrival of a fierce, dagger wielding Ezili Dantò, who (through the medium of the *manbo*) killed a black pig, distributed its blood to participants. . . . What would it mean . . . if we took seriously that the Haitian Revolution was launched not by a man or even a woman, but by *the spirit of women who love women*?" (Tinsley 2018, 11). Profound and consequential, the question will take time to answer in a substantial way. But the provocation highlights in its own way that, as has been argued by same-sex-desiring and gender-creative Haitians (not to mention the Combahee River Collective and the Black Lives Matter movement), Black freedom requires the freedom and leadership of Black queer people. Centering Black female/women's/feminine power also provides an important corrective to the *hi*story of big men in the Haitian Revolution—Toussaint Louverture, Jean-Jacques Dessalines, Alexandre Pétion, Henri Christophe, and so on—who ultimately upheld colonial patriarchal institutions.

While I do not retell their stories here, in the interest of fleshing out the symbolism of the zonbi, I relate the story of a man who battled for freedom alongside Dessalines—Jean Zonbi. Jean Zonbi participated in the defeat of Napoleon's military forces, and after Dessalines declared an independent Republic of Haiti on January 1, 1804, he brutally attempted to rid the newly formed republic of remaining white colonialists. In *Haiti, History, and the Gods*, Colin Dayan explains how Vodou incorporated revolutionary heroes—Jean Zonbi as well as many others—into its spirit pantheon: "The name zombi, once attached to the body of Jean, who killed off whites and avenged the formerly enslaved, revealed the effects of the new dispensation. Names, gods, and heroes from an oppressive colonial past remained in order to infuse ordinary citizens and devotees with a stubborn sense of independence and survival. The undead zombi, recalled in the name of Jean Zombi, thus became a terrible composite power: slave turned rebel ancestor turned *lwa*, an incongruous, demonic spirit recognized through dreams, divination, or possession" (1995, 37). Thus, one who donned the name of the living dead as a political act to conduct acts of insurgency, much like what happened with Makandal, was resurrected in Haitian religion.

Haiti was the second republic in the Western Hemisphere after the United States and remains the only nation-state to emerge from slave rebellion. Anthropologist Ira P. Lowenthal comments that the accomplishment of the Haitian Revolution cannot be adequately conveyed in these terms or even by recognizing it as the first Black republic. "Haiti was the first *free* nation of *free* men to arise within, and in resistance to, the emerging constellation of Western European empire. . . . The Revolution stands as the most serious challenge ever made to the once-inexorable expansion of a slave based plantation system [in the Americas]" (1976, 657). The importance of Haitian Vodou (inaugurated at Bwa Kayiman) ontologies and epistemologies to the success of the Haitian Revolution—to the promise of Black freedom and the development of a counter-plantation system (Casimir 2020)—cannot be overstated.

THE BLACK REPUBLIC

> There is no subject of which it is more difficult to treat than Vaudoux worship and the cannibalism that too often accompanies its rites. Few living out of the Black Republic are aware of the extent to which it is carried out, and if I insist at length upon the subject, it is in order to endeavor to fix attention on this frightful blot, and thus induce enlightened Haytians to take measures for its extirpation, if that be possible.
>
> —Sir Spenser St. John, *Hayti: Or, The Black Republic* (1884)

Immorality is so universal that it almost ceases to be a fault, for a fault implies
an exception, and in Hayti it is the rule. Young people make an experiment of
one another before they will enter into closer connection. So far they are no
worse than in our own English islands, where the custom is equally general;
but behind the immorality, behind the religiosity, there lies active and alive the
horrible revival of the West African superstitions; the serpent worship, and the
child sacrifice, and the cannibalism. There is no room to doubt it.

—James Anthony Froude, *The English in the West Indies:*
  Or, The Bow of Ulysses (1888)

My subject is Haiti, the Black Republic; the only self-made Black Republic in
the world. I am to speak to you of her character, her history, her importance
and her struggle from slavery to freedom and to statehood. . . . They tell us that
Haiti is already doomed—that she is on the down-grade to barbarism; and,
worse still, they affirm that when the negro is left to himself there or elsewhere,
he inevitably gravitates to barbarism. Alas, for poor Haiti! and alas, for the
poor negro everywhere, if this shall prove true! The argument as stated against
Haiti, is, that since her freedom, she has become lazy; that she is given to gross
idolatry, and that these evils are on the increase. That voodooism, fetishism,
serpent worship and cannibalism are prevalent there; that little children are
fatted for slaughter and offered as sacrifices to their voodoo deities; that large
boys and girls run naked through the streets of the towns and cities, and that
things are generally going from bad to worse.

—Frederick Douglass, "Lecture on Haiti" at the Chicago World's Fair (1893)

For Europe and the United States, the Black republic that emerged from the
revolution of enslaved Black people against their white colonizers was an
aberration—a "frightful blot" of Blackness in a world where divinity, mas-
tery, sovereignty, and reason supposedly were the sole domain of whiteness.
Scholars have documented how the threatening specter of Haiti was contained in various ways through lack of international recognition as a nation-
state, imposition of crushing debt to France as payment for freedom, and
suppression of the spread of radical antislavery at every turn (Dubois 2012,
Farmer 1994, Fatton 2014, Fischer 2004, Trouillot 1995).[5] Here the focus is on
another way the Black republic, an experiment of Black radical politics at an
unprecedented scale, was undermined through the transnational discourse
of Haiti as the premodern land of voodoo/vaudoux.

Within Haiti, as Kate Ramsey argues (2011), state leaders have repressed
the Vodou religion and criminalized its practitioners who *sèvi lwa* (serve
the spirits) in order to project a civilized and sufficiently modern nation in
response to racist representations of "voodoo." These discourses have also
been used to justify continued white, European imperialist domination elsewhere, as indicated in the first two epigraphs to this section. Sir Spenser St.
John, a diplomat for the British Empire in Haiti, made a case for European

colonialism by "exposing" Haiti's barbarism and detailing how the country degenerated following its independence from French colonial authority. He drew on Médéric Louis Moreau de Saint-Méry's prerevolutionary account of "fetishism" in *Description topographique, physique, civile, politique et historique de la partie française de l'isle Saint-Domingue* (1789) to state that he is "struck by how little change [in vaudoux practices], except for the worse, has taken place in the last century" (St. John 1884, 192). In his white imperialist representation, this change for the worse is one from "quaint customs and fetishism" to zombies, cannibalism, and child sacrifice—for which he provides sensationalist "evidence." Of zombies by that name, he wrote: "they [Haitians] have much superstition with regard to zombis, revenants, or ghosts, and many will not leave the house after dark; yet the love of pleasure often overcomes this, and the negro will pass half the night hieing to his lusting-place" (160). In this excerpt, the reference to the "superstitions" regarding the undead seem less troubling than the representations of Black, or "negro" (a term that St. John explains that he knows is offensive to Haitians, then uses it anyway), hypersexuality. However, *Hayti: Or, The Black Republic* includes other "real" accounts of Haitians' unnatural relationship to the dead, including one about an "unburied" woman who is seemingly reinvigorated only to be killed again and her lungs and heart cooked and eaten (219). St. John additionally relays the story of a Catholic priest who infiltrated a vaudoux ceremony but failed to save a child whose boiled bones were left on site (193–94). Sir Spenser St. John wrote about several high-profile cases of cannibalism that involved child sacrifice beyond this one. His argument—that the pervasiveness of such lurid, murderous practices that are not addressed by the police can only be attributed to the lack of white, imperialist oversight—was taken up by others, including scholar and popular author James Anthony Froude, who uses such evidence to distinguish between Haiti and supposedly civilized British colonies in the West Indies at the time, such as Jamaica.

In the United States after the Civil War, such discourses about Haiti were wielded in debates about "race relations"—particularly racist representations of Black laziness, idolatry, and capacities for violence that needed to be managed or contained. Frederick Douglass, who had been the Minister Resident and Consul General to Haiti from 1889 to 1891, knew the great stakes attached to the Black republic's reputation for Black and white people alike. In his 1893 "Lecture on Haiti," Douglass defends Haiti against accusations of widespread child sacrifice and offers an alternate representation, one of a nation-state with tremendous promise but struggling because of colonial legacies and the necessity of contending with European imperialist powers.

He chides those in the United States for such absurd accusations and reflects on the general antagonism, or as he says "coolness" toward the Republic of Haiti that permeates white U.S. culture. "Haiti is black, and we have not yet forgiven Haiti for being black, or forgiven the Almighty for making her black. In this enlightened act of repentance and forgiveness, our boasted civilization is far behind all other nations" (Douglass 1893).

Elsewhere in his speech, Douglass unknowingly foreshadows the U.S. recolonization of Haiti two decades later. He tells the audience that, with his help, President Benjamin Harrison had "asked" the Republic of Haiti for the use of Môle-Saint-Nicolas on the northern coast, a strategic site for a potential military outpost that would become all the more important for maritime commercial trading after the construction of the Panama Canal.[6] Douglass continues: "The attempt to create angry feeling in the United States against Haiti because she thought proper to refuse us the Môle-Saint-Nicolas, is neither reasonable nor creditable. There was no insult or broken faith in the case. Haiti has the same right to refuse that we had to ask, and there was insult neither in the asking nor in the refusal" (1893). He reveals connections between U.S. expansionist aspirations and the circulation of "voodoo/vaudoux" discourses that generate white anger, as an affective response to the willfulness of such a refusal. This anger is underwritten by a sense of entitlement to steal land from the Black republic, whose dark leaders cannot escape barbarism. Douglass declares that any foreign attempt to forcibly make claims on Haitian land would be met with "revolution and bloodshed," which proved true when the U.S. Marine Corps landed on Haiti's shores in 1915. It should come as no surprise that the resulting nineteen-year U.S. occupation of Haiti (1915–34) was justified by the prevalence of "voodoo."

There are also queer dimensions to the transnational discourse that rendered Haiti perverse. Even before there were implicit or explicit connections between Afro-syncretic religious practices and homosexuality, which coincides with the U.S. occupation, the stories about voodoo/vaudoux had qualities that mirror Euro-U.S. treatments of same-sex sexuality. This includes an obsession with the secrecy surrounding Vodou. The occurrence of Vodou ceremonies at night and out of the public eye, for instance, cast suspicion on the events that unfolded to the rhythmic drums that were audible at long distances. Something terrible must be transgressing, or why not have these rituals out in the open? These kinds of logics ignored the repressive context of slavery and colonization under which the religion had been forged, as well as the outlawing of *les sortilèges* (spells) in the postcolonial period that contributed to its clandestine practice.[7] The attempts to wrest voodoo/vaudoux "out of the closet" so to speak—the purpose of the "*Vaudoux* Worship and

Cannibalism" chapter in St. John's *Hayti: Or, The Black Republic* (1884)—further contributed to its demonization.

Other queer qualities can be ascertained in the themes of the maelstrom resulting from the publication of Sir Spenser St. John's "true account" of child sacrifice and cannibalism: hypersexuality, self-consumption, and child endangerment. There are hints of the first in James Anthony Froude's comments about immorality in Haiti and among Black colonial subjects in the British West Indies whose "young people make an experiment of one another before they will enter into closer connection" (1888, 303). In his estimation, the proclivity to engage in unsanctioned sexual relations—anything outside the confines of monogamous, heterosexual marriage—is a sign of weak moral character in the so-called darker races. These imperialists were citing older European discourses of Blackness focused on the primitive Black body and Black sexuality, such as those surrounding the infamous case of Sara (alternately spelled Sarah) Baartman, or "the Hottentot Venus" who was born in the 1770s in what is now South Africa. As feminist Patricia Hill Collins recounts in "The Sexual Politics of Black Womanhood" (1991), Baartman was trafficked to Europe to be commodified as a pornographic object and freak of nature. White Europeans were fascinated by her anatomy, particularly the size of her buttocks and genitals, which were scientifically translated as empirical proof of Black people's sexual baseness and closeness to animals/nature.[8] These discourses would later be used to produce postcoloniality in different ecological terms, as not *closer to* but *farther from* nature.

Self-consumption plays out in the tales of cannibalism in voodoo/vaudoux. There are erotic undertones to cannibalism—mouths ingesting human blood and flesh are not unlike the various forms of "ingestion" during sex acts. But what kinds of sex might cannibalism reference? Certainly not the prescribed missionary position of active male bodies dominating passive female ones, whose phallocentric circuits of sexuality route away from the mouth, vagina, and anus as sources of pleasure. Cannibalism is rather a reference to queer sex, that is sex for enjoyment rather than reproduction. Consumption, after all, implies using up or wasting rather than propagating. Oral sex, anal sex, and masturbation have no use value in the Christian economies of reproduction. The "self-" in self-consumption therefore slides between the meanings of species, sex, and one's own body (autoeroticism). As sociologist Mimi Sheller contends in *Consuming the Caribbean: From Arawaks to Zombies* (2003), the fascination with cannibalism and self-consumption in the Caribbean has been a strategy to mark the region's dangerous and exotic Otherness and shift attention away from violent consumption of natural resources, bodies, and histories of the Caribbean under racial capitalism.

Another prominent feature of the transnational discourse of Haiti as the premodern land of voodoo/vaudoux at this time was child sacrifice. With humans already on the sacrificial altar, why focus on children specifically? Why is this act more egregious than, say, murdering and eating an adult? As queer scholars have pointed out, "the child" is a symbol of innocence and futurity (e.g., Berlant 1997, Edelman 2004, Rubin 1984). Moral panics have been spun out with "save the children" as their goal, and homosexuals—who are assumed to be nonreproductive as well as predatory—as their target. In the instance of child sacrifice, however, the threat to children is of both a moral and mortal nature. White interest in supposed "mortal danger" to Black children is reminiscent of a case in the United States that took place a few decades before the publication of *Hayti: Or, The Black Republic*: Margaret Garner killed her child rather than condemn her to a life of slavery.[9] Those in support of slavery fixated on Garner's presumed lack of natural maternal instinct and, therefore, her lack of humanity. Abolitionists, meanwhile, used the case to condemn the brutality of the institution of slavery that would make a mother commit such an unnatural act. In the cases of child sacrifice from Sir Spenser St. John's account, Black women figure centrally: they coordinate kidnappings, approve murders, and cook children to eat at the voodoo/vaudoux ceremonies. The mother of one consumed child is suspected of being an accomplice. There is nothing redemptive about their stories, in contrast to the Margaret Garner case. Imperialist representations of the cold and callous women of the voodoo/vaudoux cult who lack maternal instinct are testament to the monstrosity of a place too far from the natural order of things. Thus, intervening in African "superstitious" practices became the perfect basis for a U.S. civilizing mission in the twentieth century.

THE FIRST U.S. OCCUPATION (1915–1934)

The phantasm of the zombi—a soulless husk deprived of freedom—is the ultimate sign of loss and dispossession. In Haiti, memories of servitude are transposed into a new idiom that both reproduces and dismantles a twentieth-century history of forced labor and denigration that became particularly acute during the American occupation of Haiti. As Haitians were forced to build roads, and thousands of peasants were brutalized and massacred, tales of zombies proliferated in the United States. [These representations] . . . helped to justify the "civilizing" presence of the marines in "barbaric" Haiti.

—Colin Dayan, *Haiti, History, and the Gods* (1995)

Here we see a strange currency in zombies, as they shift from a dread memory of slavery into a new idiom of forced labor, and then from a ghoulish monster in Hollywood movies they slip back into Haitian understandings of the U.S. occupation. Thus occupation and the American cultural consumption of the uprooted figure of the zombie serve to reinforce its power, as it is re-grounded in contemporary Haitian culture.

—Mimi Sheller, *Consuming the Caribbean: From Arawaks to Zombies* (2003)

Little more than a century after gaining independence, Haiti came under foreign control by an emerging empire that cast its imperialist ambitions in terms of paternalistic obligation, what historian Mary A. Renda describes as a "willingness to shoulder the white man's burden" (2001, 92). In 1898, from the Spanish-American War, the United States of America had acquired colonial territories (Cuba, Puerto Rico, Guam, and the Philippines), and Haiti and the neighboring Dominican Republic became places ripe for U.S. expansionism to protect ongoing capitalist interests. The formal occupation period began on July 28, 1915, when 330 Marines landed in Port-au-Prince on the orders of President Woodrow Wilson, and did not end until August 15, 1934.

For Haitians, the zonbi's signification of forced labor—particularly of the kind extracted by white masters out of brown and Black bodies—is a referent to this U.S. occupation as well as older European colonial histories. Along with assuming control of the Haitian state through a new constitution, which among other things eliminated the clause forbidding foreign ownership of land in Haiti, and waging war on the *Cacos* who organized resistance to the occupation—with the Haitian death toll number upward of eleven thousand—the United States put the reconstituted Haitian military to task instituting a *corvée* (statute labor system) between 1916 and 1918. During the official years of the corvée, the Haitian underclasses—particularly peasants—were compelled to build or repave over five hundred miles of roads. The system continued unofficially for several more years by other means, such as swelling prisons for new sources of labor.

Haitians, foreign missionaries, and—especially in the later years of the occupation—U.S. activists in solidarity movements posited the connections between colonial-era slave regimes and U.S.-instituted corvée. One who decried the violences of corvée is Lewis Ton Evans, a Baptist missionary born in Wales but naturalized in the United States. Initially, Evans had been a strong proponent of the U.S. occupation, hoping that it would aid efforts to evangelize the population. He had even written to Presidents Theodore Roosevelt and William Howard Taft appealing for U.S. involvement in Haiti (Olsen 1993, 25–28). He praised President Woodrow Wilson for finally acting and called the occupation a "godsend," although Evans quickly changed his position once he witnessed the situation firsthand. Another letter was crafted, this time to inform President Wilson of the brutalities committed by the Gendarmerie d'Haïti (Haitian military) on U.S. authority—capturing "innocent men and women, by armed gendarmes, and the roping of them together and 'marching [them] as African slave gangs to prison'" as well as the deplorable conditions of those forced to work on the roads who sometimes received no notice that they had been "contracted" (Olsen 1993, 31). Evans testified to these atrocities, which blurred distinctions between compelled "free" labor and slave labor in the context of an ongoing white occupation, at the U.S. Senate Inquiry into the Occupation and Administration of Haiti and Santo Domingo in 1921.

A decade before Langston Hughes published "White Shadows in a Black Land" (1932), an impassioned article in the *Crisis* about the injustices of U.S. imperialism based on his travels to Haiti, another African American activist and artist working for the NAACP named James Weldon Johnson made a case against the occupation in a series of articles in 1920 in the *Nation*, later published together as *Self-Determining Haiti*. Prior to working for the NAACP, Johnson had been a U.S. consul in Venezuela and then Nicaragua, facilitating U.S. military and diplomatic interests in those places. This personal history led to Johnson "urg[ing] black Americans not to jump to the conclusion that U.S. intervention in Haiti represented merely another instance of white racism, pointing instead to the clear problems of political instability" (Renda 2001, 188). Even though his contemporaries at NAACP and other Black institutions understood the occupation as the exertion of white domination in the republic that symbolized Black freedom and conjectured about its long-term implications, Johnson was slow to embrace their perspective. He ultimately arranged a two-month investigative trip to Haiti, which became the basis for the articles.

In them, Johnson denounced the public face of the occupation, troubling the portrayal that U.S. military presence in Haiti was there for the protection and political security of Haitians rather than in the interest of U.S. capital. His second installation describes the corvée as an example of the Marines' "treat 'em rough methods" during the first five years of the occupation:

> The *corvée*, or road law, in Haiti provided that each citizen should work a certain number of days on the public roads to keep them in condition, or pay a certain sum of money. In the days when this law was in force the Haitian government never required the men to work the roads except in their respective communities, and the number of days was usually limited to three a year. But the Occupation seized men wherever it could find them, and no able-bodied Haitian was safe from such raids, which most closely resembled the African slave raids of past centuries. And slavery it was—though temporary.

By day or by night, from the bosom of their families, from their little farms or while trudging peacefully on the country roads, Haitians were seized and forcibly taken to toil for months in far sections of the country. Those who protested or resisted were beaten into submission. At night, after long hours of unremitting labor under armed taskmasters, who swiftly discouraged any slackening of effort with boot or rifle butt, the victims were herded in compounds. Those attempting to escape were shot. Their terror-stricken families meanwhile were often in total ignorance of the fate of their husbands, fathers, brothers. (James Weldon Johnson 1920, 13–14)

In Renda's reading, "likening the occupation to slavery specifically in its destruction of the Black family, Johnson undermined U.S. claims to [benevolent] paternalism. Whereas pro-occupation writers figured Haiti as an orphan in need of a foster father, Johnson wrote, in contrast, 'if the United States should leave Haiti today, it would leave more than a thousand widows and orphans of its own making'" (Renda 2001, 193). He had likewise revealed to popular audiences that the U.S. "gift" of infrastructure for the "uncivilized" Haitians had been built by Haitians themselves and was fulfilled under conditions of terror similar to colonial slavery.

Although Haitian and U.S. anti-imperialist activists brought the question of Haiti into the limelight during the 1920 U.S. presidential election, it was not enough to end the occupation. With its justification of paternalism going down the tubes, U.S. imperialism in Haiti needed a public relations makeover. This was found in the spectacle of "voodoo" and the corresponding fantasy version of the "zombie," which became fixtures of occupation accounts of Haiti distributed to the U.S. public. As Haiti historian Kate Ramsey argues, "the practice of 'voudauxism' (or, increasingly, 'voodooism' or 'voodoo') is officially invoked [in the 1921 Senate Hearings about the occupation] to serve as a kind of ultimate symptom of Haitian 'disorder,' in need of American military 'cleaning up'" (2011, 130). She records that General Eli Cole's testimony about the reason for the invasion, for instance, was the issue that "Voudauxism was rampant" (130). Religious practices were suspect—associated with unsanitary, dangerous, and unearthly practices as well as the power of peasants—and Haitians who did not enforce the prohibitions against Vodou were also accused of its perpetuation and therefore the denigration of Haiti. The Marines could supposedly solve problems of enforcement and "uplift" Haiti despite the deep-rooted cultural and political deficits they posited were natural to Haitians. This position was supported by people such as J. Dryden Kuser, who published *Haiti: Its Dawn of Progress After Years in a Night of Revolution* (1921) with fantastical representations of *vaudoux* and claims that U.S.

Americans would do no wrong in Haiti, despite a preponderance of evidence to the contrary.

Associated with "voodoo"—portrayed as a demonic snake-worshipping, animal-sacrificing cult—was the zombie. As Renda documents, beginning "in the 1930s, myriad cultural forms (e.g., novels, short stories, memoirs, travel narratives, plays, and films) made use of the belief that, in Haiti, the dead could be made to rise in their soulless bodies and would then be subordinated to the will of a master. These images could be threatening: monstrous, once-dead black men rising up, embodying the white fears of black revolt at home as well as abroad" (2001, 255). These representations strengthened the association of Black Haiti with superstition and—without the more civilized influence of the United States—unbridled consumption. "If the figure of the cannibal represents European anxieties around the boundaries of consumption, then the Haitian 'zombie'—a 'living-dead' slave deprived of will and physically controlled by a sorcerer—is the ultimate representation of the psychic state of one whose body/spirit is consumed" (Sheller 2003, 145).

The figure of the zombie was introduced to popular audiences in the United States in William Seabrook's *Magic Island* (1929), which publicity materials touted as recounting the "adventures and emotional experiences of an American author in Haiti." The sensationalized travelogue includes reports about Seabrook's encounter with zombies and folkloric tales of the mythic figure represented as fact. In *Haiti and the United States: National Stereotypes and the Literary Imagination* (1997), literary scholar J. Michael Dash treats Seabrook's white fantasy of Haiti as nearly a different genre of U.S. occupation writing. While undoubtedly still part of the "colonial impulse" of revealing a true-to-nature exotic Black Haiti to U.S. audiences, Dash maintains that the "negrophile" representations in *Magic Island* differ from outright defenses of the occupation. "Unctuous racial arrogance has been replaced by an imaginative plundering of Haiti for the fatigued West—essentially an intellectual '*nostalgie de la boue*'" (Dash 1988, 25). The fantasy world of Black Haiti in the text is accompanied by highly stylized, racist illustrations by Alexander King. These illustrations amplified the perversity of voodoo and Haiti. King's illustrations of zombies and a "girl" who was transmogrified into a goat for sacrifice, depicting a ceremony similar to the ones described above, appear in figures 2 and 3. Seabrook described the event as "weird, unnatural, and unhuman" (1929, 66).

Magic Island's success spawned a whole zombie genre, including the Victor Halperin monster film, *White Zombie* (1932), which introduced a fictionalized Haiti to Hollywood. The film opens with a young, white heterosexual couple from the United States traveling by horse-drawn coach into the Haitian

"... and as she sang, she was
a daughter doomed to die."

Figure 2. "Girl," in William
Seabrook's *Magic Island*, 1929.
(Art by Alexander King)

"No one dared to stop them, for they
were corpses walking in the sunlight."

Figure 3. "Zombies," in William Seabrook's
Magic Island, 1929. (Art by Alexander King)

countryside to their wedding. Their destination is the mansion of a white man who has fallen in love with the woman and intends to thwart her marriage, a task that he accomplishes with the assistance of a heavily accented and racially ambiguous evil sorcerer (played by Bela Lugosi) who turns her—like so many others on his sugar plantation—into a zombie. The sorcerer uses a fatal poison and doll-like effigy in his magical work that creates an unfeeling shell of a person at the command of his or her master.

White Zombie associates "voodoo" and "zombie magic" with same-sex desire and, moreover, threats to white heterosexuality. Homoeroticism is implicit in the relationship between the evil sorcerer and the man (played by Charles Beaumont) contending for the young woman's affection, not in the expected relationship between the rivals—fiancé and interloper—as queer theorist Eve Sedgwick's model of triangulated desire would predict (1985, 21–27). The sorcerer—identified as Murder Legendre in the film credits—tries unsuccessfully to seduce Beaumont at every turn. When Murder Legendre realizes that his object of desire is lost in grief from zombifying his beloved, the sorcerer becomes obsessed with his torture and demise. In their penultimate scene together, Murder Legendre has Beaumont under his spell and takes perverse pleasure in the anticipation of his zombification and letting him into the intimate realm of his methods of sorcery. "It is unfortunate that you are no longer able to speak," he says. "I should be interested to hear you describe your symptoms. You see, you are the first man to know what is happening. None of the others did." Beaumont reaches out to touch the sorcerer's hand, who smiles at the gesture, noting Beaumont's earlier refusal to touch him. "Well, well. We understand each other better." This erotic interplay is eventually ended by a local white missionary—who has his own knowledge of "voodoo" since he is friendly with the "natives"—leading to the deaths of the sorcerer and Beaumont and, therefore, to the salvation of the newly married couple. The narrative conclusion contains the Black/Haitian threats of voodoo and same-sex desire for white/U.S. heterosexuality and futurity.

The tropes of zombies and homosexuality in connection to "voodoo" became a feature of anthropological scholarship just after the conclusion of the U.S. occupation. A mention of same-sex sexuality in Haiti can be found in Melville J. Herskovits's 1937 *Life in a Haitian Valley*, based on his and his wife's ethnographic research in the village of Mirebalais, which had been a hotbed of anti-occupation resistance. His treatment of Vodou and Haiti are sympathetic. Herskovits tried to provide new understandings about the spiritual system and the way it has been used to make Haiti seem freakish. His account has a couple of pages about male and female same-sex sexuality, which he said are respectively caused by a system of "plural matings" in Haiti and by women's "frigidity" (Herskovits 1937, 118–19). The section concludes with the assertion that "the most prevalent Haitian attitude towards homosexuality in either sex, it may be remarked, is one of derision rather than vindictiveness, as the term applied to effeminate men, *commères* [gossips], may suggest" (119).[10] Other than the heterocentric reasoning behind the occurrence of same-sex sexuality, this is a mild representation that has nothing to do with devil worship or other kinds of aberration. Herskovits spoke out against the "unjustifiable sensationalism" of U.S. representations of the zonbi, although he also noted that there is some basis for these accounts on which he bases a less sensationalist account with different details of how the zonbi functions in Haiti (248). While progressive in its time, Herskovits ended up reinscribing Haiti's weirdness in relation to same-sex sexuality, the undead, and other phenomena for foreign audiences already steeped in anti-Black ideologies.

These tropes are taken up again in African American anthropologist and writer Zora Neale Hurston's *Tell My Horse: Voodoo and Life in Haiti and Jamaica* (1938), based on her fieldwork in 1936 and 1937. She devotes a whole chapter to zombies and the practices of zombification, including photographic evidence of their existence. The dark rumors that U.S. Americans had been saturated with for a decade, she tells readers, are real. The technology of the photographs—understood for its truthful representations—combined with Hurston's well-respected anthropological training, brought the zombie out of the realm of fictionalized Haiti in *Magic Island* and *White Zombie*. As it happens, William Seabrook ended up using *Tell My Horse* to lend scholarly credibility to the events that unfold in his own book.

Hurston also links "voodoo," long associated with excesses of the Black body such as unbridled heterosexuality, with female same-sex sexuality.

> A woman known to be a Lesbian was "mounted" [or possessed by a spirit] one afternoon. The spirit announced through her mouth, "Tell my horse I have told this woman repeatedly to stop making love to women. It is a vile thing and I object to it. Tell my horse that this woman promised me twice that she would never do such a thing again, but each time she has broken her word to me as soon as she could find a woman suitable for her purpose. But she has made love to women for the last time. She has lied to Guedé [spirit of the dead] for the last time. Tell my horse to tell that woman I am going to kill her today. She will not lie again." The woman pranced and galloped like a horse to a great mango tree, climbed it far up among the top limbs and dived off and broke her neck. (Hurston 1938, 222)

Hurston does not say any more about the passage than to remark on the "peasants' belief" in the accuracy of such revelations. Neither does she mention anything else about homosexuality. Her ethnology leaves the passage open to interpretation. If taken at face value, it would seem that the vengeful spirits of voodoo reject female homosexuality. A more complex reading, one of which is offered by Mary Renda, would consider the woman's relationship to the Guedé, a jealous spirit that desires her devotion (2001, 290). In such a reading, lesbianism in and of itself would not be unfavorable to the spirit. While all of these are worth considering, I offer that this passage does something much more important by merely mentioning the *existence* of lesbianism in connection with other unnatural (spirits of the dead speaking through the living) and destructive (inflicting fatal harm) practices in "voodoo." It thus naturalized same-sex sexuality, "voodoo," and violence as coextensive in the dark world of Haiti imagined by imperialists.

As with other U.S. representations of zombies and voodoo, *Tell My Horse* justifies the white civilizing mission in Haiti. Hurston is known as a defender of the occupation, and parts of her text reads like the narratives of the white colonizers, including the U.S. Marines. The section on Haiti, for example, opens with the following: "For four hundred years the blacks of Haiti had yearned for peace. . . . Even when they had fought and driven out the white oppressors, oppression did not cease. . . . A prophet could have foretold it was to come to them from another land and another people utterly unlike the Haitian people in any respect" (Hurston 1938, 65). This justification was not as explicit as in the case of *Magic Island*, but it was present nonetheless.

These representations of the Black republic worked together to cover over the atrocities committed by the marines during their near two-decade occupation of Haiti, including the *corvée*, by portraying an exotic and unworldly Haiti where Black people lived in chaotic conditions, engaged in homosexual revelry, and enslaved each other through zombification. Thus the transnational discourse of Haiti as the premodern land of voodoo/vaudoux became one of the great tools of U.S. imperialism in Haiti.

EARLY YEARS OF THE AIDS EPIDEMIC (1980S AND 1990S)

Decades after William Seabrook and Zora Neale Hurston "penetrated" the mysteries of the Black republic and documented their exploits for U.S. audiences, another U.S. adventurer went to Haiti on a similar quest. Harvard ethnobotanist Wade Davis searched for the ingredients to the concoction that scientifically—rather than magically—produces zombification. His hypothesis was that this mixture of plant and possibly animal matter, knowledge of which the ancestors of Haiti carried with them to colonial Saint Domingue, slows someone's metabolic rate to the point that they appear dead for a time.

Davis cataloged his exploits in an academic text, *Passage of Darkness: The Ethnobiology of the Haitian Zombie* (1988), as well as in a novel for popular audiences, *The Serpent and the Rainbow* (1985). The cover of this international best-seller provides insight into its sensationalist content: "A Harvard scientist uncovers the startling truth about the secret world of Haitian voodoo and zombis." It was the basis for a Wes Craven horror film of the same title released in 1988. Both versions of *The Serpent and the Rainbow* represent Haiti as the premodern land of "voodoo and zombies" riddled with corruption and offer no account of histories of foreign intervention. The film differs from the novel only in that it shows the white protagonist being buried alive.

As cultural studies scholars point out, the rise of the zonbi's popularity again in the 1980s coincided with the first known cases of AIDS in the United States. They conjecture that the history of the zonbi and Vodou with its blood rituals made the Centers for Disease Control's racist identification of "Haitians" as a risk group early on in the epidemic seem like common sense (Dubois 1996, Farmer 2006). Sheller makes explicit the power structures that underlie connections between zombies, HIV/AIDS, and racialized sexuality:

> In linking stories of zombies and AIDS, I want to suggest that there is a close relation between fantasies of the primitive and fantasies surrounding what bell hooks refers to as the "willingness to transgress racial boundaries within the realm of the sexual" (hooks 1992, 22). Both the fear of Haitian zombies and the fear of supposedly infectious bodies from Haiti arise out of the racialized sexual encounters and sexualized racial encounters of (post)colonialism. . . . As hooks suggests, such border-crossing encounters serve to reaffirm the power of the dominant and to reconstitute the boundaries between Western self and Caribbean other. (Sheller 2003, 146–47)

In turn, this association between HIV and Haiti lent credibility to claims of the flesh-and-blood zonbi. J. Michael Dash notes that "it is perhaps not too farfetched to imagine that the image of the zombi became even more credible because of Haiti's general association with contaminated, ravaged physicality, the most visible symptom of the AIDS epidemic" (1997, 142). Noticeably lacking from these accounts is any mention of the predominant threat figured in discourses about the "wasting disease"—the male homosexual.

This is more than likely a continued reaction to the assertion by U.S. medical and scientific experts that HIV/AIDS was a "Haitian" epidemic introduced to gay men in the United States. The logic of this accusation, of course, posited a prevalence of Haitian men who would have sex with U.S. men. In his first book, *AIDS and Accusation: Haiti and the Geography of Blame* (1992), medical anthropologist and public health expert Paul Farmer recounts the social science literature that was used to back this theory. He quotes the following from "The Case for a Haitian Origin of the AIDS Epidemic" by Alexander Moore and Ronald D. Le Baron in its sensationalist account connecting Vodou, ritual animal sacrifice, and homosexuality:

> "In frenzied trance, the priest lets blood: mammal's (sic) throats are cut; typically, chicken's (sic) heads are torn off their necks. The priest bites out the chicken's tongue with his teeth and may suck on the bloody stump of the neck." These sacrificial offerings, "infected with one of the Type C oncogenic retroviruses . . . are repeatedly (sic) sacrificed in voodoo ceremonies, and their blood is directly ingested by priests and their assistants . . . many [of whom] are homosexual men" who are "certainly in a position to satisfy their sexual desires, especially in urban areas." (Farmer 1992, 3)

Farmer refutes this account following the lead of his informants, Haitians of various socioeconomic classes. He flips the script by concluding that gay sex tourists from the United States introduced HIV to Haiti and, moreover, extensively documents how structural violence perpetrated by the United States affects the transmission and course of the disease.

Paul Farmer's admirable anti-imperialist commitments enabled him to see and show how the exotification of Haiti through spectacular representations of "voodoo" and references to zombies renders Haiti "weird" (2006, 4). The same cannot be said for his sexual politics. In order to address the transmission route through the gay sex tourism industry in Haiti—which developed like other forms of North American tourism as a result of the United States' promotion of Haiti as an exotic Caribbean destination after the end of its almost two-decade occupation in 1934—the question remained: who was having sex with the tourists? The answer was "bisexual" men with girlfriends and wives—thus accounting for the high rates of "heterosexual transmission"—who had sex with U.S. men for money, not for pleasure.[11] Farmer cites a Haitian medical expert as saying, "'There are two groups of homosexuals. There are those who do it for pleasure and those who do it for economic reasons. In Haiti, we have economic homosexuals, people making love for money'" (2006, 261).

While this statement could have opened an analysis of imperialist power relations and transactional sex, instead it had the curious effect of defensively denying that male same-sex sexuality exists in Haiti outside of these coercive relationships. This takes several forms—from assertions by Haitians (and their allies) that there are no homosexuals/gay men in Haiti, only Haitian men who have sex with non-Haitian men for money, to accusations that the practice of same-sex sexuality was imported to Haiti through gay sex tourism.

It would be easy to discount these assertions as ignorant about the prevalence of same-sex desire and sexuality in various formations throughout time and space, as other Haitians (and their allies) have done. However, the persistence of this assertion by well-educated people with social influence—physicians, lawyers, and academics—is a cause for serious concern. *The discourse of the economic homosexual* is usually the first thing that non-same-sex-desiring Haitians, scholars in Haitian studies, and solidarity activists inquired about when I told them about my research.

This discourse makes sense given the imperialist relations that I have outlined throughout this chapter. U.S. representations of the Black republic produced Haiti's Otherness through racialized sexuality, including the "voodoo" promotion of same-sex sexual practices. As I mention above, in 1983 the Centers for Disease Control listed "Haitians" (an entire nationality) with "homosexuals" as one of the four risk groups for the newly discovered disease. This could have seemed plausible only because the commonsense imperialist understanding from the transnational discourse of Haiti as the premodern land of voodoo was that Haiti was always already sexually perverse. Debates about the origin of HIV/AIDS exacerbated the situation. What better way to respond to these imperialist representations than to locate male same-sex sexuality outside of Haiti? Paul Farmer and his contemporaries tried to cleave homosexuality from Vodou, and therefore from Haiti (perhaps an impossible task), and to represent it through the lens of respectability politics.

In doing so, they introduced an altered version of homophobia to Haiti in public health work. Same-sex-desiring Haitians pay the price for this defense that posits homosexuality as a threat to the Haitian national body politic. Beyond treating same-sex sexuality as a contagion, the discourse of the economic homosexual negatively impacts same-sex-desiring Haitians of the majority poor who confront the material conditions of grinding poverty and the accusation that their pockets must be lined with foreign money that they must be refusing to share. It becomes the basis for disownment, as the next chapter on religious sexual politics in Haiti details.

UNRAVELING IMPERIALIST IDEOLOGY

> When we are being told over and over again that Haiti is unique, bizarre, unnatural, odd, queer, freakish, or grotesque, we are also being told, in varying degrees, that it is unnatural, erratic, and therefore unexplainable. . . . The longer that Haiti appears weird, the easier it is to forget that it represents the longest neocolonial experiment in the history of the West.
>
> —Michel-Rolph Trouillot, "The Odd and the Ordinary: Haiti, the Caribbean, and the World" (1990b)

For whom and by whom has sexuality been defined in postcolonial Haiti? Sexuality for contemporary Haitians that I came to know during my field-work is shaped by the legacies of European colonialism and U.S. imperialism and, as I have argued, answering the question requires understanding racial capitalism as fundamental to Western modernity. The European colonial enterprise relied on racialized conceptions of the human. As Haitian an-thropologist Michel-Rolph Trouillot contends alongside other postcolonial theorists, "In creating 'the West,' the European Renaissance shaped a global geography of imagination. That geography required a 'Savage slot,' a space for the inherently Other . . . 'the West' is always a fiction, an exercise in global legitimation" (2003, 1). The peoples of Africa, Asia, and the Americas occu-pied this savage slot before "Haiti" could be imagined. To state the obvious, anti-Black racism and other European projections of itself and its others became globalized with the colonial enterprise and preexisted the transna-tional imperialist discourse that this chapter traces.

After Haitian independence, the transnational imperialist discourse of the Black republic as the premodern land of voodoo/vaudoux reproduced these earlier racist projections and added new fodder to the specifics of Eu-ropean projections of its Others based on investment in the failure of Haiti's revolutionary promise. Fetishism, cannibalism, child sacrifice, and other ritual human sacrifices were tropes of European colonialist discourses, which means that Haiti was not "weird" but impacted by a widespread geopolitical and economic project where "evidence" of these phenomena were used to justify the violences of colonialism. Yet the specific discourse of Haiti as the premodern land of voodoo/vaudoux is attached to what Trouillot calls "the longest neocolonial experiment in the history of the West" and therefore has served additional political purposes to undermine the Haitian postcolonial state: rationalize the continuation of European colonialism when radical an-tislavery, Black freedom, and an "afterward" to colonialism were new political possibilities; justify the U.S. occupation of Haiti and other interventions in the postcolonial period while obscuring their violent impact; blame Haitians for transmitting HIV/AIDS to the United States; and reify anti-Black racism.

Queer of color critique informs the telling of these histories here in a way that acknowledges that "race" and "sexuality" are inherently imbricated con-structions. Particularly important is Cathy Cohen's (1997) intervention calling to reshape queer politics through radical alliances between same-sex-desiring people and heterosexuals who are likewise "nonnormative" based on racial-ized constructions of sexuality. My analysis of the transnational imperialist discourse of Haiti as the premodern land of voodoo/vaudoux thinks broadly about racialized sexuality, including same-sex desire and sexuality while reaching beyond that narrow framing. Of note, same-sex desire and sexuality—oftentimes indicated through crossdressing—was a trope of European colonial discourses about other places and peoples, as in the example of the "berdache"; for Haiti, it emerges in representations connected to the advent of U.S. imperialism. The moment of this emergence is perhaps connected to the speciation of "the homosexual" in the late 1800s (Foucault 1978) and the congregation of same-sex-desiring men in urban centers in the United States during World War I (Chauncey 1994). "Queer" in the early twentieth-century United States referenced both these same-sex-desiring men as well as racial indeterminacy and marginalization; constructions of racial and sexual deviance were mutually constituted, as Siobhan Somerville elaborates in *Queering the Color Line: Race and the Invention of Homosexuality in American Culture* (2000). That is all to say that the "queer" figure of the homosexual had good company with other figures demonized though projections of racialized sexuality—hypersexual men and women who ate their own kind.

The transnational imperialist discourse of the Black republic as the premodern land of voodoo/vaudoux remains the dominant discourse about Haiti to this day, and tracing the history of its changes and continuities makes it possible to understand what sociologist Amar Wahab (2012) calls "homophobia as a state of reason" in the postcolonial Caribbean. Wahab proposes that the imagination of "always already emasculated" spaces in the West—in his article, Trinidad and Tobago—creates a "queer condition" under empire, against which contemporary forms of homophobia emerge (2012, 497). In the case of Haiti, U.S. representations that featured zombies and same-sex sexuality generated interest among conservative U.S. Protestant missionaries who were called to save Haitians from their dark roots and sinful devil worship. As I elaborate in the following chapters, these missionaries left an indelible mark on the contemporary religious, social, and political landscape of Haiti, including introducing a structure of religious homophobia that came into prominence during the time of my fieldwork.

2

THE MISSIONARY POSITION

U.S. Protestant Missionaries and Religious Homophobia

While one would hope that blaming problems in Haiti—or "Haiti's troubles"—on snake charmers, zombies, cannibals, and devil worship were a thing of the past, the transnational imperialist discourse of Haiti as the premodern land of voodoo/vaudoux has a vibrant life in the early twenty-first century. In recent history, the figures that populate the imagined realm of "voodoo" do not retain all their phantasmic glory, but there are continuities in its association with kidnappers, polygamists, bad mothers, and homosexuals. The previous chapter introduced this discourse related to European colonialism and U.S. imperialism in Haiti, with specific attention to racialized sexuality. This chapter layers that analysis by focusing on how the religious politics of empire have shaped the transnational imperialist discourse of Haiti as the premodern land of voodoo/vaudoux, and how the discourse—which remains the dominant one to this day—has in turn reshaped religious sexual politics and produced postcolonial homophobia in Haiti.

The European colonial projection of "the West" and "the rest," which placed Indigenous peoples of the Americas and Africa and eventually the nation of Haiti in the "savage slot" (Trouillot 2003) reserved for primitive—and therefore conquerable—Others, had inherently religious dimensions. As David Chidester contends in *Savage Systems: Colonialism and Comparative Religion in Southern Africa* (1996), the concept of *religion* or *religions* and the practice of comparative religion developed with European colonialism. Christians initially deemed the peoples they encountered as lacking religion (11–16), which signaled related absences, such as "the institution of marriage, a system of law, or any form of political organization" (14). Fetishism marked this absence of religion (13), and "when the existence of a religion could not be categorically denied . . . it could be demonized by being explained as the worship of the Devil" (12). Under French colonialism, the colony of Saint Domingue officially mandated Roman Catholicism as decreed by the Code Noir. The future of the Catholic institution was thrown into question by Haitian independence. The "unthinkable" revolution and emergence of the Black republic (Trouillot 1995) left Europeans scrambling to justify slavery and colonialism, and the association of Haiti with "voodoo/vaudoux" worked alongside other efforts to undermine the nation's independence. Despite the continued presence of the Catholic Church, the constitutional freedom of religion was interpreted as lack of proper religion in the European taxonomy of the time.

Understanding "sexuality" depends on an analysis of capitalism, racialization, and—as I show here—religion as they interconnect under empire in projects of colonialism and imperialism. Feminist scholars have documented the ways that institutional slavery and settler colonialism made Indigenous African and American—which is also to say "non-Christian" at the beginning of the European colonial enterprise—bodies sexually violable. Saidiya Hartman's "Venus in Two Acts" meditates on practices of representation in light of the "annihilating force of . . . description" in archives of white men's pleasure enacting violence against enslaved Black people (2008b, 6). This annihilating force relates as well to the pleasure of white European and then U.S. ethnographic descriptions of Black sexuality. Haitian independence coincided with a trend in European religious scholarship in the early nineteenth century, which Chidester, relying on the scholarship of anthropologist Edmund Leach, characterizes as "devoted to identifying the importance of sexuality, phallic cults, and the erotic dimensions of stone, tree, or serpent worship" (1996, 5). No wonder that descriptions of aberrant sexuality featured so heavily in the accounts of white Christian chroniclers of the Black republic—diplomats, missionaries, and other travelers—who produced the transnational imperialist discourse of Haiti as the premodern land of voodoo/vaudoux.

There are two iterations of this discourse related to evangelical Christianity—one explicitly religious, the other "secular" and implicitly religious—that collectively frame what I call "the (Protestant) missionary position" as they argue for foreign intervention in Haiti. To elaborate these two iterations, I draw on examples from the recent past that readers might already be familiar with: widely circulated reactions to the 2010 earthquake in popular media by televangelist Pat Robertson on *The 700 Club* and by pundit David Brooks in the *New York Times*. Despite notable differences in the Christian tenor of their representations of Haiti as the premodern land of voodoo, they had remarkably similar underlying logic that reached different audiences to herald the benefits of U.S. intervention in Haiti. However, Robertson and Brooks were far from the first to take up the missionary position; their religious/secular collusions reprised justifications for U.S. intervention beginning during the country's occupation of Haiti (1915–34).

The subsequent section of the chapter fills out this history to describe an effect of "the missionary position" over the last century—the dramatic increase in Protestantism in what had been a Roman Catholic stronghold. The U.S. occupation enabled this increase. Protestant missionaries had been in Haiti since shortly after the country's independence, but there had not been widespread interest in U.S. churches to spend their resources evangelizing heathens (by their logic) in the Black republic. L. Ton Evans, the Baptist missionary discussed in chapter 1 who spoke out against the brutality of the U.S. Marines, tried for decades before the occupation to generate ecumenical and state interest in such a project. The occupation ultimately achieved what Evans could not through the U.S. circulation of racist representations of the Black republic. U.S. evangelical missionaries proliferated in Haiti during the mid-twentieth century, evangelizing the natives and engaging in development work, to uplift a place riddled with "voodoo superstition" and an accompanying array of "cultural deficits." In the process, they brought Protestant sexual politics to Haiti.

The final section of the chapter pivots toward my ethnographic fieldwork in Haiti between 2008 and 2016 to describe the legacy of postcolonial homophobia resulting from the imperialist demonization of Haiti and the missionary position. To contextualize the social structure of Protestant homophobia, I sketch out a landscape of contemporary religious (homo)sexual politics in Haiti within Vodou, Catholicism, and evangelical Christianity. As the previous chapter describes, Vodou here is not the imagined bizarre ritualism of "voodoo/vaudoux," but an African diasporic religion, like Santería and Candomblé, that blends in elements of Christianity. The treatments of same-sex desire and sexuality vary across these three religions; as a basic distinction, Vodou honors same-sex desire and other social and spiritual relations considered non-normative by Euro-U.S. standards, whereas Catholicism and Protestantisms consider same-sex sexuality to be a sin and thus have attendant forms of religious homophobia.

However, what I learned and elaborate here is that Catholic and Protestant homophobia differ from each other. The different sects of Christianity

evaluate and act toward same-sex sexuality in ways that parallel their treatment of Vodou. Haitian Catholicism does not condone the practice of Vodou
or same-sex sexuality, yet both operate as open secrets or tacit knowledge of
the church and its followers. In popular Haitian Protestantisms, same-sex
sexuality and Vodou need to be exposed, rejected, and uprooted, which plays
out through economies of enunciation and denunciation rather than official
silences. The same-sex-desiring and gender-creative Haitians I interacted
with during my fieldwork found Catholic homophobia difficult though easier
to negotiate than evangelical Christian homophobia on a day-to-day basis.
However, as one might guess and as the following chapters illuminate, given
the increase in Protestantism in Haiti as with other places in the region and
Latin America, evangelical homophobia is becoming more prevalent and
therefore more difficult to avoid.

THE COLLUSION OF PROTESTANT RELIGIOUS
AND SECULAR IMPERIALIST DISCOURSES ABOUT HAITI

U.S. responses to the 2010 earthquake are instructive for thinking about
the interconnected histories of U.S. state, economic, religious, and social
interventions in Haiti that have resulted in a large-scale shift from Catholicism to Protestantism in the last century. I focus on two public figures—Pat
Robertson and David Brooks—who notoriously blamed the prevalence of
"voodoo" for the disaster in Haiti. These accusations respectively represent
the Protestant religious and secular iterations of the transnational imperialist
discourse of Haiti as the premodern land of voodoo. The first, espoused by
neo-evangelicals, claims that the earthquake was a form of divine retribution to punish Haiti for devil worship (or "voodoo"). The second, favored by
neoconservatives and espoused by liberals, posits instead that the earthquake
caused tremendous devastation because of a "progress-resistant" Haitian
culture that includes the practice of "voodoo." The belief in the inherent
superiority of Euro-U.S. culture and the inherent inferiority of Haitian culture replays the logic of savage systems at the heart of both iterations. Their
divergences allow the discourse underlying the missionary position to reach
audiences who would not be assumed to share political perspectives, collectively making a broad argument for (continued) U.S. intervention in Haiti.

The neo-evangelical iteration of the transnational imperialist discourse of
Haiti as the premodern land of voodoo was performed in spectacular fashion
by televangelist and former Republican presidential candidate Pat Robertson

the day after the earthquake. Robertson, a white Southern Baptist minister and founder of the Christian Broadcasting Network (CBN), hosts the network's flagship program, *The 700 Club.* He used the show as a platform for Christian humanitarianism for several decades, and thus it came as no surprise that *The 700 Club* conducted a fund-raiser for disaster relief efforts in Haiti. To contextualize the event for viewers, Robertson explained to his cohost—African American Kristi Watts, who started the "Voice of Hope" series about the complexities of Christian heterosexual dating and relationships—that the earthquake was God's punishment for the sins of Haiti's past. As he told the story,

> something happened a long time ago in Haiti, and people might not want to talk about it. They were under the heel of the French, ah you know, Napoleon the Third and whatever, and they got together and swore a pact to the devil. They said, "We will serve you if you'll get us free from the French." True story. And so the devil said, "O.K., it's a deal." And, uh, they kicked the French out. The Haitians revolted and got themselves free. But ever since they have been cursed by one thing after another, desperately poor. You know, the island of Hispanola [*sic*] is one island. And it's cut down the middle. On one side is Haiti, and on the other side is the Dominican Republic. The Dominican Republic is—is prosperous, healthy, full of resources, etc. Haiti is in desperate poverty. Same island! They need to have—and we need to pray for them—a great turning to God. And out of this tragedy, I'm optimistic something good may come, but right now we are helping the suffering people, and the suffering is unimaginable.[1] (Robertson 2010)

Ignore for a moment the blatant inaccuracies of this "true story." In his pontification, Pat Robertson posits that all of Haiti's problems—from desperate poverty to natural disasters—stem from this "pact with the devil." This story of the source of Haiti's problems—perhaps its original sin—never mentions "voodoo" directly; but since Euro–U.S. Americans represent "voodoo" as devil worship, the connection is implied. While Voodoo has no devil in its cosmology, the "pact with the devil" references the Vodou ceremony at Bwa Kayiman that initiated the Haitian Revolution, described in chapter 1. Robertson did not originate this "pact with the devil" story; as religious studies scholar Elizabeth McAlister documents extensively in "From Slave Revolt to a Blood Pact with Satan: The Evangelical Rewriting of Haitian History" (2012), this specific story about Haiti—reinterpreting the events at Bwa Kayiman—circulated transnationally for several decades before Robertson's public telling of it.[2] The evangelical disdain for "voodoo" and identification of its superstitious practices as the reason for Haiti's chronic underdevelopment and suffering rehearsed in this television segment of *The 700 Club* goes back centuries. The seemingly intractable religious and moral deficits of Haitians, Pat Robertson reminds viewers, can only be remedied through prayer and a "great turning to God" brought about through U.S. evangelicalism.

While Robertson's "pact with the devil" story may be easy for some to dismiss, the secular argument for greater U.S. presence in Haiti has widespread appeal. This is represented in conservative U.S. Jewish journalist David Brooks's op-ed, "The Underlying Tragedy," that appeared in the online version of the *New York Times* two days after the earthquake and the paper version the following day. Instead of focusing on satanism per se, the op-ed posits that the intractability of "voodoo" is part of a larger problem with Haiti that has created the tragedy of the earthquake. More specifically, Brooks makes an implicitly racist culture-of-poverty argument—borrowed from anti-dependency theorist Lawrence E. Harrison—to say that Haiti "suffers from a complex web of progress-resistant cultural influences," such as "the influence of the voodoo religion"[3] (Brooks 2010). He lists social mistrust, lack of internalized responsibility, and neglectful child-rearing practices as additional reasons that Haiti lags behind other postcolonial nations—specifically Barbados and the Dominican Republic—in terms of its development. The comparison with the Dominican Republic is particularly similar to the Robertson story, here used to make a case that the legacies of slavery and colonialism are not to blame.

> It is time to put the thorny issue of culture at the center of efforts to tackle global poverty. Why is Haiti so poor? Well, it has a history of oppression, slavery and colonialism. But so does Barbados, and Barbados is doing pretty well. Haiti has endured ruthless dictators, corruption and foreign invasions. But so has the Dominican Republic, and the D.R. is in much better shape. Haiti and the Dominican Republic share the same island and the same basic environment, yet the border between the two societies offers one of the starkest contrasts on earth—with trees and progress on one side, and deforestation and poverty and early death on the other. (Brooks 2010)

Brooks concludes by making a case for "intrusive paternalism" in Haiti to force cultural, political, and economic change (2010).

Other than the comparison of Haiti to the Dominican Republic, the op-ed and Pat Robertson's televised history of Haiti would seem to have more differences than similarities. The comments on *The 700 Club*, a Christian program averaging a million daily viewers, deployed obviously religious rhetoric to move an audience not just to pray for the suffering Haitian but to donate funds. Robertson's argument for greater Christian influences in Haiti also requires knowledge of "voodoo" as a demonic African cult that promotes "wrong" relationships to animals, nature, the body, and sexuality. According to his particular religious logics, God enacted retribution through the earthquake for the unnatural/ungodly circumstances of Haiti's independence. By contrast, the New York Times piece is moderate. It appears in one of the top three publications in the United States, with almost twice the average readers on a weekday than The 700 Club has viewers. Brooks does not use explicitly religious language to argue for more active U.S. involvement in Haiti. The closest he comes is trying to keep President Obama "faithful" to his promise that Haiti will not be forsaken or forgotten and a reference to NGOs as "doing the Lord's work"—a solution, however, that he says is not enough. In other words, Brooks puts forward a secular critique in terms of culture and economy, specifically of premodern attachment to voodoo religion and its attendant cultural deficits that hinder development: bad child-rearing practices and rampant sexual immorality.

Queer studies scholars Janet R. Jakobsen and Ann Pellegrini provide helpful guidance to understand how the secular is working in the Brooks op-ed in a way that colludes with the overtly religious. In Secularisms (2008), Jakobsen and Pellegrini elucidate how the concept of the secular emerged from the Protestant Reformation that challenged the dominance of the Roman Catholic Church, and therefore is tied to what they call the secularization narrative of Enlightenment "in which reason progressively frees itself from the bonds of religion and in so doing liberates humanity" (2003, 2). They elucidate how this secularization narrative is fundamental to U.S. nationalist discourses and unpack the binary opposition of religious/secular to assert that Protestantism is inextricable from secularisms in a U.S. context: "Our argument is not that this secularism is really (essentially) religion in disguise, but rather that in its dominant, market-based incarnation it constitutes a specifically Protestant form of secularism" (Jackobsen and Pellegrini 2008, 3). They moreover elaborate that what might be deemed religious and secular discourses of the nation—commonly represented as "two sides" or opposing viewpoints—"actually come together around the idea that civilization can be found in Europe and the United States"[4] (10).

The same applies in this case. Pat Robertson's television segment and the David Brooks op-ed collectively make a wide-reaching argument for U.S. intervention in Haiti, one that noticeably ignores that by the time of the earthquake the United States had been a major political, economic, religious, and cultural influence there for nearly a century. This exceptionalist discourse asserts that the solutions to Haiti's extraordinary problems can and should be found in the United States—an appropriately modern civilizing force to counter the premodern effects of voodoo and save Haiti from itself. The implicit anti-Black racism of this argument was only mildly tempered by the fact that President Barack Obama—who had popular support in Haiti at the time of his first election, which I watched on CNN projected on the side of a building in the public plaza of Jacmel—was the head of state at the time of the earthquake. By the time U.S. audiences were watching Robertson on *The 700 Club* and reading Brooks's op-ed in the *New York Times*, U.S. military forces were already in Haiti for Operation Unified Response.[5]

U.S. IMPERIALISM AND THE GROWTH OF PROTESTANTISM IN HAITI

At the dawn of this twentieth century, and though in close proximity to American shores—for Haiti lies between Cuba and Porto Rico, on the present direct route to our Panama Canal, and within a few hours' run of Jamaica—it is almost incredible that there should be at this moment an island five times the size of the latter and with over three times its population in such a benighted and deplorable state and without any organized efforts whatever by our great missionary societies to evangelize its heathen.

—L. Ton Evans, "An Urgent Appeal in Behalf of Haiti, West Indies" (1922)

The occupation was an experiment in social engineering. . . . It provided a context for the flourish of American Protestantism in Haiti and indirectly was responsible for reducing the prevalent influence of the Catholic church.

—Michel S. Laguerre, *The Military and Society in Haiti* (1993)

The missionary position is as old as the formation of Haiti. However, Protestant missionaries were not officially welcomed in Catholic Haiti until 1816 under the administration of President Alexandre Pétion, as was celebrated during my last summer of fieldwork in Port-au-Prince at the 200 years of Protestantism in Haiti conference. The transnational imperialist voodoo discourse compelled interest in this missionary work, though not always in ways that supported the underlying anti-Black logic. Prominent Protestant African Americans supported Haiti's independence as an example of "the capacity of the Negro race for self-governance and civilized progress" (in Plummer 1982, 126), to use the words of Rev. James Theodore Augustus Holly, the first African American bishop in the Protestant Episcopal Church who emigrated to Haiti in 1861. However, as documented in historian Brenda

Gayle Plummer's "The Afro-American Response to the Occupation of Haiti, 1915–1934" (1982), Rev. Holly also engaged in a campaign against voodoo as impeding the progress of the Haitian nation, which he envisioned as a much-needed example to counter deeply entrenched anti-Black racism, and he sought instead to instill "Anglo-African" values through Protestantism.

While Rev. Holly and other missionaries founded churches during the nineteenth century, evangelicalism did not make inroads in Catholic Haiti until the twentieth century.[6] A century after Haitian independence, Rev. Lewis Ton Evans lamented the lack of "organized efforts . . . by our great missionary societies to evangelize its heathen" (see epigraph to this section). He had traveled extensively before taking on the station of general missionary to Jamaica, Haiti, and Santo Domingo (the Dominican Republic) in 1892.

> In Haiti [Rev. Evans] observed what appeared to be depravity of the worst kind. He worked diligently at assessing the effort he felt would be required to evangelize a largely illiterate and rural Haitian population. From his perspective, Haiti was one of the most spiritually-backward, and therefore challenging, fields he had seen. Evans deduced that Haitian spirituality comprised a mixture of Voodooism (Vodun) and Roman Catholicism. He claimed that "the present state of the island is most deplorable, the densest darkness prevailing; Romanism in its worst forms; women devotees . . . connected with Voodooism . . . or . . . devil worship, . . . fowls and beasts . . . and human lives are offered up . . . and blood drunk . . . and cannibalism practiced." (Olsen 1993, 25–26)

Rev. Evans assumed the missionary position and attempted to generate interest in large-scale Baptist missionary work in Haiti. Over the years he issued appeals in letters to Presidents Roosevelt, Taft, and Wilson for U.S. intervention on the island of Hispaniola, and thanked President Wilson for his Christian moral diplomacy of initiating the U.S. occupation (Olsen 1993, 26–30). However, Rev. Evans eventually denounced the brutality of the marines and publicly challenged the occupation as enacting extreme violence against Haitians.

Perhaps ironically, the U.S. occupation of Haiti did more to generate Protestant interest in "evangelizing its heathens" than any previous campaigns by missionaries like Rev. Evans. The proliferation of U.S. popular culture, scholarly, and state representations of voodoo—many described in the previous chapter—played a crucial role. This is particularly true after the 1921 U.S. Senate Inquiry into the Occupation of Haiti and Santo Domingo, in which the U.S. (Protestant) mission to uproot voodoo in the Black republic was a major thread. An excerpt follows of an exchange between a U.S. senator (Medill McCormick of Illinois) and a Haitian Roman Catholic bishop

(Jean-Marie Jan) during the hearing, transcribed in Vodou scholar Patrick Bellegarde-Smith's "Resisting Freedom":

> SENATOR: Your comments on the U.S. occupation of Haiti?
> BISHOP: The occupation was an act of kindness . . .
> SENATOR: The war against the Americans, how do you explain it?
> BISHOP: The people were pushed to desperation by (American) arbitrariness, injustice and mistreatments. It proclaimed its right to self-defense. Does the United States want to impose Protestantism by force?
> SENATOR: The Washington government will never attack Haiti's (Catholic) faith. Can you provide information on Vodun, its practices and status? Has it diminished since the occupation?
> BISHOP: It has increased. . . . The greatest cause for this is that the bocors (bokò) were the soul of the insurrection.
> (Bellegarde-Smith 2006, 111)

Here, bocors—regarded as "voodoo sorcerers"—are positioned as spreading voodoo as well as insurrectionary spirit. The U.S. occupation was portrayed as an effort to quell their influence. It continued for more than a decade after the Senate hearings, and an uncoordinated large-scale public-relations campaign ensued to portray Haiti as progress-resistant and riddled by the satanic African cult of voodoo and all its freakishness—child sacrifice, cannibalism, overt sexual displays, demonic possession, and eventually stories about zombies and homosexuality.

Bishop Jean-Marie Jan's concern that the U.S. occupation would increase Protestant influence in Catholic Haiti turned out to be well-founded. This evangelizing work began in earnest in the 1920s, but by 1930 only 1.5 percent of the Haitian population was Protestant. The following decade this had increased to almost 5 percent, then doubled during the 1940s. The election of President François "Papa Doc" Duvalier in 1957 facilitated this process even further. This notorious dictator was closely aligned with the Vodou religion. But he is also known as the father of Protestantism because he welcomed missionaries, who he figured would challenge the authority of the Catholic Church but pose no threat to his own power. These missionaries also benefitted from the developed circuits of travel that the United States had established between the two countries for the purposes of attracting North American tourism to Haiti. By the end of the 1970s, more than 20 percent of the Haitian population was Protestant.[7]

The promotion of monogamous heterosexual marriage was a key strategy of Protestant missionary development in Haiti in the mid-twentieth century.

The institution of marriage was already linked with colonialist legacies because the French Code Noir (1685) legislated marriages and extramarital relationships to discourage miscegenation. After the U.S. occupation period, "premarital" and "extramarital" sexual relationships—known within Haiti as *plasaj* (multiple partnerings in nonlegal unions)—became a source of fascination for U.S. social scientists and a primary site of intervention for U.S. missionaries (see Allman 1980 and 1985, Bastien 1961, Comhaire-Sylvain 1958, Herskovits 1937). As sociologist James Graham Leyburn describes the issue, "nowhere else in the Western World has there been so little actual marriage in proportion to the population as in Haiti" (2004 [1941], 187). Protestants sought to remedy this problem and reached out to the majority poor Haitians to promote marriage by, for instance, offering church services for wedding ceremonies at no cost. Missionaries slowly implemented these civilizational reforms in the sphere of profligate sexuality—always already racialized—to the point that monogamous, heterosexual marriage would become commonsense, even if not widely practiced.

These mid-century missionaries initiated other human development projects, particularly in the realms of education and health care, that were within the scope of bringing Christianity to the Black republic. These projects would come to have a larger than expected impact as Haiti became a laboratory for neoliberalism, or as Jean-Claude "Baby Doc" Duvalier called it, turning the country into the "Taiwan of the Caribbean" through post-Fordist manufacturing and benefits to attract foreign business while diminishing any potential of developing a social safety net for the Haitian population. U.S. policies after the ousting of the younger Duvalier in 1986 continued this trend, and faith-based and other NGOs grew tenfold during the 1990s. As anthropologist Mark Schuller argues, this was both a product of general global trends that included the "distrust of states and a preference for private-sector initiatives and the elusive concept of 'civil society,'" as well as specific policies enacted by the United States, most prominently the Dole Amendment, which prevented the U.S. Agency for International Development (USAID) from funding any projects directed by the Haitian state (Schuller 2010). Instead, funding to Haiti was channeled through projects directed by U.S.-led NGOs, thereby radically transforming the landscape of aid and promoting an increase in foreign presence as well as foreign control over assessment of needs in Haiti and implementation of new projects. Because of their history engaging in development projects since the 1950s, Protestants had positioned themselves to be major contenders for this U.S. foreign aid funding for Haiti.

By the time I initiated my fieldwork in 2008, an estimated 33 to 40 percent of the Haitian population was Baptist, Pentecostal, Adventist, Presbyterian,

Episcopal, or affiliated with another non-Catholic denomination of Christianity, such as Mormonism. Protestantism had long been successfully "nativized" through missionaries' dedication to the use of Haitian Creole language, recruitment of Haitians to church leadership, and the dynamic of instilling a work ethic whose proof was witnessed in the Haitian takeover of U.S. missionary projects in orphanages, schools, and clinics. While the nativization of Protestantism happened long ago, U.S. missionaries have continued to flock to Haiti. Most are compelled by a general sense of Christian humanitarianism to help the needy, though some have specifically targeted Haiti because of voodoo and its so-called "demonic entrenchment" (McAlister 2012). They often stay for short durations to ferry supplies for schools, orphanages, and clinics; learn about the struggles of the "developing" world; and thus acquire a kind of religious cultural capital for partaking in modern missionary efforts with natives who had already converted (DeTemple 2006). It is clear from years of having casual conversations with the often loud, matching T-shirt-clad U.S. Americans who fill flights to and from the Toussaint Louverture International Airport in Port-au-Prince that the majority of these missionaries have no idea that they travel well-worn routes or that their missions are intimately connected to U.S. statecraft.

Despite this demographic shift over the last century, Haiti is still imagined to be a Catholic country rife with voodoo witchcraft. However, while Catholicism is still widely practiced, the country's social and political landscape has been significantly transformed by the missionary position and the growth of Protestantism. Evangelical Christianity has left an indelible mark in Haiti beyond the influx of missionaries. During the years of my fieldwork, it felt like an unavoidable part of day-to-day life. For example, I was subjected to singing amplified from the churches that seem to saturate all neighborhoods; engaged in conversations about Christ while walking the streets or riding popular transportation; and offered "educational" pamphlets and books about Christianity when people learned that I was not a missionary. I regularly encountered sidewalk preachers and trucks and cars blasting sermons as they wound through busy city streets. And I would have to endure—I say because it felt tedious compared to *konpa* music, *futbòl* match coverage, and news reporting—Christian radio and television programs, particularly when I was running errands and visiting people's homes.

Offering a full account of the Protestantization of Haiti (and its diaspora) might well be an impossible task, and it is in any case beyond the scope of this book. Clearly there are many factors beyond those that I have considered in this section, such as developments in Haitian state politics and the conditions that created individuals' openness to the possibility of converting. The crucial point for my purpose here is to recognize the multiple ways U.S. imperialism facilitated this religious shift over the last century and therefore shaped contemporary sexual politics in Haiti.

RELIGIOUS SEXUAL POLITICS IN HAITI: VODOU, CATHOLICISM, AND PROTESTANTISM

This religious shift in Haiti catalyzed and in many ways facilitated by U.S. imperialism—and more broadly the transnational imperialist discourse of Haiti as the premodern land of voodoo—has been accompanied by the growing prevalence of Protestant homophobia. This social structure is distinct from Vodou and Catholic treatments of same-sex sexuality. I detail all three here to situate readers in a complex landscape of sexual politics in order to better understand the impacts of postcolonial homophobia. The extant academic work about Haitian same-sex sexuality and transgender embodiments overwhelmingly focuses on Vodou contexts, and scholars of Vodou have weighed in on the topic of same-sex sexuality (e.g., McAlister 2000 and 2002; Lescot and Magliore 2002; Strongman 2002, 2008, and 2019; Conner 2004; Michel, Bellegarde-Smith, and Racine-Toussaint 2006; Tinsley 2011 and 2018; Chapman 2019; Nwokocha 2019). However, there is a dearth of scholarly—particularly ethnographic—information about these topics in Catholic and Protestant contexts, which I hope to rectify here. Not meant to be a comprehensive overview of religious cultures and sexual politics in Haiti, my analysis focuses on some of the kinds of omofobi that Haitians with whom I interacted perceived to make the most difference in their daily lives. Although I outlined my methods in the introduction, I want to begin by providing a fuller picture of how I collected the data for this overview of contemporary religious sexual politics in Vodou, Catholicism, and Protestantism.

Before initiating my fieldwork in 2008, I had read and watched everything I could locate about same-sex sexuality in Haiti and its diaspora, which required learning about Vodou. I crafted a research project that would extend beyond Vodou contexts, since little was published about the lives of same-sex-desiring and gender-creative people's lives otherwise. But within an hour after arriving at the arts school where I would live in residence for the first part of my fieldwork, FOSAJ, I was whisked away by same-sex-desiring and gender-creative Haitians and a U.S. American to a Vodou ceremony. It was late in the evening of Fèt Gede (the day of the dead), and we traveled by foot on city streets lined with tin can oil lamps dimly lighting our path to a ceremony that was just beginning. My hosts offered food, a joint, and my first taste of *kleren* (moonshine rum) after I settled on a raised platform to one side of the square temple arranged around a colorful *poto mitan* (central pillar). My U.S. host inquired if I had exchanged currency, and when I told him I had not had the time, he pressed coins into my hand and told me that I should give the *goud* to any spirits who requested money of me. Despite everything I thought I had learned about Vodou, I felt unprepared for—and daunted by—such a task. It was one thing to read about spirit possessions and watch them in documentaries, and quite another to interact with the *lwa* (spirits) in embodied form. I was so focused on performing this small bit of spiritual work—which I did with helpful guidance from the lwa and nearby human company—that I was unaware of most of the events that unfolded at the ceremony before I stumbled back to FOSAJ and fell asleep on a palate covered by a stack of hay and a sheet.

Thankfully, I had many more opportunities to learn. I attended Vodou ceremonies or related rituals as often as I could when I was invited. The following year at Fèt Gede, I participated in the four-hour-long procession around the city to the cemetery where Bawon Samedi and Maman Brijit (patron spirits of the dead) were waiting by a gigantic black cross. I barely had time to recover from a day spent in the sweltering heat when a band of *gede* (spirits of dead individuals) danced bawdily through my neighborhood; I joined with friends and we were treated to several blocks of sexual humor in song and playfully promiscuous dancing.[8] The final event of the evening was a ceremony similar to the one I attended when I first arrived, it unfolded over a long night and therefore I abstained from alcohol and took a large mug of coffee. Many of the Vodou ceremonies and rituals I attended took place like this within a single day or single night; however, some lasted much longer over many days, and I would attend for periods of time in between doing the rest of the things I needed to do.

As a non-initiate, I was mostly limited to public ceremonies and rituals, though along the way I witnessed other activities from a limited perspective. I often lived with Vodou practitioners, friends who would tell me about ceremonies like the *lave tèt* (head cleansing) and *maryaj lwa* (spirit marriage) to the level they considered appropriate to a sympathetic outsider. A handful of times I participated in the behind-the-scenes labor for ceremonies with other women: gathering supplies at the market, cooking food for participants, turning chunks of raw cotton into candle wicks, arranging furniture and ceremonial objects, and so on. I also paid for private consultations or "readings" with *manbo* (priestesses) and *ougan* (priests) who interpreted messages for me from the lwa in playing cards, which facilitated spiritual learning and—perhaps less importantly—contained a series of correct predictions: I would pass my comprehensive exams, birth one child, divorce my wife, and write a book about Haiti.

There were two periods when, for reasons of proximity rather than purposefully seeking it out on my own, I received the gift of training in Vodou practice. For three weeks over a summer, I lived with a manbo and her family while I attended the University of Massachusetts Haitian Creole Summer Institute. She is an excellent teacher who has attracted scholars of Black studies, Haitian studies, and religious studies wishing to learn more about Vodou. I attended formal training sessions at her house for and by the scholars and informal sessions that happened constantly during meal preparation, on our way to and from Haitian dance classes in Cambridge, and lounging around the living room with the Disney Channel playing in the background. I learned about the labor performed by manbo and their families from her, her children, and the various kinds of people who made house calls. She continued to teach me during the times we overlapped in Jacmel, including the weeks of *kanzo* (initiation). The other period is when I accompanied members of the performance troupe Lakou on regular visits to an *oungan Ginè* (Vodou priest) who lived on a large piece of land with his many wives and children in the countryside outside of Jacmel, a location that required a half-hour moto ride followed by an hourlong climb up mountain paths. The oungan and his family member apprenticed the Lakou founders, who they considered to be performing spiritual work as artists, teaching them (and therefore me) about things like identifying and using medicinal plants as well as cooking methods to feed the lwa.

Unlike learning about Haitian Vodou, which I largely enjoyed, it felt like a chore to go to church. Sitting on the uncomfortable wooden pews of Cathédrale Saint-Jacques et Saint-Philippe recalled all the times my parents dragged me to church under protest, though compared to those of my childhood, the inside of this church was remarkably austere—hospital pastel with few icons. I only went to Sunday mass at the striking yellow-and-white cathedral across the street from the open-air market a half dozen times before the structural damage caused by the earthquake rendered it unsafe. But in this particular church close to my home and centrally located in Jacmel, rather than any others that I attended, is where I observed that the congregation included a noticeable amount of people I had seen or interacted with at the previous night's Vodou ceremony. They, like the members of Lakou who had taken me to mass, were dressed in their finest church clothes and seemed not to have to fight off the urge to sleep caused by the droning priest, like I did. However, over the years of my fieldwork, I came to appreciate the familiar rhythm of the Sunday mass delivered in Kreyòl whether I was in a permanently constructed building or a makeshift church of folding chairs under tarps.

My other occasion for going to Catholic religious services, other than for Sunday mass or holidays, was to attend funerals. I have attended more funerals in Haiti than I have in the whole rest of my lifetime, and the ages of those who died—sometimes friends, sometimes friends or family members of friends—have tended to be far younger. The news of someone's death usually circulates with a fund-raising request, as funerals are extraordinarily expensive, costing a minimum of $500 while others cost upward of $1,000. Though these figures may not seem high by U.S. standards, they are nearly impossible for majority poor Haitians to pay at one time. The funeral services start with an open-casket wake and a memorial mass. Men carry the casket and sometimes women, who are given over to mourning in fits of crying, wailing, and fainting. After the services, everyone leaves in their black and white church clothes to form a funeral procession with the hearse. This procession moves by foot to the music of a brass band to the place where the casket will take up residence for as long as the family of the deceased can afford to rent space in the cemetery.

I have admittedly far less direct experience with services at Haitian Protestant churches, except for Episcopal ones that are quite similar to Catholic services. In 2008, I was invited by a white U.S. scholar for a trip to the famous Episcopal Cathédrale de Sainte Trinité in Port-au-Prince, primarily to admire its murals. I also accepted offers from white U.S. Americans I knew in Haiti to visit their congregations. But I never attended services at Baptist, Seventh-day Adventist, Pentecostal, or any of the neo-evangelical churches in Haiti. The two reasons for this are shaped by the focus of my research on the daily lives of same-sex-desiring and gender-creative Haitians. The first reason is that I spent most of my time with these same-sex-desiring and gender-creative Haitians who took me to Vodou ceremonies and Catholic churches. Those who were practicing Protestants did not invite me to attend their churches; the sincere invitations always came from straight people. The second reason is that, based on what I was learning about the sexual politics of these churches as I describe below, I was nervous to attend even if I would have learned a lot through the process. My experiences with evangelical Christianity were generally limited, as previously described: as a regular feature of the Haitian visual and sonic landscape encountered through street preachers and missionaries.

Some of the most important insights about religious sexual politics and homophobic social structures came from the individual interviews I conducted with more than seventy same-sex-desiring and gender-creative Haitians. Notably all of the interviewees were believers—mostly, but not exclusively, Christians. I have only ever met one atheist in a decade of fieldwork in Haiti. The last summer of conducting fieldwork in Port-au-Prince, I accidentally outed this person as an atheist to one of his coworkers, Daniel, and a couple of our friends on an evening when we were having dinner at my home. Since I had known for years that this person was an atheist and wrongly assumed that other people did as well, I casually mentioned it in conversation, and everyone at the table stopped eating. "Really?!! Really?!!" Daniel said in surprise. "I am shocked. I thought I knew him. Where is his heart? How can someone not believe in God? It's like he is not even human." The depths of Daniel's disbelief and the subsequent conversation led me to the realization that there is something even more *dwol* (strange) or queer—even outside the realm of possibility—than same-sex sexuality in Haiti.

The data I collected during my initial fieldwork period between 2008 and 2011 revealed two notable trends in the ways that interviewees described their experiences with violence based on their same-sex desires and practices, which correlated with whether they had grown up in Catholic or Protestant households (or interfaith households with a Protestant parent). This created the possibility for me to delineate distinct social structures of homophobia in Haiti—Catholic homophobia and Protestant homophobia—and how they have changed over time. Broadly, the culture of Catholic homophobia *demands discretion*: that people not publicly discuss same-sex desires. Protestant homophobia, by contrast, *demands public discussions of homosexuality*: that sinful desires and practices be exposed for sinners to be saved. Elizabeth Lapovsky Kennedy and Madeline Davis's five-to-ten stories method used by queer oral historians and anthropologists held true for this project; that is, "between five and ten narrators' stories need to be juxtaposed in order to develop an analysis that is not changed dramatically by each new story"[9] (2014, 23). In the years since I initially recognized the patterns of Catholic and Protestant homophobia from the stories people shared about their lives in interviews, I have been able to correctly anticipate what others tell me in interviews, on less formal occasions, and eventually in court testimony for asylum petitions as an expert witness.

Protestant homophobia became nationally prominent throughout the years of my research, a shift that has forced same-sex-desiring and gender-creative Haitians to develop new strategies for contending with omofobi personally and politically. Daniel, a committed organizer and advocate for same-sex-desiring and gender-creative people who worked as a peer facilitator for an MSM/LGBT human rights organization, stated:

> You know, the Catholic Church does not like gay[10] people and there is homophobia, but we are in the church without too many problems. But Protestants, they really do not like gay people. They are mean . . . and throw their family members out on the streets without any resources. They say, "You are gay!" and throw people out of their churches. They just do not care about people because they learned in their churches to do stuff like that, that it is better . . . and they want to do that for all of Haiti.

In the following sections, I elaborate what Daniel sketches here as the differences between Catholic and Protestant homophobia in their familial and institutional forms. There is ample evidence that, as Daniel indicates, some evangelical Christians want all same-sex-desiring and gender-creative people out of Haiti. That goal is attempted by "saving" these people though destroying their indulgence in sinful activities, by exterminating them (sometimes in an effort to "save" them), or—through a politics of attrition—by creating a climate so hostile that same-sex-desiring and gender-creative Haitians want or need to leave.

HAITIAN VODOU

Before outlining these two forms of religious homophobia in Haiti, I offer the contrast of Vodou treatments of same-sex sexuality. Vodou welcomes all people, as is encapsulated in the philosophy "tout moun se moun" (everyone is a person, or all people are equal). Scholarly consensus is that Vodou provides space for queer practices and possibilities that extend beyond acceptance of same-sex sexuality and transgender embodiments.

One of Vodou's queer qualities is spirit possession or "mounting," often during religious ceremonies. Female practitioners may be mounted by lwa who are understood to correspond to "men," while male practitioners may be mounted by lwa who are understood to correspond to "women." The lwa themselves express a range of gender presentations that affect the mounting, which can be seen across the family of "women" spirits closely linked with same-sex desire, Ezili. Ezili Freda, the spirit of love and beauty, is a high femme who notoriously prefers to mount masisi. Ezili Dantò, the Black mother of Haiti and spirit of maternal love, is masculine and revered for her participation in the Haitian Revolution. She is the patron lwa of madivin ("my divine" or lesbian). Practitioners of any sex embodiment can be mounted by a feminine or masculine "woman," like these two manifestations of Ezili.

Another queer quality is the range of sexualities expressed within the spirits. Haitian Vodou scholars have written about Ezili Dantò as madivin and refer to "the words of Audre Lorde and other Black feminists" to call that spirit "a 'woman-identified-woman,' a lesbian" (Michel, Bellegarde-Smith, and Racine-Toussaint 2006, 70). Two Haitian women—one in Jacmel and one in the diaspora (whose human relationships are exclusively with straight, non-transgender men)—told me that they were married to this lwa. These spiritual unions are everlasting and require commitments from the lwa and the human involved. Vodou practitioners can have multiple spirit marriages in addition to their human lovers and spouses. This twist on the concept of marriage is far outside the realm of what is sanctioned by the Haitian state and Christian religious institutions.

Same-sex-desiring and gender-creative Haitians also consider Vodou an essential part of their queer lineage in relationship to masisi and madivin spirits as well as human ancestors—parents, grandparents, and members of their extended spiritual family—who engaged in same-sex relationships. For instance, three of my informants had remarkably similar stories about their grandmothers who were manbo. In response to a question I asked Marc, who grew up in the upscale suburb of Pétion-Ville, about his family's perception of same-sex sexuality, he responded matter-of-factly:

> It's a tradition to be gay. . . . My grandmother was a lesbian. You don't believe me! [*Laughs*] It's true! Well, she was married to my grand-father and had children. But she also had several lovers who were women. After my grandfather died . . . one of her lovers moved in, and they lived together as husband and wife until my grandmother died. . . . They raised their children together. They had many children, even other people's kids sometimes. Everything was normal. [My grandmother's lover] is family. I never knew my grandfather, only [the two women].
>
> *Did they ever have any problems?*
>
> Like homophobia? No, no—everyone treated my grandmother respect-fully.

One of the other grandmothers had several wives like the two "lesbian priest-esses" that religious studies scholar Elizabeth McAlister met while conducting research on Vodou, "who each had several sexual partners, in the polygamous style of the rural Haitian man" (2000, 135).

These queer aspects of Vodou contribute to the collective sense among same-sex-desiring and gender-creative Haitian *vodouizan* that same-sex sexuality is not tolerated in Vodou, it is honored. In the words of Femme Noir, a young lesbian in Jacmel who grew up in a Masonic-Catholic-Vodou religious household: "Most religions do not love people who are masisi and madivin. They use these words as maledictions. But Vodou loves them. The spirits make people like that. . . . People who love strongly." Another young Jacmelian, Mirabo, comes from a family of vodouizan. He told me, "There is a place for masisi in Vodou. Yes, that is why so many masisi and madivin are vodouizan [and] more than 90 percent of ougan and manbo are masisi and madivin." Mirabo's cousin is a manbo who presided over several ceremonies that we attended together. Manbo M told me: "The lwa appreciate masisi. . . . Because they're good looking. [*Laughs*] Well, Vodou is about creating balance where there is imbalance. That balance is the core of masisi who is neither a man nor a woman exactly, but a mélange. You understand? Because of this balance, they have a respected role in spiritual work."

I have found over the years that, while it is true that same-sex-desiring and gender-creative people have a "place" and a "respected position" within Vodou, there is also a tendency—particularly among converts and outsiders—to romanticize its queerness. The spirit pantheon transmits knowledge in its own way of variation in general, and specifically "a concept of benign (sexual) variation" (Rubin 1984), as well as that "people are different from each other" (Sedgwick 1990). Lwa tastes, desires, and affinities vary greatly, even within families and nations. While some lwa prefer and protect masisi and madivin, others have neutral or even antagonistic relationships. As Mirabo said, "some lwa do not care for masisi."

Moreover, in the temples I have visited over the years, the topic of same-sex sexuality was still sometimes discussed in low tones or by insiders speaking in code. Those who draw too much attention to themselves or announce their same-sex desires are verbally chastised and become fodder for gossip. The imperative to exercise discretion in some Vodou ceremonial contexts is likely related to Catholicism.

ROMAN CATHOLICISM

Vodou and Catholicism are very much woven together because of the historical conditions of French colonialism. I have heard and read various ways of describing the relationships between the two: as syncretic—Vodou as a *melanj* (blend) of Catholicism and other spiritual and religious influences; as in dialogue with each other; as existing simultaneously in a way that is complementary; as parallel religions; as Catholicism being the outward face of Vodou because the latter has been outlawed throughout most of Haiti's history; and as religious studies scholar Terry Rey says, "two intertwined trunks of a single religious tree" (2004, 332). Without privileging one of these explanations, I emphasize that, when I talk about Catholicism in Haiti, it is always in relationship to Vodou.

During the time of my field work, the Roman Catholic Church opposed same-sex sexuality, and its religious leaders at every level of the patriarchal hierarchy reiterated church doctrine against homosexuality and LGBT rights. However, what I found in practice is that the Catholic Church is an important institution for Haitian same-sex-desiring and gender-creative people—to have a relationship with God, to fulfill familial and other obligations, and to form and enrich social relations. That is not to say that same-sex sexuality is accepted; rather, it is treated in a similar way as Vodou: as a kind of open secret. Same-sex sexuality is generally tolerated as long as it is not declared or otherwise expressed outside of the confessional, in the context of certain public celebrations like Kanaval (McAlister 2002), or in intimate queer settings—in the lap of a lover or among friends.

Same-sex-desiring Catholics told me that their family members, coworkers, and even fellow congregants know about their same-sex desires and/or lovers. Moreover, they know how these people regard their sexuality even when—as was most often the case—they never discussed it. In our exchange, Michel, a young man from the Delmas neighborhood of Port-au-Prince, gives a sense of this phenomenon:

Have you ever had problems at work because you are masisi?
No, there is no tension at work.
Is that because they don't know?
No, everyone knows! They see/perceive it. How couldn't they know?
Do you ever talk about it with them?
I will never talk about it with them. I always use discretion.
What do you mean when you say "discretion"?
Well, I do not want to cause any problems. If I told them I was masisi, then there would be problems. It might be impossible for me to stay there because it would affect everyone. So . . . sometimes I say "gay" when I am talking with friends. People do not know what that means. [The word] *masisi* makes everyone mad. You have to know your environment.
What about your family?
My family. My mother knows, and she does not agree. My sister knows, and she is cool.
What have they said to you?
Nothing. They communicate it in other ways.

I had innumerable similar conversations: people know that others know about their same-sex desires but rarely broach the topic directly. During the early years of my fieldwork, that was true even for most antihomophobic social service workers and activists. Daniel, a peer facilitator at an organization in Port-au-Prince, told me that his family knows that he is gay as well as that he worked with same-sex-desiring and gender-creative people, but they have never explicitly addressed those topics in a discussion. Catholic same-sex-desiring Haitians like Michel and Daniel do not pretend to be heterosexual; rather, they perform *discretion* in a social field where everyone already knows. Discretion in this context means that they observe the prohibition against announcing same-sex sexual desires and practices in certain publics.[11]

These Catholic Haitians are "tacit subjects" whose same-sex sexuality is "already understood or assumed—tacit—in an exchange. What is *tacit* is neither secret nor silent" (Decena 2011, 19). In Carlos Ulises Decena's ethnographic research with tacit subjects in the Dominican diaspora, he notes that same-sex-desiring immigrant men "assumed that many people had the requisite skills to recognize and decode their behavior" (20). At the same time, the lack of a verbal declaration of one's homosexuality maintained established social relations in what is presumably another Catholic context, though Decena does not focus on religion. "When the terms were violated and people confronted one another . . . what may fall, break, or get disordered was the very glue of sociality that made survival possible for these men and the people they loved" (21).

Similarly, there can be social consequences for Haitians who declare their same-sex desires outside of prescribed contexts. Beyond immediate forms of censure to bring people in line with norms, negative consequences include the deterioration of important relationships with family, friends, and neighbors. Same-sex-desiring Haitians who prefer to maintain discretion may also cut off ties from people who do not. These forms of social isolation particularly impact Haiti's majority poor who rely on developed social networks for jobs, housing, food sharing, and more.

Yet even the bourgeoisie fear the ostracism of Catholic homophobia, despite the fact that they are not economically dependent on social relations in the same way. A Jacmelian middle-class professor, Jean-Élie Gilles, and I have regularly discussed this topic over many years—usually in the late evenings over tea, wine, and brown sugar missionary cookies on his rooftop. It is the primary subject of his cultural work. Asked about his inspiration to write a novel about male same-sex sexuality in Haiti, *Sur les pas de Diogène* (1995), he responded:

I was inspired by all the hypocrisy and lies that one cannot only find in society itself but among some gay Haitians who can be very aggressive toward
gayness, [but] when with their friends while behind closed doors they are so
whorish and passionate about getting it on with other gays that it's insane. This
hypocrisy is mainly found among the bourgeoisie and the intellectual classes
who have always something to preserve . . . : honor, pride, political clout, etc.
. . . Haitian gay men love anonymity and prefer their closet.

In the fictionalized version of Jean-Élie's life experiences as a bisexual man in
Haiti who attended seminary, he represents ways that male same-sex sexuality flourishes alongside other social institutions—in the nooks and crannies
of family homes, in the otherwise unoccupied spaces of the Roman Catholic
Church, and alongside traditional heterosexual marriages. The main character, Diogène, has various male lovers, and their system of mutual discretion
allows for more opportunities to seek out sex and develop relationships in
homosocial spaces. However, the persistent threat of exposure looms: homosexual intimacies among boys are met with private rebuke, and among
men it can mean the devastating loss of reputation.

What of the assertion, then, that "Haitian gay men love anonymity and
prefer their closet"? Historical and ethnographically based LGBTQ studies
scholarship has helpfully situated the closet as a spatial metaphor of sexuality attached to the political projects of U.S. gay liberation beginning in the
late 1960s that does not travel well in other historical, geographical, and cultural contexts (e.g., Chauncey 1994, Decena 2011, Kennedy 1996, Manalansan
2003). This is true in Haiti, as I learned when my literal translation of closet
(*armoire*) was met time and again with a mixture of confusion and giggles.
Gilles was familiar with the metaphor of "the closet" from his years of living
in the United States, but if Haitians who had not had this exposure to U.S.
framings of sexual politics were to reference a somewhat related concept in
Kreyòl, they would say *kachè* (hidden).

It is necessary to note that Jean-Élie's assertion is specifically not performing a comparison where, in terms of attitudes toward same-sex sexuality,
Haiti is traditional and homophobic and the United States, France, or the
Dominican Republic for that matter, is more liberated and modern. Rather,
he is criticizing the cultural capital of a privileged few whose discretion affects
many same-sex-desiring people's material circumstances and creates barri-
ers for social change. Jean-Élie chose to return to Haiti after living abroad
and, like many others, he is fiercely dedicated to improving daily life in the
country. "If I had to choose [where] to be born again, I would choose Haiti

because that's the only place where I can live because of the struggle with each other, the resilience, the generosity and the smartness of my people. I love Haitians. . . . We just need to love each other better." One of his strategies to intervene in Catholic homophobia has been to break with norms of discretion to positively portray same-sex sexuality and to raise awareness about the impacts of this homophobia in his social networks and in the media, particularly surrounding his book. However, these strategies do not have the same impact in the context of Protestant homophobia, as I detail next.

PROTESTANTISM

There is a range of Protestant perspectives on same-sex sexuality across, and even within, denominations. However, the most populous churches in Haiti—Baptist, Pentecostal, Seventh-day Adventist, and Assembly of God—engage in fervent proselytizing against homosexuality and related sins. Evangelical Christianity treats same-sex sexuality in a parallel way that it treats Vodou, just as Catholicism does, albeit differently, as I detail above. In Protestant contexts, both are considered sinful lifestyles outside the favor of God. Repentance requires a full rejection of both same-sex sexuality and Vodou, with the intent never to practice them again. In exchange for repentance, the churches offer homosexuals and vodouizan grace; this leads to transformation in God's forgiveness and the ability to become truly Christian.

The evangelical Christian compulsion to bring sinners to salvation results in an emphasis on revealing one's own as well as other people's same-sex desires rather than ignoring them. Individual same-sex-desiring Protestants told me that they "liked" or "preferred" the practice of discretion in order to remain members of congregations that consider same-sex sexuality to be a sin, especially because they understood that church doctrine considers their actions deceitful, which is potentially worse than the sinful acts of human nature. But discretion is not an option. Protestant homophobia works through economies of enunciation (pronouncing one's own or another's same-sex sexuality) and denunciation (publicly condemning homosexuality).

One of the frequent life stories of same-sex-desiring Haitians who grew up in Protestant households included the experience of being subjected to the inquiry: *are you homosexual/masisi/madivin?* By contrast, only one person recounted being asked this question by a Catholic family member. Norh, a young man from Jacmel, recalled being surprised by the question when he ventured from his Catholic household into the realm of evangelical Christianity. He had been fascinated by a Baptist service that he attended with his uncle.

"I liked the way that they adored God, and so I stayed." However, people at the church and then his uncle and extended family members started asking Norh if he was homosexual. His affirmation initiated rounds of arguments and proselytizing. "I did not like the drama, but I learned how to defend myself." Nevertheless, he stopped going to the church.

Active participants in evangelical Christian churches often deny engaging in same-sex sexual activity when confronted. Junior, a gay Baptist in Jacmel, said: "It's my business, but people are suspicious because I am not married and do not have a girlfriend." Lovers of any kind seemed to be rare in his life, which his friends speculated came from struggling with homophobia. A gay teenager in Port-au-Prince, Star, told me that his family repeatedly asked if he was masisi, and they even arranged for the pastor at their Baptist church to perform some sort of religious intervention, the details of which he did not disclose. Star insisted to them that there was not a problem, and he strategized to bring one of his good friends from school—a girl who knows that he is gay—to his house more often.

The accusation of same-sex sexuality is often outright rather than couched in a question. Johanne, a woman in Jacmel who attended the same church as Junior, told me that she had flings with other girls during her preadolescent years, but when she became romantically involved with a slightly older girl from school as a teenager, her mother scolded her by saying they were acting like *bouzen* (sluts). The intensity of these accusations prompted Johanne to move in with her aunt and uncle until she married a man with whom she had two children. Johanne's marriage opened the possibility of reconciling with her mother, and no one since has questioned whether she might be madivin even though she continues to have short- and long-term relationships with women. Her situation and those similar can often be dangerous, as husbands rarely accept their wives having women lovers or being labeled as sluts or lesbians.

While it is important to recognize that part of what distinguishes Protestant homophobia from Catholic homophobia in Haiti is that it works through economies of enunciation and denunciation, there is another remarkable feature to this social structure: its virulence. For all his critiques of the Catholic Church, Jean-Élie Gilles saves his most scathing remarks to decry "religious bigotry, hypocrisy, . . . [and] exploitation of the poor by the Protestant churches who keep illiterate people by the guts by feeding them, owning them, and making them become religious nuts who are fucking other people's lives in the name of JESUS!" Jean-Élie understands the loss of reputation that can come with expressing that one engages in same-sex sexuality, though he understands this (Catholic) homophobia as qualitatively different than "fucking other people's lives in the name of JESUS!" Other same-sex-desiring and gender-creative Haitians have felt the full weight of this statement, as Protestant homophobia negatively impacts people's daily lives and material circumstances.

Haitians who grew up and lived as adults in Protestant households experienced significant homophobic violence from their family members. I rarely saw this violence firsthand, though it was a regular feature of interviews, focus groups, and the day-to-day life of people with whom I interacted. The most common story is one of public disowning where—as Daniel noted previously—people were temporarily or permanently cast out of family homes. A high percentage of the service seekers at the organization where he worked had this experience and would either move in with other family members or live without stable housing. His organization eventually implemented emergency housing into the array of services it provides while same-sex-desiring and gender-creative people came up with informal ways to meet this need, like the Peace House in Jacmel that serves as temporary shelter for people after these disownings.

Protestant homophobia also takes the form of physical and emotional abuse, violence often couched in terms of families trying to "save" their loved ones by exterminating their same-sex desires and gender-creative inclinations. A young transgender woman named Lovely from a village in northern Haiti showed me scars on the soles of her feet where her parents had applied hot coals to try to "burn the masisi out" of her. A gay man in Port-au-Prince, Joseph, confided in me that he lost an eye because his father beat him with a stick. A young man named Junior had his wrists bound with rope and was dragged behind a truck when he was thirteen years old, after his uncle found him having sex with a boy from school. Shirley, a bisexual woman in her thirties, endured several years of marital abuse after her husband learned that she was attracted to women. He stalked her, read her emails and social media messages, and beat her in front of their children "for being a dirty lesbian." When Shirley's husband mistook her colleague from work to be one of Shirley's lovers, he raped Shirley. Each of these brief examples deserves more attention, though I gather such accounts together here to give a sense of the vast archive of Protestant homophobia as it is lived in familial contexts. In a sociological sense, this religious structure of homophobia impacts Haitians across lines of economic class and rural/urban divides, with the one remarkable difference in how it is experienced being based on sexed embodiment for those assigned male or female at birth. This violence marks the bodies of same-sex-desiring and gender-creative Haitians with scars, lost eyesight, missing limbs. It became clear to me over the years of working in Haiti that this form of religious homophobia was extremely harmful and sometimes fatal.

Jean-Élie Gilles not only helped me to understand Catholic discretion but also the increase in Protestant homophobia. At forty-eight years old when we first met, Jean-Élie was one of the oldest of my informants who are men, and one of my questions for him was: over the course of your life, do you think that Haiti has become more or less tolerant of homosexuality? He answered: "Haiti has become very intolerant toward homosexuality. Homosexuality in Haiti has always been a reality, and homophobia is a new thing. . . . In the 19th and 20th centuries . . . they did not talk about it. Homosexuality was considered by some people as a vice [that] gay men could not help themselves." In this reply, Catholic homophobia operates as a cultural norm and way of life, an unfortunate but negotiable disdain of (male) same-sex sexual practices. Homophobia as "a new thing," however, refers to evangelical Christian religious homophobia. In Jean-Élie's memory, the pejorative versions of the terms masisi and *madivinez* did not become popular until after the uprooting of the younger Duvalier's regime in 1986, and he blames the influx of Protestant missionaries for the change in cultural attitudes toward homosexuality.

A TWIST ON CONVERSION THERAPY: RECLAIMING VODOU AND CATHOLICISM

At a time when Protestantism (and therefore Protestant homophobia) had been significantly increasing in the general population, same-sex-desiring and gender-creative Haitians who grew up in evangelical Christian households were converting to Vodou. They expressed to me feeling more welcome in Vodou spaces than in Protestant ones. Not all were direct targets of Protestant homophobia, though generally they were turned off by the denunciation of same-sex sexuality in their families and churches. Such negative experiences played an important role in decisions to reclaim Vodou and therefore Catholicism since, for many, they are practiced together.

These formerly Protestant Haitians initially had to surmount the false perceptions of the religion that they had learned from intimates during their upbringing. Essentially, in Protestant formulation, Vodou is devil worship and its practitioners are dangerous people—homosexuals, criminals, kidnappers, rapists, poisoners, and cannibals—in league with demons who seek to destroy not only individual lives but the well-being of the Haitian nation.

Shared by evangelical Haitians and missionaries, as well as those outside of Haiti, this perspective considers Vodou a powerful and corruptive force that is necessary to contain and expel. It inspires hatred and fear and requires constant spiritual vigilance to resist its temptations. Embracing Vodou goes against everything Protestants have been taught in their lifetimes. Below I describe some of the common ways that these Haitians were reintroduced to Vodou.

Three gay Haitians described that they were invited to rethink their relationship with the religion through folkloric dance, which is a popular style based on Vodou ritual. As Jean Appolon recounted, "As a kid in Port-au-Prince, I was scared of the drums. My family taught me to fear them . . . [they were] very religious." I asked Jean what had changed. "I just knew that I needed to dance, that the desire was in me. But dancing in Haiti is also associated with homosexuality. When I got a scholarship to dance, I hid it from my family. I eventually told my mom, and she has been very supportive, but my father's side of the family was not." Jean now teaches Haitian dance in Boston, New York, and Port-au-Prince, where he runs a no-tuition institute to expose young people to Haitian tradition through dance education.[12] "Haitian culture breathes through tradition. This is precisely the missionaries' concern with music and dance—it will bring people back to Vodou."

Jean's story had similarities with those of two men still living in Haiti—Juni and Junior. Both described having a feeling or desire for dance, which was seemingly off-limits to them because of its associations with Vodou. Now they teach as well as perform—one in a prominent troupe that regularly tours internationally (making it difficult to not tell his family that he is a dancer) and the other in a group he created with friends that performs only in Haiti. Through their creative endeavors, these three men reclaimed Vodou and eventually Catholicism because, as Junior said, "the lwa (spirits) lead people to church."

It was far more common for lovers and friends—trusted intimates outside of the family—to introduce people to Vodou ceremonies. Lele, a Jacmelian lesbian in her mid-twenties, was invited by friends. "I was very afraid the first time that I went to a ceremony. I heard the music inside, and I thought that I was going to die!" When I asked what happened, she replied, "Well, they didn't eat me! [Laughs]" I was surprised by her answer since by the time we met she had initiated and was immersed in studying Vodou. She, like other converts from Protestantism, enthusiastically supported education and re-education about Vodou and carefully taught me about its rituals, principles, and meanings. "It brings me closer to my culture and history as a Haitian."

Reclaiming Vodou—and Haitian history—often coincides with embracing one's own same-sex desires or reconfiguring one's relationship to male homosexuality, as was true for Lele. Her Baptist upbringing with a family actively involved in the church had been very positive. Lele was well aware that the church did not approve of homosexuality; however, she thought that the general messages of the church did not concern her desires because the antihomosexual sermons singled out *pederas* (pederast, also a pejorative term for male homosexuals). But once she started meeting some of these "pederas" through her ex-girlfriend, Lele realized that they had commonalities. "My aunt and a couple of her friends told me bad things about them. They said, they are masisi! Do you know what kinds of wicked things they do? . . . They were criminals and [infecting people with] AIDS. I told them these things were lies." This exchange made Lele wonder what her aunt might do if she found out that the niece she had raised as her own child is a lesbian. It also opened up the possibility to question church doctrine because, as Lele said, "God loves everyone, without exception. I realized that even though I learned that from the church, they find reasons to discriminate against people and treat them like garbage. But Vodou loves everyone. It has an open philosophy toward gays and lesbians."

Esther, a generation older than Lele, who had grown up in Cap-Haïtien, also had to contend with antigay expressions, in her case from her in-laws. After moving near her husband's family in Delmas, she befriended men her in-laws (correctly) suspected to be masisi. These in-laws derided the men who helped Esther with her children and taunted Esther by calling her masisi as well. She expressed to me that she was unsure whether her in-laws felt threatened by the way that she defended her friends or if they knew that she had romantic relationships with women (to use her description) before marrying her husband. Esther found the whole situation insulting, not just because they used "masisi" against her. Her in-laws bent over backward to ignore or reframe her husband's sexual indiscretions and abuse of Esther and one of their children, and she could not understand why "[same-sex-desiring] men and women just living their lives" could arouse such vitriol when her husband's violence did not. Esther bravely left her husband and the Baptist church. She tried other churches, including the Seventh-day Adventist Church and the Church of Jesus Christ of Latter-day Saints, though ultimately—after her previous experiences—their emphasis on patriarchal heterosexuality turned her off. While she did not consider herself to be a feminist, she critiqued the way church doctrine put men in charge of women, "as if we are slaves!" Esther finally affiliated with Vodou, where she found that women are honored spiritual leaders along with men.

Reclaiming Vodou has powerful effects for men, as well, as was true for a mid-twenties man from Jacmel named Avadra who grew up in a Baptist household. His mother had converted from Catholicism when she married Avadra's father, and he described her to me as someone totally immersed in church life. He first heard the term "masisi" from his mother, but in the context of men who have sex with other men for money. During his teenage years, Avadra's mother started inquiring if he was a masisi. Unfortunately, his friends also made a game of asking him if he was homosexual, to which he would reply, "It's not important, guys." He asked the question of himself, as he had already been having sexual encounters for years with other young men. This prospect in the context of growing up in a household and congregation that "hated gays" produced internal conflict, and Avadra seriously contemplated suicide. Someone he knew from work—a heterosexual boy several years younger than him—reached out to offer support, and he introduced Avadra to someone who would become his long-term lover. This man, Franck, a well-respected artist who had lived many years abroad, taught Avadra about the divine aspects of masisi in Vodou, and he invited Avadra to attend ceremonies. This conversion formed the groundwork for later queer anti-imperialist political organizing, inspired by the first wave of widespread attacks against same-sex-desiring Haitians that included a nearly fatal attack on Franck in their home.

POSTCOLONIAL HOMOPHOBIA AS THE (HOMO)SEXUAL POLITICS OF EMPIRE

This chapter illuminates some of the wide-reaching effects of United States imperialism in Haiti over the last century in terms of religious sexual politics. Two decades of U.S. occupation on the island of Hispaniola aimed to bring Haiti and the Dominican Republic within the sphere of U.S. empire, coupled—as I discuss here—with the missionary position, created the possibilities for and generated interest in U.S. evangelizing missions to a much greater degree than there had been previously. The religious shift in Haiti from having an almost nonexistent Protestant population to almost 40 percent by the turn of the century had significant impacts in the intimate realm of sexual politics and introduced a kind of evangelical Christian homophobia to Haiti that has become the norm, infiltrating all aspects of Haitian life from family and interpersonal relations to political and social structures.

During my fieldwork, there were three moments when Protestant homophobia spiked in Haiti and verbal and physical assault against same-sex-desiring and gender-creative Haitians became widespread: in 2008, when the nominee to the position of prime minister faced public accusations of being a lesbian; in 2010, when Protestants scapegoated homosexuals for the earthquake by supposedly making Haiti fall out of favor with God; and in 2013, when evangelical Christians staged marches in major metropolitan cities to oppose same-sex marriage. It happened again in 2016, when the government shut down the country's first scheduled LGBTI film, arts, and performance festival, Massimadi. These are discussed further in the following chapters. Based on my knowledge of these cycles and the increasing popularity of Protestant participation in national politics, I anticipated that elected Haitian leaders might enact a law criminalizing same-sex sexuality, which was set in motion in 2017. As I assert, these events and the general spread of Protestant homophobia means that Catholic practices of discretion no longer work to protect same-sex-desiring Haitians as well as they used to and, therefore, life for them is becoming increasingly difficult.

2008

3

EVANGELICAL CHRISTIAN HOMOPHOBIA AND THE MICHÈLE PIERRE-LOUIS CONTROVERSY

I make it a point to thank all those who have shown both their support and their solidarity toward me by rising up against the slander and disinformation campaign launched against me and my family since President Préval called on me to lead the next government.

Special thanks to the youths, the peasants, the monks, the intellectuals, the artists, the Vodou followers, the women's organizations, the human rights organizations, the members of the poor neighborhoods, the Haitian diaspora, the press, the private business sector, the international community, and all of my friends here and there for their support and their civic commitment at this difficult juncture of our national life. I thank my family, which surrounds me with its unwavering affection, in particular my daughter, who just gave me my first grandson.

Since 1986, I have received several invitations to be part of the government or to accept a post in a public institution. I always refused, because I wanted to continue to work to strengthen civil society through the youths, the peasants, the unions, the human rights and women's organizations, the churches, the artists, and the artisans. As indicated on my resume, I worked in the private and para-governmental sector on numerous development projects financed by almost all the national and international agencies throughout the country. My morals and ethics were always recognized by all.

Today, I have answered Préval's invitation to serve my country in a difficult juncture. I have agreed to do it with my head held high, knowing that I am committing to the political field, which is the field of collective interest and common good. I know that I must arm myself with courage and wisdom to overcome the multiple challenges I will have to face, but I will never allow myself to be led into a debate centered on disinformation and slander. The solidarity movement that has emerged since my designation shows me that I am not alone in this fight. Let us work together and urgently in order to bring lasting solutions to the multiple problems facing the country. (Michèle Duvivier Pierre-Louis, radio address 2008)

President René Préval nominated educator, economist, and human development leader Michèle Duvivier Pierre-Louis to the position of prime minister of Haiti on June 14, 2008, around the time I started the research project that resulted in this book. The parliament, tasked by the 1987 constitution with ratifying presidential nominations for the position of prime minister, had rejected Préval's first two nominees—Haiti's representative to the Inter-American Development Bank and the Secretary of State for Public Safety—on the basis of state citizenship and residency requirements. As with the other nominations, Michèle Duvivier Pierre-Louis was a close associate of Préval's; the two had worked together and for a time co-owned and managed a bakery. By the time of her nomination, Pierre-Louis—originally from the coastal city of Jérémie in western Haiti—had an impressive resume and qualities that would make for an excellent prime minister. She had earned a master's degree in economics from Queens College of City University of New York, and—in addition to running a small business with President Préval—held a variety of positions that gave her insight into bureaucracies and neoliberal political economies: deputy director at the National Airport Authority, Director of Credit at the Bank of Nova Scotia, and officer of Administration and Human Resources for the Haitian Development Finance Corporation. She had long been involved in literacy and education efforts in Haiti, including teaching at the Université Quisqueya in the Department of Educational Sciences at the time of her nomination.

Perhaps most importantly, Pierre-Louis cofounded and served as director of Fondasyon Konsesans ak Libète/Knowledge and Liberty Foundation (FOKAL). She established FOKAL in 1995 as a branch of the Open Society Foundations (OSF), a philanthropic project of Hungarian American billionaire George Soros. The executive director of OSF (then the Open Society Institute) had worked in Haiti and asked Pierre-Louis to participate in a witnessing trip to South Africa during the political struggle to end apartheid. He ended up extending an invitation to her to create what would become FOKAL, with the understanding that the institution would be guided by her vision and priorities. By the time Pierre-Louis was nominated as prime minister, FOKAL had become a major player in Haitian development in the realms of the arts, culture, education, and environment.

Unlike the previous two nominees for the position of prime minister, Pierre-Louis's role as FOKAL director garnered her popular appeal in a country with an understandable distrust of elites. At the helm of a well-respected institution within Haiti, Pierre-Louis made it a point to attend FOKAL events rather than stay behind the scenes. Her visibility reached across the deep socioeconomic divides in the country and became associated with an institution that made a concerted effort to work with the majority poor as well as those in privileged-class positions. I know many people—particularly artists—from downtown Port-au-Prince, the countryside, and other areas marked by lack of access to financial resources who have benefitted immensely from the opportunities created by FOKAL: performances, artistic exhibitions, lectures, conferences, classes, and workshops. These people remarked on Pierre-Louis's accessibility, affability, generosity, and trustworthiness in addition to her intelligence and the usual array of leadership qualities. One person described her as someone who did not grow "fat"—or personally profit—from the foreign donations to her organization.

Pierre-Louis's popular appeal made her an ideal nominee for prime minister in the wake of the so-called "global food crisis" in spring 2008. The astronomical rise in cost of food staples around the world plunged an estimated three billion people who had already been experiencing food insecurity into slow starvation. Majority-poor Haitians had been made vulnerable to such price fluctuations through the influence of structural adjustment and other U.S. neoliberal economic policies, such as the one championed by President Bill Clinton requiring Haiti to drop tariffs on imported government-subsidized white rice from the United States. Haitians substituted this once low-cost "Miami rice" for Haitian rice, and by the time of the global food crisis, relied heavily on this import for everyday nourishment. When the cost of white rice, additional food staples, and imported products for daily use like oil doubled in a matter of months, Haitians already struggling with food insecurity suffered from "Clorox hunger" that seemed to eat away their insides. Meanwhile U.S. news media circulated stories of people eating "mud cookies," taking poverty pornography to another level, alongside stories of political unrest in Haiti that rarely discussed the role of the United States in generating the problems. There was good reason for majority poor Haitians and their allies to take to the streets, and the mass demonstrations led to the parliament ousting the prime minister, Jacques Édouard-Alexis, with a vote of no confidence.

Despite Pierre-Louis's demonstrated leadership qualities and strong base of support, not everyone reacted positively when Préval nominated her for the position as her radio address—transcribed above—indicates. Her nomination was mired in "slander" and "disinformation" (to use her words) meant to keep her from assuming office. While it would be likely that anyone with foreign funding and connections—even though commonplace among the elite—would come under suspicion, the slander and disinformation was levied vis-à-vis sexuality that cannot be untangled from these other dynamics. Rumors that Pierre-Louis was gay, lesbian, madivin, *madouda* (another pejorative Kreyòl term for same-sex-desiring women), and homosexuelle circulated through the transnational Haitian *teledjòl* (rumor mill) in the weeks following Préval's announcement. The evidence wielded as "fact" about her sexuality was Pierre-Louis's cohabitation with a woman in one of Haiti's elite families, rumored to be her long-term lover and the reason for Pierre-Louis's divorce from her husband. Eventually, Pierre-Louis was asked directly if the content of these rumors were true, and she declined to comment. This controversy culminated in explicit attacks on the content of her "moral character" as a potential state representative of Haiti. It was to these attacks that she eventually responded in the national radio address once it was clear that Pierre-Louis would become prime minister.

This chapter provides a feminist and queer analysis of the controversy about Michèle Duvivier Pierre-Louis's nomination in Haiti and the diaspora, a controversy that centrally concerned sexuality and therefore highlights important dynamics of postcolonial homophobia. Haitian feminist organizers considered the tarnishing of Pierre-Louis's reputation to be a strategy for keeping women out of leadership, because the accusation of lesbianism marked her as morally unfit to be head of government. Given the various forms of homophobia that anyone targeted would face in Haiti, the truthfulness of the accusations—of which I am not certain—did not matter. (At that time *no* country in the world had a head of government who openly identified as gay, lesbian, bisexual, or same-sex-desiring by another name.) Feminists knew the political punch that these accusations had on women, exacerbating an already difficult path to public leadership that is predominantly the domain of men.

To layer this analysis, I document that the Pierre-Louis controversy inaugurated a period of intensified evangelical Christian homophobia within Haiti—what I refer to as a flare-up of postcolonial homophobia to connote the underlying structural conditions and the cyclical pattern of violence that escalates around major events. Same-sex-desiring Haitians remarked to me in casual conversations and formal interviews that the controversy marked what felt to them like a new public discourse about same-sex sexuality, and lesbianism in particular. Starline, a woman from Jacmel who worked in a restaurant and was about my age—mid-twenties at the time, stated this directly in one of our interviews.

> There have been changes in Haiti.
> *Can you say more?*
> Well, last year there was a lot of drama about the prime minister . . .
> *Michèle Pierre-Louis?*
> Yes, people were saying bad things about her . . . that she is a lesbian. But they said it differently.
> *Well, what do you think?*
> I can't determine if she is a lesbian. I would have to meet her myself.
> *No, I mean, how is that part of the changes in Haiti?*
> I have never never never heard such a public discussion like that.
> *Like what?*
> You know, about lesbians. People should let other people do what they want.

I met Starline through her girlfriend who danced with a group I got to know well because they practiced at the arts center where I lived when I moved to Haiti for fieldwork. She was understandably reluctant to be associated with me—a white U.S. American researching, as I would say, "gender" and "sexuality"—though she warmed up over time as we found each other again and again in overlapping social circles in the small city. She and others maintained that while gossip between individuals had been par for the course in terms of managing information about one's own sexuality, it was different to see such a public figure as the prime minister nominee not only subjected to widespread speculation, but directly asked if she is homosexual and outrightly accused of lesbianism. It offended their sense of how to act respectfully in relationship to other people and countered familiar (Catholic) norms about speaking about sexuality in public, using words like "new," "different," "changes," "never before," and "weird" to describe the controversy. While the Pierre-Louis controversy may or may not have marked something entirely "new" or "different" in Haiti, it was the first time many of my younger interlocutors felt the widespread effects of clashes between Catholic and Protestant systems of sexuality. Both the question posed to Pierre-Louis—"are you a homosexual?"—and the presumption of revealing her true sexual inclinations exemplify Protestant homophobia through the evangelical Christian emphasis on enunciation and denunciation that I described in chapter 2.

The Pierre-Louis controversy is a case study in postcolonial homophobia. Thinking long-term about connections between the transnational imperialist discourse of Haiti as the premodern land of voodoo/vaudoux, the American occupation and evangelical Christian missions in Haiti, and the growing prevalence of Protestantisms and their sexual politics, provides necessary context for understanding the incitement to discourse about homosexuality surrounding the controversy and its effects on the lives of same-sex-desiring and gender-creative Haitians. As I document, the controversy generated a violent backlash against Haitians known—or even perceived to be—masisi, madivin, homosexuelle, gay, lesbian, or otherwise same-sex-desiring. Verbal and physical assaults spiked in the wake of the events. However, a small group of same-sex-desiring Haitians, who experienced this violence and witnessed Michèle Pierre-Louis respond to the accusations in the radio address by refusing to either confirm or deny that she is a lesbian, fomented public and organized queer resistance in Haiti.

HOMOPHOBIA AND HETEROPATRIARCHY

When President René Préval nominated Michèle Pierre-Louis as prime minister in summer 2008, I was interning at a Haitian organization while attending the Haitian Creole Language and Culture Summer Institute at the University of Massachusetts, Boston. One day while the staff and interns ate our bagged lunches together, the executive director, Madeline inquired what I thought about the Pierre-Louis accusations and mentioned that she had been asked to comment publicly on them. When I said that I knew little about the situation, Madeline provided a basic description and noted:

> You know, we have this problem in Haitian society, and we see the effects of it here every so often. Like recently we had a young woman, a teenager, come to us whose family threw her out of their house because she prefers women. There is so much that we need to do to change homophobic attitudes. But the problem is bigger than that. When people run for political office in Haiti, they are always subject to rumors and speculation, but people are brutal towards women. I do not think that this is only about sexuality, it is a way of keeping women out of leadership.

She introduced homophobia "in Haitian society" to me through these two examples as an interested outsider—and relevant to the story, as someone who as a teenager had been thrown out of my home for being a lesbian. Importantly, my first explicit conversation about homophobia in Haiti and its diaspora centered women's experiences with violence. Madeline clearly considered addressing homophobia within the scope of the work of her grassroots Haitian organization. Because homophobia harms Haitian women, Madeline told me, it fractures families and communities. So as I learned about the social problem of homophobia from her, it was in the context of Haitian heterosexual women's antihomophobic work—envisioned as a reparative project for cultivating positive social relationships in Haiti and the diaspora.

Because the Pierre-Louis controversy was taking place during the first year of my field work, I came to know that women's rights organizers in Haiti affiliated with Kay Fanm (Women's House) and Solidarite Fanm Ayisyèn (Haitian Women's Solidarity) shared Madeline's analysis: homophobia is a way of "keeping women out of leadership." The evidence they offered was that men—even ones who they were aware had sexual relationships with other men—had not faced such public scrutiny, yet women leaders regularly had to contend with unseemly rumors about their personal lives. Haiti had already had two female heads of state—President Ertha Pascal-Trouillot (1990–91) and Prime Minister Claudette Werleigh (1995–96). These women held only interim positions during times of political change, consistent with women leaders at the national level whom political scientist Jane S. Jensen describes as "temporaries, tokens, and ceremonial leaders" (2008, 63). Both Pascal-Trouillot and Werleigh were subject to what women organizers considered to be gender-biased charges against their leadership. The controversy about Michèle Pierre-Louis was the latest iteration in this trend targeting women leaders with any ammunition—trumped up or fabricated—that might work to disempower them.

Lesbian and queer women have theorized the relationship of homophobia to sexism and patriarchy in ways that are helpful to understanding this phenomenon with regards to the Pierre-Louis controversy. In *Homophobia: A Weapon of Sexism*, lesbian social justice activist Suzanne Pharr describes what she terms "lesbian baiting," a kind of homophobia that operates as a weapon of sexism:

> If lesbians are established as threats to the status quo, as outcasts who must be punished, homophobia can wield its power over all women through lesbian baiting. Lesbian baiting is an attempt to control women by labeling us as lesbians because our behavior is not acceptable, that is, when we are being independent, going our own way, living whole lives, fighting for our rights, demanding equal pay, saying no to violence, being self-assertive, bonding with and loving the company of women, assuming the right to our bodies,

insisting upon our own authority, making changes that include us in society's decision-making; lesbian baiting occurs when women are called lesbians because we resist male dominance and control. And it has little or nothing to do with one's sexual identity. To be named as lesbian threatens all women, not just lesbians, with great loss. And any woman who steps out of role risks being called a lesbian. (1997, 19)

Women like Michèle Pierre-Louis and others in Haiti who are positioned to have a great effect on state and national politics—regardless of their political agenda—are at risk for lesbian baiting. As Pharr suggests, this is because women attempting to make changes where patriarchy is the norm are inherently threatening.

Patriarchal rule in Haiti, as with so many places, is a product of European colonialism closely associated with the dominance of the Roman Catholic Church. Yet, as feminist Haitian studies scholarship describes, this male-dominated institution has existed alongside and in tension with Vodou, in which women are respected spiritual leaders and women and men must serve the spirits alongside each other. However, patriarchy—like homophobia—has renewed force because of the spread of evangelical Christianity connected to U.S. imperialism, which both reinforces male supremacy and mandates that converts reject Vodou—although whether they do or not and to what degree are different questions. As previous chapters elaborate, this religious shift in Haiti from Catholicism to Protestantism exacerbated the other condition of lesbian baiting: the devaluation of same-sex sexuality. That is to say that homophobia is not *reducible* to a weapon of sexism or "keeping women out of leadership" even when these dynamics are at play. As I have been showing, homophobia needs to be taken seriously in its own right because of how it structures and is structured by ongoing foreign intervention and people's daily lives in Haiti.

Suzanne Pharr goes on to say that part of what makes lesbian baiting such an effective tool for sexism is that it is a difficult charge to defend yourself against because *any* woman could potentially be a lesbian, or rather have same-sex desires for other women that she may or may not act on (1997, 20). Evidence of heterosexuality is not enough to discount the claim that one is a lesbian, and in Haiti, where the majority of same-sex-desiring women with whom I have interacted have both men and women as sexual partners, this is certainly the case. In my close reading of Pierre-Louis's defense in the next section, I show how she navigated this situation of lesbian baiting through *reproductive* heterosexuality—having children and grandchildren—that ameliorates some effects of homophobia on Haitian women. The defense she mounted worked insofar as she became the prime minister, but she was deposed after serving little more than a year. Moreover, the taint of the accusations against Pierre-Louis served as a warning to other women of the kind of struggle that might ensue should they pursue state leadership positions.

While Pharr is primarily interested in the effects of lesbian-baiting and homophobia on women as a kind of sexism, queer theorist Ann Pellegrini elaborates in "S(h)ifting the Terms of Hetero/Sexism: Gender, Power, and Homophobias" (1992) that homophobia has broad implications for upholding a two-sex system and its attendant gender norms.[1] "Sexism provides the social context within which the hatred of lesbians and gay men can flourish; in its turn, homophobia reinforces gender asymmetries" (48). Or, put another way, the social structure of homophobia is a key component of the interplay between heterosexism and patriarchy, which lesbian performance studies scholar Lynda S. Hart (1994) calls heteropatriarchy. Feminist scholars such as M. Jacqui Alexander (1997) and Kamala Kempadoo (2004) as well as grassroots activists brought the term into prominence in ways that connected a critique of heteropatriarchy to a project of decolonization in the Americas.

M. Jacqui Alexander's scholarship focuses on the postcolonial Caribbean context of the Bahamas and has deeply shaped this project about neighboring Haiti. In *Pedagogies of Crossing: Meditations on Feminism, Sexual Politics, Memory, and the Sacred*, Alexander argues that "*heteropatriarchy* is useful in continuing to perpetuate a colonial inheritance . . . and in enabling the political and economic processes of recolonization [in the present moment]," that is, "the ways in which political and economic strategies are made to usurp the self-determination of the Bahamian people" (2005, 24–25). The Bahamas had been a colony of the British Empire, and in 1973 it became an independent commonwealth nation. Recolonization refers to the triangulation of the postcolonial nation to its former colonizers and newer forms of imperialism, such as that exerted by the United States through various means that do not necessarily include military occupation, as in Haiti's case. These processes of heteropatriarchal recolonization happen at the juridico-discursive level (in the law), through "material and ideological processes initiated by the state" such as tourism, and at the level of the body-mind by naturalizing social hierarchies (Alexander 2005, 25–27). As Alexander contends, lesbians and "sodomites" (the term used in the Bahamas) bear the greatest burden of this recolonization—they are subjects who are discursively produced as being outside the postcolonial nation as it becomes "configured as heterosexual" (40). Alexander, like many queer theorists, does not explicitly theorize homophobia within the context of her book. Here I complement her work by illuminating the ways that structures of homophobia are part of heteropatriarchal recolonization—what I have been calling postcolonial homophobia. A product of homophobic sexual politics imported from the United States, the Michèle Pierre-Louis controversy in Haiti worked to disempower a highly qualified and popular woman leader *and* intensify the oppression of same-sex-desiring and gender-creative Haitians.

STATE PERFORMANCES OF SEXUALITY: MICHÈLE PIERRE-LOUIS

While accusations had hounded women who breached the male-dominated political sphere other than Michèle Pierre-Louis, as Haitian women's organizers and feminists pointed out, the attacks against her were particularly virulent and aided in their dissemination by new media—such as blogs, Facebook, and YouTube. The accusations that Pierre-Louis was a lesbian sparked a transnational debate in Haiti and the diaspora that extended beyond her leadership qualifications. It was what philosopher Michel Foucault called an "incitement to discourse" about homosexuality (1978, 17).

Unlike the context of an incitement to discourse that Foucault theorizes in *The History of Sexuality* (1978), the Pierre-Louis controversy was situated in a Haitian context characterized by a restrictive economy of language pertaining to sexuality vis-à-vis Roman Catholicism. Whereas rumors about politicians had circulated in the past, the direct question (*are you or are you not a homosexual?*) and public assertions that Pierre-Louis is a lesbian, or at least a woman-loving-woman by another name, broke long-established Catholic norms about when, where, and how conversations about sexuality in general—and homosexuality in particular—should take place. The controversy was discussed and disputed throughout Haiti and the diaspora: *well, is she or isn't she? why does it matter anyway, isn't it a private issue? why aren't you more concerned about the morality of our leaders? who says homosexuality has anything to do with morality?*

Pierre-Louis artfully negotiated this minefield shaped by Protestant homophobia. Less than a month after her nomination, when her dossier was still under consideration in the senate, Pierre-Louis addressed the Haitian nation over the radio about the concerns. She had tried multiple avenues of damage control by that point, beginning with her website as well as Préval's. *Le nouvelliste*, one of the highly circulated reputable newspapers in Haiti, reported that Michèle Pierre-Louis told Haitian political leaders in closed-door meetings that the accusations of her homosexuality were unfounded (Claude Gilles 2008). Yet, even if this information about "unfounded accusations" was available on the Internet (a technology that was becoming popular in Haiti with the proliferation of Internet cafés) and in the newspaper (accessible to a small percentage of the population who can read French), it reached a limited audience. The radio, on the other hand, served as a popular venue for staging political performances in Haiti because it is a technology accessible to the majority.

In only twelve sentences—the ones opening this chapter—Pierre-Louis skillfully positioned herself as the leader of the future government of Haiti. She began by thanking those who have risen up with her against the slander and reminding people that President Préval *called on her* to lead the next government. Her approach included hailing a motley crew of supporters under the rubric of civil society or what George Soros has called an "open society"—including international organizations, feminist groups, the Haitian diaspora, and practitioners of Vodou—to serve the country alongside her at a "difficult juncture in national life." Pierre-Louis used this phrase—"difficult juncture in national life"—twice in the speech's short duration in order to invoke a national crisis to which her leadership was the answer. In addition to the famine produced by Clinton administration policies that resulted in her predecessor's ouster, the Pierre-Louis controversy overlapped with the worst hurricane season on record at the time—with severe flooding in the city of Gonaives and the decimation of an estimated 70 percent of the crops grown in the country.

As a state performance of sexuality, the rhetorical strategy of Pierre-Louis' performance is interesting because, even though most heterosexual Haitians and Americans that I have spoken to remember the address as a denial of lesbianism, Pierre-Louis never explicitly denied being a lesbian or engaging in homosexual acts. In her speech, she uttered none of the terms used to condemn her—*madivin, madoda, homosexuelle*, lesbian. She instead shifted the burden of responsibility for accountability on the accusations themselves, calling them "slander" and "disinformation." Pierre-Louis responded to the accusations sideways, without mentioning their content. First, she recounts her successes working in the private and para-governmental sectors with national and international organizations. Early in the speech, Pierre-Louis noted her track record working in these sectors: "My morals and ethics were always recognized by all." Referencing her universally recognized ethics situated her in favorable relation to the general distrust of politicians and government representatives. Her mention of morals, however, was a thinly veiled response to the sources that accused her of being morally unfit to be prime minister based on her alleged same-sex sexuality.

Second, Pierre-Louis tried to negate the allegations by repositioning herself as a mother and grandmother. After nods to President Préval, civil society, and friends early in the speech, she devotes a whole sentence to her family: "I thank my family, which surrounds me with its unwavering affection, in particular my daughter, who just gave me my first grandson." Invoking her daughter evidenced heterosexual sex in a way that her prior marriage to a man could not in and of itself, and it performed proper Catholic women's subjectivity through reproduction. However, since Pierre-Louis was rumored to have had an affair with a woman after the birth of her daughter, this strategy could only be slightly effective in terms of countering the rumors. On the other hand, the reference to her grandson places her in an extended line of reproductive heterosexuality. As a sixty-one-year-old grandmother, she was also able to draw on ageist conceptions that older people, especially older women, are asexual. This effectively countered the rumors since, for most people, "lesbian" and "homosexual" imply the need for engagement in sexual activity. If anything, Pierre-Louis projected that she was married to her work.

This strategy worked to the effect of securing Pierre-Louis's position as prime minister by framing the Haitian nation as a site of reproductive heterosexuality. In no small part, this was also possible because Pierre-Louis operated within familial frameworks of government, where she acted as the figurative (grand)mother-leader of the Haitian nation at the side of Papa Préval. The "coupling" of the prime minister and president through proximity anchored the leadership of Pierre-Louis in traditional patriarchal authority, making her associations with feminist groups and rumored lesbianism less threatening. Imagine if the president of Haiti had been a woman; the coupling of the prime minister and president would hardly discourage rumors of Pierre-Louis's homosexuality or mitigate the impact of postcolonial homophobia. But it was not just that Préval was a man that facilitated Pierre-Louis's path to the prime ministry, it was also his particular kind of masculinity. He was sixty-five when he nominated Michèle Pierre-Louis, with a full gray beard and distinguished air. Unlike his successor, Michel Martelly or "Sweet Micky"—at one time known for his youthful, explicitly sexual antics—Préval was stalwart and proper. Next to him, Michèle Pierre-Louis could perform the respectable heterosexuality that was necessary for her public appointment.

In the end, Haitians seemed to be assured enough of Michèle Pierre-Louis's heterosexuality (or potentially her ability to exercise discretion), and she was installed as prime minister on 5 September 2008. Her term lasted only fourteen months, however, and she was ousted in November 2009 after a vote of no confidence. Though Pierre-Louis's time in office was short, it was a period of major changes for same-sex-desiring and gender-creative Haitians. Next, I elaborate the various ripple effects of the Pierre-Louis controversy. These effects included a flare-up of homophobic violence and, at the same time, the emboldening of Haitians of the majority poor who were negatively impacted by postcolonial homophobia to stage their own acts of intervention in national politics.

THE QUEER AFTERLIVES OF PIERRE-LOUIS'S STATE PERFORMANCE OF (HETERO?)SEXUALITY

The Michèle Pierre-Louis controversy had negative effects on the daily lives of same-sex-desiring and gender-creative Haitians. The intensity of anti-homosexual discourse and physical violence against people perceived to be masisi and madivin escalated in the ensuing months. My informants noted that their daily life included more exposure to derogatory comments during mid- to late 2008. Many of these were in direct reference to Michèle Pierre-Louis. Medline told me, for instance, "people sent me bad words over text messages about Michèle Pierre-Louis after the radio announcement." When I asked what words she was referring to, Medline responded, "They called her a liar and said that she is madivin. I do not like that term at all. It sounds so . . . bad." A lesbian woman named Flore who would take the tap-tap to and from her family's small restaurant where she worked each day told me that Pierre-Louis was a regular topic of conversation. The benign versions included passengers' speculations about what causes someone to be homosexual. "One man said that it is the devil's influence, and there was a quarrel. [*Laughing*] People said, 'No, no, no! It is such-and-such or such-and-such.'" I asked if Flore said anything in response. "Oh! Who me? No, that was their drama." I asked if they said anything that bothered her. "Not them. Later I was with some men [on the bus], and they were making jokes about how Michèle Pierre-Louis is a whore. That made me really angry because Pierre-Louis is educated . . . and working hard to make a difference for our country." People told me about these lewd comments and public debates about same-sex sexuality in other settings as well—shopping in the marketplace, walking between school and home, and at work at a hotel—although not necessarily in direct connection to Michèle Pierre-Louis.

For some people the negative comments were directed at them. Several young Jacmelians whom I mentioned in the last chapter had never faced this kind of homophobia before because they practiced discretion. Those who were still in secondary school, for instance, had classmates who taunted them with insults like *masisi*, *madivin*, and *bouzen*. Even though Norh did not have the most feminine outward appearance or comportment, many of the slurs against him had gendered connotations, such as calling him "madame." Norh, who also ended up having problems at home, needed to repeat the year because of the stress. One young woman, Lady, faced such persistent harassment that she asked her aunt living in Florida, who was funding her education with remittances, if she could move there to be with her. "I love my mother and my brothers and sisters. I love Jacmel, too. But I was sick all the time. I did not want to eat. I did not want to go to school. I had always believed that I would go to college." She ended up dropping out of school.

This is also the moment when Starline, whose family is Catholic, told me that her mother asked her directly about her same-sex desires. "You know, the people of Jacmel talk. They were saying all kinds of bad things about me . . . that I was *madivin sal* [dirty madivin]. My family knew, but my mother asked—'what they say, is it true?' I did not say anything. . . . It was better that I did not say anything because it's my business." Her mother, with whom Starline expressed previously that she is close, seemed to have asked out of concern rather than accusation. Her mother nonetheless breached the Catholic norms in Haiti around explicit discussions of homosexuality, which Starline rerouted by not saying anything.

Two men—one self-identified as masisi and the other one gay—told me that they had each faced more serious physical violence. The two had little in common other than being effeminate and having access to few economic resources as part of Haiti's majority poor. The first—Dorme—was one of a few male cosmetologists in Jacmel. Within a span of a month and a half, one group of men that he knew from around the neighborhood had thrown rocks at him when he was returning home from work and then yet another cadre had chased him with sticks saying, "We will get you, masisi!" He has considered that the second of the two was an attempted robbery, since "everyone thinks that masisi are rich. They see my nice hair and my nice clothes, and they think that I have money. But I don't!" The other man, Charles, had actually been injured in the physical altercation started by the aggressive comments of two strangers. "I fought the homophobes, but thank God my neighbors saw what happened . . . [otherwise] it could have been worse."

The most extreme situation happened to Avadra and his boyfriend, Franck, right after they moved in together. Three men came into the house late at night when Avadra was not there and beat Franck with a hammer and an ice pick. The men broke his skull and three ribs, and they ruptured his liver before leaving him for dead. Franck miraculously survived after being found by a neighbor in the morning and immediately taken to the hospital. His well-resourced family immediately blamed Avadra, and the police arrested him for the crime. Avadra declared his innocence to the police and told them that someone else had beaten his boyfriend. "I was one of the worst people in their eyes because I am gay," he told me before recounting how he was subject to extreme physical violence by the police and other prisoners. After ten days in which his family, friends, and internationals like myself advocated for his release, Avadra was released.

While Franck was recovering from major surgeries, he did not know that his family was making plans for him to leave the country to live in Africa in a kind of exile. Once that plan was executed, Avadra and his boyfriend were no longer able to connect in the same way as they had before, although they stayed in touch and would rendezvous in the Dominican Republic. Avadra told me in one of our interviews: "It was the worst experience of my life, but I also learned more from it than anything else. If you are masisi or do not have money, you are nothing in Haiti. Justice will not be served." It was radicalizing for Avadra in many ways, and because of this experience, he committed to fight for a better life for *ti masisi* and *ti madivin*—masisi and madivin of Haiti's majority poor.

It is perhaps unimaginable that anything positive could come from these experiences, and yet they did. The prominence of *madivin* in national discourse had some unintended enabling effects. In *Excitable Speech: A Politics of the Performative*, queer theorist Judith Butler elaborates the unanticipated effects of hate speech aimed at minoritarian subjects in the United States: "One is not simply fixed by the name that one is called. In being called an injurious name, one is derogated and demeaned. But the name holds out another possibility as well: by being called a name, one is also, paradoxically, given a certain possibility for social existence, initiated into a temporal life of language that exceeds the prior purposes that animate that call. Thus, the injurious address may appear to fix or paralyze the one it hails, but it may also produce an unexpected and enabling response" (1997, 2). Many same-sex-desiring Haitians had avoided the terms *masisi* and *madivin* because they had known them only in a pejorative sense. As readers have seen throughout, my interlocutors repeatedly stated that they did not like these terms, that they were associated with nastiness; one man told me that when people used it against him, it made him feel like he was dead. They preferred other terms of self-description—such as gay, lesbian, and *se* (sister)—because they were not laden with negative connotations and also because they afforded a certain amount of discretion. However, as people talked about their experiences of being hailed by these terms in Jacmel, they started to imagine a collective social existence and came together to organize a response to the proliferation of Protestant homophobia. This was the beginning of Lakou, a performance troupe started by Avadra, his by then long-distance boyfriend, and a small group of masisi in Jacmel.

Moreover, these ti masisi and ti madivin recognized an ally of sorts in Michèle Pierre-Louis. Many people asserted that Pierre-Louis is a lesbian, without offering specific evidence when I inquired. They would tell me, "I know that she is a lesbian." As I elaborated earlier, this form of knowing references a kind of queer knowledge that is transmitted without being declared. Some people had twice-removed interactions with Pierre-Louis that informed their intuition that she is a lesbian—they heard about her doing something that sparked their intuition. Busy, an artist and mother living in downtown Port-au-Prince, told me that Pierre-Louis had helped one of her friends in need when his wife died. She told me, "I know that Michèle Pierre-Louis is a lesbian because she is generous. All gays are generous, different than other people."

But the majority of these references went back to the way that Pierre-Louis performed her speech on the radio. The rhetorical strategy of her speech enacted Haitian political discourse connected to Vodou called *pwen* (points), that are "defined by Karen McCarthy Brown [an anthropologist and author of *Mama Lola: A Vodou Priestess in Brooklyn*] as 'anything that captures the essence or the pith of a complex situation' and presents it figuratively" (McAlister 2002, 167). As McAlister coveys in a section of her book titled "Pwen: Indigenous Theory of Magic and Communication," pwen operate politically and rely on shared knowledge to understand complex situations and unpack coded meanings. Pierre-Louis refused the "points" thrown in her direction meant to derail her leadership, and she responded with her own pwen that repositioned herself as the right person to assume leadership as prime minister. Same-sex-desiring Haitians read the speech as covertly transmitting queer knowledge, as expressed eloquently by Norh: "They read a letter on the radio to affirm that Michèle Pierre-Louis is not a lesbian. She did not confirm that she was a lesbian. She did not deny it. But it was like the blood calling the blood. From what she said in the letter, I know she is a lesbian." In Norh's reading, when Pierre-Louis came up against a Protestant system of sexuality wherein people were demanding that she enunciate her lesbianism, she adeptly rerouted the vitriol by maintaining discretion. Therefore Norh, and others like him who grew up in Catholic families, recognized queerness in what was said, and more importantly *what was not said* in the speech.

Pierre-Louis' performance worked on multiple registers and can be considered what José Esteban Muñoz called a "queer act." In "Ephemera as Evidence: Introductory Notes to Queer Acts" he elaborates: "Queerness is often transmitted covertly. This has everything to do with the fact that leaving too much of a trace has often meant that the queer subject has left herself open for attack. Instead of being clearly available as visible evidence, queerness has instead existed as innuendo, gossip, fleeting moments, and performances that are meant to be interacted with by those within its epistemological sphere—while evaporating at the touch of those who would eliminate queer possibility" (1996, 6). For "those who would eliminate queer possibility," her speech sounded enough like a denial of lesbianism through association with tropes of reproductive heterosexuality that she was inaugurated. Yet she never in fact denied that she is a lesbian. Her same-sex-desiring and gender-creative audience tuned into this signal as "fleeting evidence" of queer possibility and read her as either one of their own or at least as someone who would act to their benefit. Not surprisingly, some—predominantly Protestants—expressed to me or others that they would have preferred that Pierre-Louis either affirm or deny that she is a lesbian. Medline said, "It would help Haiti if Pierre-Louis declared that she is a lesbian. If the prime minister can stand up, there will be more respect for homosexual people."

These readings of Pierre-Louis's performance—as queer, as performing Catholic discretion against the annihilating force of evangelical Christian homophobia—bolstered the confidence of same-sex-desiring and gender-creative Haitians to stage their own act of intervention in an era of sexual politics dominated by Protestant homophobia. I highlight this act of intervention in the next chapter: a performance by the troupe Lakou from Jacmel at the 2009 Ghetto Biennale, a few weeks before the earthquake. Titled "Zonbi, Zonbi," this queer undercommons performance used the trope of the zonbi and the medium of Vodou to stage a critique of postcolonial homophobia connected to U.S. imperialism in Haiti.

4

"ZONBI, ZONBI" AT THE GHETTO BIENNALE

A Queer Act of Intervention against Postcolonial Homophobia

In the wake of the Michèle Pierre-Louis controversy, same-sex-desiring and gender-creative Haitians staged a queer act of intervention against postcolonial homophobia in Haiti. The performance troupe staging this act, Lakou, was associated with the arts center FOSAJ in the southern coastal city of Jacmel where I worked—and even lived for a time—from 2008 to 2010. In their "Zonbi, Zonbi" performance, Lakou creatively highlighted their experiences with homophobic violence as same-sex-desiring and gender-creative Haitians of the majority poor. In the performance, the Lakou artists reclaimed the figure of the zonbi in a queer anti-imperialist critique, following in the Haitian tradition of cultural workers who use this figure to meditate on the conditions of European colonialism, U.S. imperialism, and other forms of foreign domination. Unlike anti-imperialists who adamantly avoid the reviled and debased figure of the zonbi precisely because of the way "zombies" have been used to project a nightmarish Haiti in the transnational imperialist discourse of the Black republic as the premodern land of "voodoo/vaudoux," the queer critique worked against the grain of these normative respectability politics that harm same-sex-desiring and gender-creative Haitians (see chapters 1 and 2). Moreover, Lakou's mobilization of antihomophobic politics stands out from those that do not embody anti-imperialist critique or that work in the mode of identity politics since the performers did not announce themselves as "gay" or same-sex desiring. This chapter describes the "Zonbi, Zonbi" performance at the inaugural Ghetto Biennale in late 2009, provides background about the founding of Lakou and their conception of the performance, elaborates why the zonbi is an effective figure for anti-imperialist critique in relationship to Frankétienne's novel *Dézafi*, and analyzes the queer aspects of Lakou's act of intervention into postcolonial homophobia.

The inaugural "Ghetto Biennale: Salon des Refusés for the 21st Century" stretched over three weeks in November and December 2009 and transformed the crowded Leanne neighborhood in downtown Port-au-Prince into an international arts destination. The neighborhood had long been a workspace and home for craftspeople and visionaries, including a collective of Afro-futurist Vodou-inspired sculptors who dubbed themselves Atis Rezistans.[1] Atis Rezistans imagined the Ghetto Biennale as a response to the bordering practices of an art world whose elite could not or would not contend with the limited mobilities of Haitian artists of the majority poor even though their creations traveled all over the world.[2] The sculptors turned the tables by inviting the rest of the art world to their ghetto for an event that has turned out to be part of an emergent movement of biennales in the global south. The Ghetto Biennale was an experiment guided by a question that riffs off Chicana lesbian feminist Gloria E. Anzaldùa's description of the borderlands (1987, 25), calling artists to consider: "What happens when first world art rubs up against third world art? Does it bleed?"

I visited the Atis Rezistans ateliers in Ghetto Leanne once—in fall 2008—before Haiti-based artists invited me to participate in their projects for the Ghetto Biennale. My role in "Zonbi, Zonbi" was modest: I participated in conversations about the performance as Lakou developed it, attended choreography sessions and rehearsals, bought and ferried supplies, traveled with Lakou members to Port-au-Prince to check out the performance site, and documented the project with photo and video. Three of us involved in "Zonbi, Zonbi" worked on another project envisioned by the director of the FOSAJ arts center, Flores "Flo" McGarrell, a cinematic adaptation of Kathy Acker's *Kathy Goes to Haiti* (1978). Flo was moved by the novel about a young white woman from New York who travels to Haiti and fucks a lot of men; he considered it a work of twisted genius even though—or maybe especially because—Acker hated it and scrawled on the proofs, "This is a piece of garbage."[3] At the time, I had neither read the book nor worked on a film before, though I was happy to be recruited to the project since I enjoyed assisting the FOSAJ artists while I served as a "researcher-in-residence."[4] Filming *Kathy Goes to Haiti* and attending Ghetto Biennale events meant that I started to build relationships with the people—particularly women and kids—who lived in the Leanne neighborhood where I had been repeatedly instructed not to go by middle-class and diasporic Haitians who considered downtown Port-au-Prince unsafe. The residents challenged these generalized classist conceptions of their ghetto, and Busy—who has become a longtime friend—said to me at the time, "I bet you were not expecting to meet anyone here who is open to gay and lesbian people. There is homophobia here like there are other problems, but we take care of each other too and welcome people from the outside."

After a busy month of project work and events, the day of the Ghetto Biennale opening—when Lakou was scheduled to perform "Zonbi, Zonbi"—arrived with fanfare. The Leanne neighborhood buzzed with excitement as artists put the finishing touches on their projects. A freshly painted sign on the facade of a concrete building announcing "Ghetto BIENNALE" greeted everyone at the entrance to the neighborhood from Boulevard Jean-Jacques Dessalines, with portraits of resident artists Eugène and Louco on a building surrounded by Atis Rezistans sculptures. The likeness of Eugène wore sunglasses that showed the reflection of glowing skulls, evoking Bawon Samdi, the patriarch of the gede and overseer of the cemetery. The *vèvè* (ritual symbol for Vodou spirits) for Papa Legba, who opens the doors to the spirit world, appeared under Louco. People poured into the neighborhood, arriving on foot from surrounding neighborhoods and by *moto*, car, or tap-tap from farther away. I had arrived early in the day and was talking with an older FOSAJ artist, Destin Domond, about his mural-size canvas filled with stick- and machete-painted "nations" represented at the Ghetto Biennale—with Mexico, Jamaica, Germany, Canada, and the United States all appropriately dwarfed by Haiti—when the members of Lakou filed by in their street clothes to prepare for "Zonbi, Zonbi." I followed Lakou through to the Atis Rezistans sculptor Eugène's courtyard to assist with setting up—clearing the performance space of small stones, moving framed Vodou flags to clear space for the drums and musicians, and hanging a piece of canvas between the art pieces on the back walls of the courtyard.

The performance was scheduled for 5 p.m., though no one circulated paper programs to indicate when to show up. However, as the Lakou members changed into costumes for the performance, a steady stream of Ghetto Biennale attendees filled Eugène's courtyard, following the sound of the drums. Before long the courtyard was packed with people, and some audience members climbed to sit or stand on the outside walls for a better view. Zaka, the FOSAJ assistant director and my roommate, and I were responsible for holding open the performance space in one section of the courtyard, but I relinquished the task because it required a certain degree of authority that I was uncomfortable asserting as a white U.S. American in a predominantly Haitian crowd. Instead, I moved to stand behind a cluster of children who had parked in the "front row" to await a performance that had been more than half a year in the making.

The "Zonbi, Zonbi" drummers finished setting up in a line against the wall directly across the performance space from me and started teasing the audience with snippets of rhythm on their wooden Haitian drums. The audience talked loudly over the sound, even as a break in the drumming signaled the entrance of the first noninstrumental performer. This performer pushed assertively through the excited crowd. People looked with surprise and amusement at the figure that had emerged with white-painted face, arms, and legs and white clothes to compliment an otherworldly appearance: a knit-band crown (or exercise headband in another context) and a long t-shirt that had been cut to hang loosely from the body to resemble a skeletal structure. Contrasting with the white, a black knit chain looped around the performer's head and torso. The performer's slight, androgynous frame did not stand out against the boisterousness in the courtyard until their resonant voice filled the air. "Nou rive nan lakou an . . . Mape mande si pa gen gran moun—ohhhhh—nan lakou a . . ." (We have arrived in the *lakou*/courtyard . . . I am asking if there are elders in the *lakou*/courtyard . . .). The *chantè* (singer) welcomed everyone into the sacred space of the performance with this traditional Vodou song, also popularly performed by the Haitian konpas group Magnum Band. The chantè turned around to face everyone while he was singing: "Bonjou manman. Bonjou pitit yo. Bonjou papa. Bonjou pitit yo" (Hello, Mother. Hello, my children. Hello, Father. Hello, my children). The energy became palpable as the Haitian audience exclaimed with excitement, everyone talking and leaning in to get a closer look. The chantè repeated the verses while gliding barefoot across the rubble of the courtyard to climb onto a platform to the left of the drummers, remaining there like a ghostly guardian—upright against the sunset, swaying slightly, and singing with the beat of the drums.

A few minutes later, a set of three performers wove through the thickening crowd into the ever-shrinking performance space: another androgynous barefoot figure followed by a couple adorned in vibrant red-and-black knitted costumes (fig. 4). The lone figure was recognizable as a zonbi, at least to the Haitian audience. It had a painted-white face like the singer, was cloaked in a white sheet bound in tight loops of black knitted rope, spoke in the recognizable high and unearthly tones of spirits of the dead, and moved through space by bouncing or creeping rather than walking. The two other performers followed behind, figured in a composition similar to the painting *Zonbi* (1939) by Haitian artist Wilson Bigaud, which portrays head-bent figures clad in sheets being led with tethered ropes by a peasant man with a whip (fig. 5). In the "Zonbi, Zonbi" scene at the Ghetto Biennale, however, a clearly gendered man and woman with painted-red skin wearing ornate horned headdresses escorted the zonbi. The zonbi master was shirtless, wearing only pants and black socks with white polka dots (a detail that made me giggle). The zonbi mistress wore a sleeveless red shirt, black belt, and red skirt. Although only the zonbi master wielded a whip, the dance movements he made with the mistress worked together to corral and guide the skittish zonbi around the courtyard. At one point, the zonbi curled up against my body like a pitiful dog that was hot and panting, and I was unsure what to do in the brief moment before it was retrieved by the master's strong arm pulling back on its shoulder. During several such attempts by the zonbi to seek refuge or break through to the "outside," the master cracked his whip, though the sound was barely audible over the roar of the commentary from the crowd. The message of the performers' movements was clear: the zonbi had no chance to escape under the attentive gaze of the masters, and the only possibility was submission.

A final set of performers entered with barely enough time for the quieting of the drums to announce their arrival. Six figures dressed in skeletal costumes with black ropes similar to the initial performer—although with women's head wraps instead of a crown—lined up perpendicular to me and the drummers facing the audience. I was drawn in by their stillness after all the commotion of the zonbi and its masters, at least until an audience

Figure 4. An early scene from Lakou's performance of "Zonbi, Zonbi," 2009. (Video still by author)

Figure 5. Wilson Bigaud's *Zombies*, 1953, oil on Masonite, 24.1 cm x 21.5 cm. (Collection of Figge Art Museum, City of Davenport Art Collection, Friends of Art Acquisition Fund, 1990.41)

member shouted out in Kreyòl, "Hey! Look! Look at the zombies!"—inciting laughter and further loud comments from the peanut gallery. The performers were unflappable. They left the line two at a time, walking to opposing corners of the space then returning to the line to complete triangle shapes across the dusty "stage." The zombies went through a series of synchronized and repetitive movements—kneeling on the ground and bowing in reverence, "running" over and over again to the outer edge of the performance space (falling into slow movements as if being held in molasses, finding no place to go), crossing their arms across their bodies like bats, then in unison unfolding arms stretched outward, bending over with their hands bound together behind their backs. These movements clearly signaled cohesion, as well as something deeper. The group performance deemphasized the individual, as each zonbi traded places with another again and again to provide the sense of the lack of value and importance of their particular (undead) lives. In this way, they performed the function of something akin to a chorus, an understanding supported by their unified chanting—speaking with one kinetic voice about the unfolding events and their miserable state (fig. 6).

After performing for five minutes, the chorus of zonbi circled in front of the crowd and then lined up against the back wall, this time facing away from the audience. The master, mistress, and lone zonbi reemerged from the sidelines. The chorus did not initially engage the other performers; they were quiet and still as the lone zonbi and its devilish masters moved across the space. By this time, the sun had nearly set, casting a darkened haze over the performance since there was no electricity to light it up. The crack of the whip broke the evening air and the lone zonbi—the most visible of all the characters because it was clothed from head to toe in white—tumbled through the performance space. Eventually the chorus members would look up in recognition as the zonbi passed, one then another, until they exclaimed together: "Nou tout se zonbi!" ("We are all zonbi!").

Figure 6. Zonbi chorus in Lakou's performance of "Zonbi, Zonbi," 2009. (Video stills by author)

The predictable geometric movements of the zonbi chorus then started to have a different effect, interrupting the space between the lone zonbi and its masters. They created obstacles with their bodies, breaking the connection between the two and eventually weaving through the audience to use them as well. One of the zonbi chorus members with a headdress resembling a large white chef's hat danced in a circle around a few of us standing up front, inching us into the performance space. Another came soon after, then another, until the zonbi chorus had created enough space to dance their way through paths in the audience, moving all of us into the performance. I stood watching the unfolding events until one of the zonbi grabbed my hand in an invitation to dance, and I gladly followed the zonbi movements. All around me, I noticed that other audience members took up invitations from other zonbi chorus members. Through these movements, the zonbi and the audience members overtook the now-powerless masters, relegated to the sidelines. The performance culminated in a *bonboch* (rowdy party) of zonbi–humans–zonbi–humans–zonbi that lasted more than half an hour. Without electricity, which never came on during opening night, much to the frustration of Ghetto Biennale artists, we danced in the dark with only the ambient glow of moon and the occasional flash from our cameras as we took selfies to document our collective sweaty experience of "Zonbi, Zonbi" at the international arts festival.

LAKOU

Four men gather together to plan a performance for fall in one of the second-floor studio spaces at the FOSAJ arts center. I sit with them on folding chairs next to their new drums, close to the window for the light because the electricity has not yet come on. Before beginning to plan, however, the leaders of Lakou discuss the tension they are experiencing with the other artists who live and work in the space. They are aware that a few of the artists want them out, for a variety of interpersonal reasons that include that their performance troupe members are known to be *masisi*. One of the four men calls them a bunch of homophobes and begins to list the infractions that they have committed, a series of aggressive acts that make the members of the troupe feel uncomfortable practicing in the space. Another of the men who has been taking a lead role in organizing the troupe and outlining its political and artistic position stands up to say that there is more to their homophobia than those exclusionary actions intended to make Lakou find another space to gather. "Homophobia is their whole world. It's their worldview and their mentality.

They are ignorant about homosexuality and bisexuality, so all they know is homophobia. They think like heterosexuals . . . their minds are colonized!" (Field notes, July 2009)

The performance troupe Lakou was founded in late 2008 and early 2009 by five Haitian men who had lived in Jacmel and been engaged in cultural work for many years—theater, musical performance, dance, and visual arts. It was inspired by Avadra's experiences in the wake of the Michèle Pierre-Louis controversy: the brutal attack on his boyfriend, Franck; blame and imprisonment for the violent crime; and feeling left behind when his boyfriend was exiled by his family. The Avadra that I knew before these experiences— whose greatest wish was to emigrate to the Dominican Republic so that he and Franck could create art and have a family together—was transformed into a revolutionary who committed himself to the political struggle of ti masisi and ti madivin, same-sex-desiring and gender-creative Haitians of the majority poor. He invited creative collaborators who he believed would promote this vision, mostly other men open to embracing the denigrated terms of "masisi" and "madivin."

Avadra convened these men for the first time in the public plaza of Jacmel. It was a test to see if they would openly affiliate with a known masisi under the watchful eye of street vendors, futbòl players, library patrons, and passersby. Three men accepted the invitation: the slight-of-build dancer Mirabo, his friend Legba with a slightly bad eye given to him by his father who tried to beat out his femininity, and the much-shorter saxophonist, Anri, who could usually be found at the classical music school. Avadra shared his vision with them of assembling a performance group to "set a good example for Jacmel" by challenging the homophobia that affected their city and country. They knew Avadra's story and had likewise experienced homophobia to different degrees; even the heterosexually identified Anri cited examples of job opportunities he had missed because someone misperceived him to be masisi. There was a consensus that things needed to change to improve their lives and that a performance troupe could be the agent of that change.

The four men decided to meet at FOSAJ, housed in the Boucard & Co. building on Rue St Anne along the waterfront that allegedly had been a coffee warehouse built in the 1800s. It is where I met Avadra at the 2008 Fèt Gede celebration, the first event organized by my friend Flo McGarrell as the incoming director of FOSAJ. Avadra's boyfriend, Franck, was the one who shyly woke me up from my hay-bale and pallet bed at FOSAJ the following morning to escort me, my then partner, and my stepson to their house for coffee and comfortable accommodations. Avadra and Franck—who by the time of the performance troupe's founding was a remote participant—knew that Flo would let them meet in the space free of charge and also support the group's mission. It was a convenient place for me because Flo had set me up there with the aforementioned "researcher-in-residence" position based on the model of their artist residencies, where I taught workshops and paid $5 (U.S.) a day to stay in a tent in the attic, accessed by ladder from the second-story office where the assistant director slept in a hammock. Despite the unusual set-up, I was committed to living in the center of things with the artists, at least for a time. I could see all the activity on the second floor from my platform (and everyone could see me), which means that I had a great deal of intimacy with the artists—all men—who lived at FOSAJ and used the center for their work. We ate the one meal available together each day from the collective kitchen (cooked in a large pot over an open fire in the back yard by women employed by FOSAJ for domestic labor), worked alongside each other in the nooks and crannies of the warehouse, hosted Haitian and foreign visitors in the gallery space on the first floor and in the second-floor studios, had late-night talks over tea in the bar area around the tiny "kitchen" (consisting of a sink, a water cooler, and a fridge that was subject to the frequent power cuts), and—in the way only people with that much intimacy can—generally annoyed each other. From this location I was only a few steps away whenever the burgeoning performance troupe met or practiced, and I was privy to interactions between the group's members and the rest of the FOSAJ artists, and privy to gossip about the performance troupe and its activities.

At their first meeting at FOSAJ, Avadra, Mirabo, Legba, and Anri decided to call the performance troupe Lakou. Often translated as "yard" or "courtyard" in English, *lakou* refers both to an arrangement of space (a courtyard surrounded by habitations) and the social relationships between the people—often familial—who share this space. As historian Laurent Dubois documents, the lakou structure became popular in Haiti after independence; modeled after African settlement patterns, the circle of buildings around a common courtyard guarded against attack and against plantation spatial arrangements for visual "oversight" of slaves. The lakou system contributed to the flourishing of Vodou as practitioners shared a ceremonial space. Three historic lakous in the north of Haiti—Lakou Souvenance, Lakou Soukri, and Lakou Badjo—continue to serve as important spiritual spaces and sites of Vodou pilgrimage. By taking on the name Lakou, the performance troupe's founders grounded their cultural work in histories of Black resistance with explicit Vodou connections. *Lakou* also signified queer kinship and belonging for the same-sex-desiring and gender-creative Haitians (several of whom had been kicked out of their familial homes) who participated in the performance troupe.

The Lakou founders came up with a concept for an antihomophobic performance before recruiting new members, each of whom were instructed by one of the founders—usually Avadra or Mirabo—that their intention was not just to showcase Haitian culture through dance, but to intervene in cultures of homophobia. Lakou staged these interventions in the cultural realm because they knew the power of performance to create social change. As Elizabeth McAlister contends in *Rara! Vodou, Power, and Performance in Haiti and Its Diaspora* (2002), performance is one of the most productive sites of public discourse in Haiti and the diaspora, especially among the majority poor. Her book briefly documents same-sex sexuality and gender creativity in relationship to two kinds of public performance: bands for Kanaval (Haitian Carnival celebrations similar to those for Mardi Gras, Fat Tuesday) and Rara (a festival of roving bands during the season of Lent originating in the Haitian countryside). As she notes, there is a tradition of cross-dressing and singing about masisi and madivin in these performance contexts. "In keeping with the popular license on [irreverent] vulgarity" in Kanaval and Rara, they are both socially sanctioned spaces for the public display of nonnormative gender and sexual performances as well as spaces where masisi, madivin, and related subjects are produced through *betiz*—humorous innuendo, often referencing gender and sexuality (McAlister 2002, 75–76).[5]

Lakou considered themselves to be in dialogue with Kanaval bands in particular, whose antics they considered homophobic for treating homosexuality as fodder for comedy. They moreover considered the performance of queerness for public consumption through gender-bending drag and making masisi and madivin the butt of the joke to be connected to an antipathy towards homosexuals. For one of their members, Femme Noir, this perspective came out of her two-year involvement as a singer for one of the bands in Jacmel. She told me, "They do not want people like that [lesbians] in their group. They were always singing songs like that, about masisi and madivin. One time I went to Port-au-Prince with a girl—just a friend, and when I came back they gave me a letter uninviting me from the group. They did not say why. But people around town were talking about the reason why, calling me a lesbian." Femme Noir reported that, at the time, it was the only discrimination she had experienced in terms of her lesbian sexuality. While she actually did not know until later that many of the members of Lakou were masisi and madivin, when she learned about their *travay anti-diskriminasyon* (antidiscrimination work), she decided to sing with them. Most Lakou members—whose numbers ranged from a dozen to fifteen—were likewise drawn to the group because of the founders' public denouncements of oppression, including discrimination against women and people with disabilities.

Their antidiscrimination philosophy was rooted in the spiritual system of Vodou—particularly the values of the inherent worth of all people, generosity, and balance. All but one of the founders and the majority of the members were vodouizan. The founding member of Lakou who did not serve the spirits still attended Vodou ceremonies because, as he told me, he likes Haitian culture. The Lakou founders took their commitment to Vodou seriously and, in addition to participating in ceremonies, would pass time in the countryside learning about Vodou with an oungan Ginè who constructed their drums. Unlike the Haitian elites of the mid-twentieth century who turned to Vodou as a cultural reservoir of "African-ness" during and after the U.S. occupation, here the spiritual system was a way for these mostly dispossessed urban poor in Haiti to connect to the living practices of their ancestors that are supportive of masisi, madivin, gays, lesbians, and other same-sex-desiring and gender-creative Haitians. For Avadra, the Lakou founder who made the pronouncement about homophobia at the planning meeting, Vodou was a welcome relief from the evangelical Christian homophobia that had wreaked devastation in his life: harassment, depression, physical violence, imprisonment, and psychic trauma. He, like others who had grown up in evangelical Christian households, was particularly zealous when it came to the subject of Vodou, which he considered to be a radical space of belonging that was distinctly Haitian. Vodou, moreover, informed his queer, anti-imperialist politics.

Avadra often spoke about homophobia as a *mond* (world), as in his comment that "homophobia is their whole world." "World" is used in queer theory in ways that have some interesting points of connection with Avadra's theorization of homophobia. In *Epistemology of the Closet*, Eve Kosofsky Sedgwick (1990) discusses the twentieth-century "world-mapping" projects in which everyone is designated not only a gender (girl/boy) based on their sexed body (female/male), but also a sexuality based on the homo/hetero binary.[6] World-mapping, or cartography, is an epistemological practice with strong ties to colonization—as a technology of "discovering," "exploring," and "charting" new worlds for the purposes of white European conquest. The first map of what would come to be called the Americas featured the northern coastline of present-day Haiti, a tool for Spanish colonization in the Caribbean. By using the term "world-mapping," Sedgwick draws on these productions of self/Other to highlight the inherent violences of other binary definitions that determine so much of our lives. Avadra likewise references the violence of homo/hetero definition as a kind of psychic colonization—"Tèt yo kolonize!" (They/their minds are colonized!) Here *kolonize* marks the binary inherent to homophobia—because it differentiates kinds of people who are then de/valued in relationship to one another—as a product of European and U.S. intervention in Haiti.

Homophobia as a world, especially one in which people "think like heterosexuals," also seems akin to what Michael Warner, in his introduction to *Fear of a Queer Planet: Queer Politics and Social Theory* calls heteronormativity. Heteronormativity is the norming of all things related to heterosexuality or a kind of "heterosexual ideology, toward a totalized view of the social. . . . Het culture thinks of itself as the elemental form of human association, as the very model of inter-gender relations, as the indivisible basis of all community, and as the means of reproduction without which society wouldn't exist" (1993, xxi). Catholicism and Protestantism are inherently heteronormative, although some same-sex-desiring believers have subverted the passage from Genesis before the differentiation of male from female and God's command to "be fruitful and multiply" through heterosexual reproduction—that is, "God made man in his own image"—to argue that the occurrence of same-sex sexual desire in humans is also natural and part of His plan.

Avadra claimed that this heteronormativity produces ignorance, as in "they are ignorant about homosexuality and bisexuality." Avadra's use of the term "ignorant" here is less a classist judgment about formal education (as is so often implied in its deployment), since his politics are rooted in the plight of Haiti's majority poor, but rather an assessment of distance from nonnormative perspectives, or what Michael Warner calls queer worlds. Warner asserts that "heteronormativity can be overcome only by actively imagining a necessarily and desirably queer world" (1993, xvi). Warner and his collaborator Lauren Berlant described queer worlds this way: "The queer world is a space of entrances, exits, unsystematized lines of acquaintance, projected horizons, typifying examples, alternate routes, blockages, incommensurate geographies. . . . Queer and other insurgents have long striven, often dangerously or scandalously, to cultivate what good folks call criminal intimacies. . . . Making a queer world has required the development of kinds of intimacy that bear no necessary relation to domestic space, to kinship, to the couple form, to property, or to the nation" (Berlant and Warner 1998, 558). "Queer" includes same-sex desires and sexuality, since this quality deviates from the projected horizons of heteronormativity, but is a much more expansive political project of "more thorough resistance to regimes of the normal" (Warner 1993, xxvi).

Black queer activist scholars have theorized queer as an outside, beyond, or blockage not only to heteronormativity but other imbricated regimes of the normal—capitalism, patriarchy, and white supremacy. The vision of queer politics articulated by political scientist Cathy Cohen (1997) pushed beyond the identitarian "gay/lesbian/same-sex-desiring" versus "straight" to imagine forging alliances—criminal intimacies—between, for instance, "punks, bulldaggers, and welfare queens." Caribbeanist literary scholar Omise'eke Natasha Tinsley contends that Haitian Vodou has been doing this work since its formation. Citing Cohen's political vision of queer, she noted in relationship to particular Vodou celebrations that they "offered a promiscuous meeting point for what Cathy Cohen describes as 'relationships which have been prohibited, stigmatized, and generally repressed' and that trace 'spaces of shared or similar oppression and resistance'" (Tinsley 2018, 22). Across her scholarly work she also shows that the *lwa* Ezili (a family of women spirits), assembles a motley crew of those dispossessed by regimes of the normal as her "children"—the poor, single mothers, same-sex-desiring people, women, and Haitians in general (Tinsley 2011 and 2018).

In *Ezili's Mirrors: Imagining Black Queer Genders*, Tinsley explores the possibility of the lwa as Vodou epistemology that "offers more conceptual and spiritual space for expansive gendered and sexual practices than western European epistemologies circulating in the Caribbean" (2018, 10). For this reason, she notes that Haitian and other Black cultural workers, whether or not they are Vodou practitioners, "mediate their reflections on gender and sexuality through the epistemology of this spiritual practice" (9). My project is aligned with Tinsley's in that it considers Vodou to be an inherently queer epistemology and world-building project that counters regimes of the normal in the way it values Blackness, African transplanted traditions, women, same-sex-desiring people, the majority poor, and much much more.

With these considerations, it is no wonder that Lakou used Vodou as a medium for queer resistance to postcolonial homophobia. Their performance created at FOSAJ that ultimately premiered at the Ghetto Biennale combined *fòklò* (Haitian folkloric performance based in Vodou ritual) with conceptual art.[7] As the title of the piece—"Zonbi, Zonbi"—suggests, Lakou reclaimed this figure, which has been used in Euro-U.S. imperialist discourse to pervert the Black republic. In doing so, Lakou was not entirely unique; the artists tapped into a lineage of Haitian anti-imperialist resistance that has used the zonbi as metaphor or allegory. In the next section, I review one classic example—Frankétienne's *Dézafi* (1975), the first novel written entirely in Haitian Kreyòl.[8] This novel provides context for "Zonbi, Zonbi," with which it shares many qualities. It also helps illuminate how Lakou performed a specifically queer understanding of Haiti's modern monster and anti-imperialist resistance.

DÉZAFI AND ALLEGORIES OF U.S. IMPERIALISM IN HAITI UNDER THE DUVALIER DICTATORSHIP

> Integrated into this most essential Haitian belief system [of Vodou], the zombie offered a fitting vehicle for intellectuals interested in affirming their commitment to Haiti's popular culture as well as an ideal metaphor through which to condemn Haiti's social and political ills. The zombie thus proved highly exploitable as a literary device and, perhaps more significantly, proposed a distinctly Haitian contribution to the world of francophone literature.
>
> —Kaiama L. Glover, *Haiti Unbound: A Spiralist Challenge to the Postcolonial Canon* (2010)

Dézafi is characteristic of the late twentieth-century spiralist movement in Haiti—dense, abstract, chaotic yet rhythmic, and fundamentally concerned with the human condition—in which Frankétienne and this novel played a significant role.[9] It is about those whose "life [is] worse than being in a coffin" (Frankétienne 1975, 26): self-imposed shut-ins terrified of being re-enslaved and zonbi endlessly laboring on a rice plantation with a ruthless overseer, Zofè. Frankétienne describes their abject existence in excessive and grotesque terms that produce a kind of miasmic mise-en-scène that literary scholar Kaiama L. Glover calls "sensorily offensive and even nauseating" (2010, 158). The regime of terror represented by the novel refuses to be contained in the pages of the book.

The plot turns on the relationships between the megalomaniac zonbi master Sintil, his daughter Siltàna, and the zonbi Klodonis who is "a young student whose educated 'impudence' threatens [Sintil's] power. . . . In so 'zombifying' [Klodonis], [Sintil] effectively issues a warning to any and all who would oppose him, and so solidifies his control over Bois Neuf" (Glover 2010, 61). Sintil's power, however, cannot be absolute even though the world of his creation is seemingly inescapable. Siltàna becomes enamored with Klodonis and troubled by his lack of reciprocation. Since her gendered domestic duties include feeding the zonbi on the plantation, she feeds Klodonis salted broth to free him from his unresponsive and unfeeling zonbi state. He, in turn, brings the other zonbi to consciousness by distributing salt, and they rise up to slay Sintil and Zofè. Instead of a celebration for what might seem like an act of justice, however, the novel ends with the caution that there will always be another Sintil, another Zofè, another regime of terror in the making. "In order to chase away paralyzing indolence, lethargy, and death, we must—everywhere and at all times—learn to live for the sharing of salt" (Frankétienne and Glover 2013, 73).

Scholars of Francophone literature describe Klodonis as a hero who overthrows Sintil's tyrannical order. However, Glover—drawing on the literary criticism of Régis Antoine—offers another reading that aligns with my interpretation. She remarks that for Antoine, the figure of the zonbi is "the antithesis of characters marked by 'the idea of happiness and the will to live fully'. . . in accordance with ideas of collective liberation. . . . He thus understands the zombie as polar opposite of the romanticized hero portrayed in the Indigenist novel and of the noble peasant extolled in Indigenist theoretical writings" (Glover 2010, 57). Glover builds on this by noting that the zonbi is therefore the perfect character to express the organized chaos of human conditions that the spiralists represented. "A de facto antihero, the zombie exposes the limits of any rationalist metaphysical order and fully embraces a destabilizing uncertainty. Physically present but absent of soul, inspiring pity yet devoid of emotion, effectively subjugated but smoldering with the potential for rebellion, the zombie personifies the state of centrifugal-centripetal tension that characterizes the spiral" (61).

Klodonis is objectified, first by Sintil and his overseer Zofè, who reduce him to basic bodily functions in order to extract his labor, and then by Siltàna. She works to free him because of pure self-interest rather than out of disgust at the zonbi's debased conditions or any grander sense of justice. The moment of Klodonis's "heroism" comes as he is coming to consciousness, supposedly making the individual choice to free the other zonbi. Yet Frankétienne seems to imply that there is no other option than to "awaken them with salt" as the overwhelming urge of the awakening zonbi is to seek revenge in whatever way possible. Moreover, the zonbi—including Klodonis—have been joined together and speak as one. The reader gets a sense of their interiority as they struggle with trying to connect to memory through the body, each sentence beginning with "nou" (we). For example: "We fall asleep drunk. We awake senseless. We understand nothing. We grimace under a deck of double sixes. We've become entirely bewildered, stunned stupid under the heavy weight of the burden we bear. We swallow the potion in a long dream smeared with evil spirits, a dream torn apart by a cacophony of rusty knives, sharp machetes, and broken glass" (Frankétienne, Lamour, and Glover 2013, 63). We who are reading cannot help but understand ourselves as part of this "we," an interpellation aided by the double sense of "nou" in Kreyòl, which means both "we" and "you all." Franketienne proclaimed to the novel's Haitian audience, then, that "we/you all" are zonbi who will—by some means—come to consciousness and destroy our master or masters.

Dézafi is an allegory about life under the brutal Duvalier dictatorship (1957–86); it is one of several examples of cultural work that used the figure of the zonbi to explore the miserable conditions under François "Papa Doc" Duvalier's tyranny. In an interview, Franketienne notes that "*Dézafi* . . . symbolically exploited the phenomenon of zombification in order to denounce the horrors and alienation bred by all forms of tyranny and totalitarianism," and he goes on to say that it foreshadowed the uprooting of the Duvalier regime in 1986 (Rowell 1992, 389). Duvalier's election rode on anti-U.S. sentiment. A medical doctor and ethnologist who valued Haiti's African roots and a promoter of the Black nationalist movement *noirisme*, he had popular appeal among the majority poor Haitians who—with vivid memories of the U.S. occupation—were ready to throw off Euro-U.S. masters. Unfortunately, however, he used his knowledge of Vodou over the people—creating a symbology around himself as a kind of divine authority and declaring himself "president for life" in 1964. His dictatorship is most often associated with the paramilitary force he created—the Volontaires de la Sécurité Nationale (National Security Volunteers), commonly called the Tonton Macoutes—devised from forces who had been trained by the United States during the occupation. These "boogeymen" (as the term is often translated into English) carried out a regime of terror to squelch possible threats to Papa Doc and later his son Jean-Claude "Baby Doc" Duvalier's power. The Tonton Macoutes killed an estimated thirty to sixty thousand people, sadistically tortured many more, and created a general paralysis among the Haitian population.[10]

The United States, interested in maintaining a Caribbean ally during the Cold War, backed the Duvalier dictatorship and thus continued its imperialistic influences in Haiti. J. Michael Dash illuminates how the allegory of the zonbi in *Dézafi* references this relationship: "In [Franketienne]'s novel Haiti is symbolized by the cramped and viscous world of Bois-Neuf, in which a malevolent 'houngan' Sintil rules over the unprotesting passivity of his zombified community. . . . Behind Sintil there can be discerned the shadowy presence of American interests—the railways of the Mac-Donald Company and the sisal fields of SHADA" (1988, 125). The novel reflects the United States' and Haiti's ongoing relationship, in which the former levied significant amounts of international aid money to pursue its state and commercial interests in Haiti—predominately experiments with economic restructuring—with devastating consequences. For example, USAID conducted the disastrous wholesale eradication of the black "creole" pig because of a limited outbreak of swine flu, replacing them with pink pigs from the United States that could not survive conditions in Haiti. This action undermined peasant economies and caused spiritual disturbances, since the black pig was a critical, well-adapted element of the environmental and food ecosystems and was also used in Vodou ceremonies to feed lwa.[11] This period also set the stage for other neoliberal reforms in Haiti whose effects have only escalated in recent years.

As many critics have pointed out, there are no references to this historical period within the context of the novel—it is, in some sense, timeless. Glover remarked on the "spatio-temporal incoherence" of *Dézafi* as a way of representing "the profound dispossession and uprootedness that have historically plagued New World post-slavery communities" (2010, 157). The spiralists' conception of time, she notes, was characterized of course by the spiral and aptly described by the Francophone Caribbean writer and literary critic Édouard Glissant. "We have a conception of time in a spiral that corresponds neither to the linear time of Westerners nor the circular time of the Precolumbians or Asian philosophers, but that is a sort of combination of the two, that is, a circular movement, but always with an escape from that circularity towards something else—that is what constitutes the spiral" (Glissant quoted in Glover 2010, 157). The figure of the zonbi is perfect for this genre, a way of showing that the past—slavery and colonization, the Haitian Revolution, and the first U.S. occupation of Haiti—is never "dead," because it carries forward into the present. *Dézafi* is about the reoccurrence of, in Frankétienne's words, "tyranny and totalitarianism" in Haiti and those who struggle to overthrow it.

Whereas the circularity to be escaped in the novel is Duvalierism, Lakou created their performance for a twenty-first-century Haiti under *new conditions* of U.S. imperialism, including neoliberal economic regimes and foreign militarization. The majority of the troupe's members—like a significant percent of the current Haitian population—were young children during, or even born after, the ousting of Baby Doc and his family in 1986, a time known as the *dechoukaj* (uprooting or political upheaval). This generation therefore has a different sense of U.S. imperialism in Haiti. Some of their earliest memories are of the 1990 election of President Jean-Bertrand Aristide, the former Catholic priest who was a proponent of liberation theology and candidate for the leftist political party Fanmi Lavalas (lit. "the flood"). However, before he could make any wide scale changes in Haiti, President Aristide was overthrown in a CIA-supported coup d'état in 1991. The U.S. government, which publicly decried the coup, immediately imposed economic sanctions on Haiti. The three years of the *anbago* (embargo)—when material conditions in Haiti declined tremendously, especially for the majority poor—firmly associated U.S. influence in the country with extreme deprivation (Garfield 2002, Gibbons and Garfield 1999). Thus there was already widespread anti-U.S. sentiment in Haiti when U.S. military forces touched down in 1994 for Operation Uphold Democracy, the half-year mission to restore Aristide's presidency. Operation Uphold Democracy was transitioned into Operation New Horizons to support the installation of the United Nations Mission in Haiti (UNMIH), and the UN maintained a presence until 2000. Haiti was once again under foreign military occupation, this time under the guise of a "peacekeeping mission," and these missions paved the road for future interventions.

In early 2004, a more conservative President Aristide was deposed in yet another coup d'état. As he maintains, and as the majority of Haitians I know believe whether or not they liked what he did during his presidency, U.S. and French officials forced his resignation and then coerced him to leave Haiti under the threat of violence. U.S. defense officials offer a different account, contending that they helped "stabilize" Haiti by sending in the Marines, who were joined by a multinational force. This mission, Operation Secure Tomorrow, laid the "peacekeeping" groundwork for the United Nations Stabilization Mission in Haiti (MINUSTAH), approved by a UN Security Council resolution in mid-2004, that remained in place until 2017. When I started my fieldwork in 2008, MINUSTAH had been going on for four years and marked the landscape of Haiti—white armored tanks and trucks full of blue-helmeted soldiers, barbed-wire compounds, and armored watchtowers—particularly in Port-au-Prince. Lakou members had therefore lived the majority of their lives under some form of foreign military occupation. While "Zonbi, Zonbi" shares the quality of timelessness with *Dézafi* in that there are no explicit references to this period of U.S. imperialism in Haiti, the context is implicit in their performance as I describe below.

LIVING UNDER POSTCOLONIAL HOMOPHOBIA: BONDAGE AND RESISTANCE

Lakou's performance of the zonbi and their masters is meant to be understood in terms of Haitian history in much the same way as *Dézafi*. "Zonbi, Zonbi" activates what performance studies scholar Diana Taylor (2003) would call a repertoire, an embodied performance of cultural memory—in this situation, the interplay of foreign domination and popular resistance so common to Haitian experience. Lakou's performance rehearses and holds a space for the history of slavery in the colonial period, the Haitian revolution, and U.S. interventions during the postcolonial period. This history is brought to bear as a critique of the present moment. Lakou, like the spiralists for a previous generation of Haitians, critiqued the "shadowy presence of American interests" behind the armed UN soldiers from Brazil and Jordan—as well as their compatriots in the Haitian National Police—in more subtle ways than the anti-UN manifestations and graffiti described in the introduction. The UN soldiers and the Haitian National Police are the newest manifestation of the Tonton Macoutes, the gendarmes, and the overseers. Lakou's performance moreover critiqued homophobia as an import associated with these kinds of violent foreign oversight.

While the cast of characters in "Zonbi, Zonbi" was similar to those in *Dézafi*, Lakou queered the script. In the novel, heterosexual desire is the catalyst for change and the zonbi's coming to consciousness. Siltàna is compelled by her sexual attraction to feed Klodonis the salt that wakes him up, an action ostensibly not taken out of love, but the need for reciprocation. Feeding Klodonis salt—in an astute commentary on the ways in which people's actions have unintended consequences that can either dismantle or support empire—sets off a chain of events that upends the reign of terror by violent means. In Lakou's performance, by contrast, heterosexuality was associated not with a cure to the zonbi state, but rather with its creation and perpetuation in the forms of the zonbi master and mistress. This couple is paired together in all but one scene of the performance—he wielding the whip and she herding the bound zonbi. They work together to impose force over the always potentially rebellious zonbi. The zonbi, on the other hand, are queer—or queered—by this relation to the master and mistress. This queerness is signaled in the effeminate comportment of the roped-up chantè who opens "Zonbi, Zonbi," the gender ambiguity of the lone zonbi, whose body is totally wrapped in cloth and who is noticeably not relegated to the gendered tasks of plantation life, and in the homosocial world of the chorus whose female zonbi express intimacy in their unison.

Lakou's performance theorizes heterosexuality as linked to the masters, the French colonialists and U.S. imperialists of Haiti's history. These forms of foreign domination, as the first two chapters detail, are respectively associated with heteronormative Catholicism—legalized in the Code Noir—and evangelical Christianity. The master's whip and the mistress's control of the zonbi's movement are different manifestations of homophobia. The Haitian audience is meant to identify not with institutional heterosexuality and homophobia, but rather with zonbi, who are enslaved by their workings. In the performance, the zonbi are not just homosexual, they are a motley crew who stand in for all kinds of desire, kinship, and spiritual alliances—criminal intimacies not sanctioned by colonial regimes, the Haitian state, or postcolonial religion introduced by U.S. missionaries.

Through the dramatic structure of "Zonbi, Zonbi," the Haitian audience is meant to recognize that their liberation is bound up with same-sex-desiring people and that they—everyone in Haiti—are rendered queer in relationship to foreign domination. The chorus, who most represents pèp-la (the people), do not initially engage the other performers; they are quiet and still when the lone zonbi and its masters move across the performance space. Yet as the performance continues, they gain greater proximity to the lone zonbi and begin to recognize, "Nou tout se zonbi!" ("We are all zonbi!"). The "nou" here works in the same way as in Dézafi, both in terms of a "we" that includes the Haitian audience but also in terms of a "you-all" that more directly interpellates them. The movements of the chorus then begin to interrupt the space between the zonbi and its masters, and eventually weaving through the audience to draw their bodies into the performance.

The powerful assertion of this performance—tout moun se zonbi (everyone is a zonbi)—riffs on the radical principle in Vodou that tout moun se moun (everyone is a person). In its message and through interrupting the spaces between performers and audience, "Zonbi, Zonbi" created not just a commons within the space of the lakou, but an undercommons in response to the ongoing conditions of U.S. imperialism in Haiti. Undercommons, as conceived by Stefano Harney and Fred Moten (2013), are alternative forms of sociality connected to the Black radical tradition, extended here to encompass Vodou and its connections to the Haitian revolution. They are the fleeting spaces of queer connection where we can find ways of relating to one another that are not overdetermined by colonial and neo-imperialist postcolonial relations. The consciousness gained from such relationality is what will enable us to do the hard and necessary work of studying and planning together—men and women, Black and white, heterosexual and homosexual, prudish and kinky, and all the wonderful variations in between—to overthrow systems of domination.

In sum, "Zonbi, Zonbi" reworked the transnational narrative of Haiti as the premodern land of voodoo that has been used to negatively queer the Black republic for more than a century. Rather than countering this portrayal by projecting respectability and sufficiently modern (secular/Protestant) sexual subjectivity, Lakou embraced Vodou as a site of queer Black Haitian resistance. The performance troupe remakes the zonbi—connected as it is to U.S. representations of "voodoo" in Haiti that have justified military, religious, and other cultural interventions—as metaphor for racialized sexuality in postcolonial Haiti. Their message to the primarily Haitian audience of "Nou tout zonbi!" signals that it is not just homosexuals contending with the effects of religious homophobia, but all Haitians who are queered under conditions of U.S. imperialism and foreign military occupation. This recognition invited by the audience joining the performance is the "sharing of salt" to overthrow the tyranny and totalitarianism for a new generation.

Lakou had intended to perform the anti-imperialist critique of "Zonbi, Zonbi" to more audiences, but they suffered a series of major setbacks that prevented them from doing so. The earthquake happened less than a month after the Ghetto Biennale, and they lost some of their biggest advocates in the devastation. None of the Lakou members died, but they—like millions of others in the metropolitan areas of Port-au-Prince and Jacmel—were thrust into survival mode. In the following chapter, I show how global LGBTQI human rights responses to assist Lakou ended up causing major problems within the group that resulted in the split. What remains of this original constellation in a new form, Gran Lakou, no longer had an anti-imperialist politics but rather operated as an "inclusive" dance troupe in Haiti with the aim of LGBT visibility.

2010

5

THE SEXUAL POLITICS OF RESCUE

The Global LGBTQI and Postcolonial Homophobia
after the 2010 Earthquake in Haiti

> Where it appears palpable or deemed locatable, empirically and experientially, the designation of homophobia produces a geopolitical mapping of neoliberal power relations in the guise of cultures of sexual expression and repression. Debates regarding which communities, countries, cultures, or religions are more, less, equally, similarly, or differently homophobic miss a more critical assessment regarding the conditions of its possibility and impossibility, conditions revolving around economic incentives, state policies on welfare and immigration, and racial hierarchy, rather than some abstracted or disengaged notion of culture per se.
>
> —Jasbir K. Puar, *Terrorist Assemblages: Homonationalism in Queer Times* (2007)

Thus far, this book has considered postcolonial homophobia in its manifestations as Catholic and Protestant homophobias in Haiti, the former a legacy of European colonialism and the latter a legacy of U.S. imperialism. In this chapter, I detail an important dimension to postcolonial homophobia in the twenty-first century as the compounded effects of both historical and contemporary Western imperialist biopolitical interventions to regulate, manage, control, govern, and *liberate* (homo)sexuality and (trans)gender embodiments. Unlike the biopolitical interventions of Christian missionaries, however, here I focus on those staged by global human rights organizations following the 7.0 magnitude earthquake that devastated the country in 2010. During the course of earthquake relief efforts, these organizations expressed concern about the importation of religious homophobia into Haiti. As articulated in an article by Amnesty International, "[in] Haiti: attitudes to LGBTI people have become increasingly hostile since the 12 January 2010 earthquake, when a number of religious groups providing aid to Haiti claimed homosexuality had led to the natural disaster" (Amnesty International, 2014). While this short excerpt implies that homophobic hostility in Haiti predated the earthquake, this account and the ones of global human rights organizations differ greatly from the one that I offer in the first two chapters about how the U.S. occupation (1915–34) laid the groundwork for conservative evangelical Christianity in Haiti, accompanied by a virulent form of Protestant homophobia. Instead, as I detail below, global human rights organizations constructed Haitian culture—by virtue of the prevalence of Catholic (colonial) but not Protestant (postcolonial) religiosity—as essentially homophobic. The earthquake, therefore, marks a shift in the way U.S. imperialist discourses produce the Haitian nation in relationship to racialized sexuality, from more than a century being perverted or queered in relationship to "voodoo/vaudoux" (still the dominant narrative) to being a hotbed of intractable homophobia (the emerging narrative).

This shift was produced through the influence of a subset of global human rights organizations and foundations whose mission is to end oppression based on sexual orientation and gender identity wherever it occurs. While there is great diversity among these organizations and foundations in terms of their contexts of origin, political frameworks, and their strategies to extinguish homophobia and transphobia, I refer collectively to them and their mission to promote lesbian, gay, bisexual, transgender, queer, and intersex or "LGBTQI" rights as "the global LGBTQI." In "Re-Orienting Desire: The Gay International in the Arab World," Joseph A. Massad dubs these Western organizations with the agenda to universalize gay rights as human rights on an international scale "the Gay International" (2007, 160–61). "The Gay International" refers to the organizations' "missionary role . . . to defend the rights of 'gays and lesbians' around the world and to advocate on their behalf" as well as "the discourse [of human rights] that produces them" (160–61). I am indebted to Massad's scholarship that illuminates the Orientalist impulse of the Gay International that produces Muslim and Arab cultures as exceptionally homophobic (161). However, I update his language to reflect these organizations' terminology of LGBTQI for most of the years of my fieldwork (though the "Q" was dropped in the later years) and to use the liberal discourse of "global," which is more in line with their politics than "international" with its leftist/communist/Black radical connotations.

Haiti became a place of interest for the global LGBTQI because of the earthquake, and their identity politics framework gave the International Gay and Lesbian Human Rights Commission (IGLHRC, now Outright Action

International), the Astraea Foundation for Lesbian Justice (Astraea), and others a purchase on how to help in the context of an otherwise unwieldy crisis—by reaching out to Haitians who were subject to homophobia and transphobia in the context of the disaster. In so doing, the global LGBTQI performed "selective recognition," medical anthropologist Erica Caple James's term for when "during a crisis or emergency the humanitarian gaze tends to focus on certain forms of victimization or victim identities deemed emblematic of acute suffering" (2010, 90).

In the process of enacting humanitarian projects to help Haitians, the global LGBTQI produced an "LGBT community" in Haiti where there had not been one previously. To be more precise, same-sex-desiring and gender-creative Haitian social networks and institutions existed before 2010 as discussed in previous chapters, but none used the discourse of LGBT community. The great array of English, French, Spanish, and Kreyòl terms that people used to signal same-sex sexuality and transgender embodiments when I started my ethnographic research in Haiti in 2008 were replaced in late 2010 and early 2011 with the marker "LGBT," which shifted again between 2014 and 2015 to "LGBTI."[1] This linguistic signal of "LGBT community" clued me into the acceleration of metropolitan Haitians' enmeshment with the global LGBTQI, the constitution of LGBT Haitians as a population in the course of disaster relief efforts, and their production as intelligible to foreigners through transnational identity politics when they had previously lived more or less off the radar. Rather than mourning the loss of those various forms of Haitian subjectivities to the somehow less authentic or at least more monolithic discourse of LGBT community, my purpose is to document how this shift in sexual and political subjectivity coincided with the imperialist imperative of rescue. I do so with ethnographic evidence from my fieldwork in Jacmel and Port-au-Prince, interviews with staff and volunteers at IGLHRC and Astraea, documents from these organizations, as well as French- and English-language media.

I argue that one of the effects of this enmeshment with the global LGBTQI was the legitimization of projects to "save" LGBT Haitians. Transnational feminist scholarship has called our attention to the phenomenon of the imperialist imperative of rescue, which includes the ways that imperialist archives are constructed through the relationship of "white men . . . saving brown women from brown men" (Spivak 1999, 284) and the global feminist imperative—in the register of women's rights as human rights—that "construct[s] 'American' feminists as saviors and rescuers of 'oppressed women' elsewhere within a 'global' economy run by a few power states" (Grewal 2005, 152). I build on this work as well as the work of queer postcolonial scholars within this field who illuminate the power dynamics of the United States and of U.S. organizations supposedly "saving" queers from the homophobic confines of their hopelessly traditional societies.[2]

Here I bring these transnational feminist/queer analyses together with Haitian studies scholarship about the broader politics of "rescue" and NGOs. In *Killing with Kindness: Haiti, International Aid, and NGOs* (2012), Mark Schuller elucidates that humanitarian patterns of aid after the earthquake are part of a several-decade trend in Haiti, in line with the kinds of day-to-day "rescue" missions that feminist and queer postcolonial scholars critique as part of the legacy of imperialism. As Schuller elaborates, one particular policy that continues to have a tremendous impact is the 1995 Dole Amendment (Schuller 2010). Intended to bolster the embargo of Haiti, the Dole Amendment prevented the U.S. state—including the USAID—from funding any projects directed by the Haitian state. Instead, the Dole Amendment encouraged USAID to fund projects in Haiti that were directed by foreign nationals, especially U.S.-led NGOs. The Dole Amendment radically transfigured the landscape of aid and promoted an increase in foreign presence as well as foreign control over assessment of needs in Haiti and implementation of new projects. Before the post-earthquake influx of aid in 2010, for example, the number of registered NGOs had already risen 500 percent since 1986 (Schuller 2010). As Schuller argues, one of the most detrimental impacts of U.S. involvement in Haiti is undermining the capacity for the Haitian state to meet the needs of its people before and after the earthquake, thus rendering the country "the Republic of NGOs." Therefore, the humanitarian operations around the earthquake—what Giorgio Agamben calls a state of exception (2005)—were in many senses business as usual. A growing body of scholarship illuminates the negative impacts of this relief work, which enhances neoliberal projects by bolstering foreign-determined structures of aid that are not accountable to the Haitian state or population, from distributing pharmaceuticals without medical supervision to the highly publicized U.S. Baptist kidnapping of Haitian children.[3]

The rescue, relief, and recovery work of the global LGBTQI took place in this broader context of NGOization. In particular, the IGLHRC took a central role in knowledge production about gender and sexuality in Haiti after the earthquake, partnering with an HIV/AIDS outreach organization in Port-au-Prince called SEROvie, one of my research sites. IGLHRC produced and circulated research briefings, press releases, and other media that narrated that Haiti is a bad (failed) state that exists only in its repressive form—that is, in ways that promote violence and homophobia. The solution to these issues,

IGLHRC posited in these documents and in their actions, can be found in intergovernmental organizations like the United Nations and NGOs that are supposedly working in the best interests of LGBT people. This liberal narrative of Haiti's modernity disavows the effects of colonialism, imperialism, and ongoing militarization and promoted solutions in harmful neoliberal processes that have undermined Haiti.

THE EMERGENCE OF LGBT COMMUNITY IN HAITI

At the start of this project in 2008, the acronym "LGBT" had a life in the diaspora, in organizations such as the Haitian Gays and Lesbians Alliance in New York City founded in 2007, but not in Haiti. People in Port-au-Prince and Jacmel used words in multiple languages to signal same-sex sexuality and transgender embodiment with different effects and meanings (for example, homosexual, gay, masisi), but "LGBT" was not among them. Despite the omnipresence of "LGBT" and its various iterations (e.g., LGBTQ, LGBTIQ, LGBTTIQQA) in the United States, it caught my attention the first time that a friend in Port-au-Prince referred to "LGBT in Haiti" in a conversation in summer 2010. Because the friend had lived abroad in Canada with her exiled mother, it was not until others began to regularly use "LGBT" in the following months that I realized that the term was trending in Haiti. Men and women alike started talking about themselves as LGBT (using the full acronym instead of just gay, lesbian, bisexual or transgender as a self-description), referring to LGBT groups and organizations, and referencing an "LGBT community" and "Haiti's LGBT." In most of these instances, LGBT had been creolized; the familiar roughness of each punctuated letter in English replaced with the Kreyòl pronunciation that had the quality of melting the letters into one another: *el-jeh-beh-teh*. By early 2011, "LGBT" was seemingly omnipresent in Haiti.

The confluence of identity politics encapsulated in "LGBT" did not travel alone to Haiti after the earthquake; it was attached to *the romantic discourse of "community"* (Joseph 2002). Seemingly overnight there were so many references to the *kominote LGBT* (LGBT community), particularly by residents of Port-au-Prince and neighboring zones, that it would seem that it had existed all along. While the occasional expat or other *blan* (foreigner) might invoke an LGBT community in Haiti before that time, this discourse did not previously circulate among same-sex-desiring and gender-creative Haitians in Port-au-Prince and Jacmel. Even though there were Haitians who used the self-descriptors gay and lesbian and, more rarely, bisexual and transgender, these people did not necessarily conceive of themselves as being "in community." The constituencies of the few groups and organizations for same-sex-desiring and gender-creative people also did not think of themselves as LGBT, although these constituencies would come to be hailed as the LGBT community. The discourse of "LGBT community," however, traveled along certain routes. Just as I found in my initial interviews in 2008 and 2009 that people who used "gay," "lesbian," and especially "transgender" as self-descriptors had more access to Internet technologies than those who used *masisi, madivin, yon fi ki prefere fi* (or the gendered-male iteration), those using "LGBT" after 2010 were more likely to be connected in some way to a group or organization in Haiti with funding from and other connections to the global LGBTQI.

This shift was particularly evident at SEROvie. SEROvie developed from Grasadis, a small group of homosexual men formed in 1999 to provide HIV and AIDS prevention services to men who have sex with men (MSM).[4] In 2009, the organization had the same mission, although its staff included a heterosexual ally who had been friends with the founders of Grasadis. Despite having many foreign connections through social and funding networks—hence its use of the MSM language that came out of HIV/AIDS organizing in U.S. communities of color and was then dispersed through the transnational AIDS industrial complex—the ten-year-old organization did not consider itself to be of or for the LGBT community. All of the nineteen men who regularly attended SEROvie meetings and events whom I interviewed before the earthquake used the term "gay" as a self-descriptor and referred to SEROvie as a gay program.

While keeping MSM as the focus, SEROvie started describing itself as an organization by and for the LGBT community after the earthquake. Every segment of the description from the "About Us" section of the SEROvie website, for instance, was peppered with the acronym LGBT—an LGBT population, LGBT individuals, and Haiti's LGBT community.

> SEROvie is the sole institution in Haiti providing services to MSM, bisexual men and women, lesbian and transgender individuals (LGBT). The organization has a dual focus on health and rights, seeking to empower its clients to break a cycle of discrimination, poverty, and HIV infection.

> SEROvie initially began its involvement in HIV/AIDS programming by focusing on educating SEROvie staff and partners, providing them with a strong foundation of HIV/AIDS knowledge, and supporting them to share that knowledge with others. Since then, SEROvie has established and maintained a local resource center for information and documentation on sexual

health and sexual rights, available to local NGOs as well as to the LGBT population in Port-au-Prince.

> SEROvie has developed significant expertise in community-based and peer-led initiatives that respond to the unique needs of these populations. SEROvie provides direct HIV and AIDS prevention and support services to over 3,000 LGBT individuals and sex workers throughout five geographical departments in Haiti and offers a safe, educational and supportive space for Haiti's LGBT community to meet, organize and provide mutual support.[5]

The way that "LGBT" is used here articulates with the organization's mission before the earthquake, namely to provide HIV/AIDS outreach and other services to MSM. "Gay," as just noted, was already widely used within the organization, and in this description, "MSM" is able to stand in for the "gay" element of LGBT because these two have been used interchangeably for so long. The new "LGBT" framework overlaid onto SEROvie's previous work in other ways as well. SEROvie understood that many of the "gay" men—or MSM—in its constituency also had relationships with women, so even though these men did not use the term "bisexual," this term was understood to describe them.[6] The enumeration of "transgender individuals" within LGBT also solved conflicts within the organization about whether transgender women, a few of whom used SEROvie's services before the earthquake, were included within the scope of the organization's mission.

However, "LGBT" also signaled a new way of thinking about the organization's scope and aims. The executive director of SEROvie, Steve Laguerre, discusses the LGBT framework as an achievement for the organization. Laguerre had the following exchange with Caribbean studies scholar Angelique V. Nixon in an interview published in the online platform, *Theorizing Homophobias in the Caribbean: Complexities of Place, Desire, and Belonging*:

> *Are there any services [at SEROvie] targeted for Lesbian, Bisexual and/or Transgender people, or do you mostly focus on HIV/AIDS?*
> Our services are primary interventions for men who have sex with men. We have nine networks across Haiti. But last year, we started a new initiative to directly involve women. And about 17 women here in Port-Au-Prince came to us and wanted our support to create their own organization. We can now call ourselves a *real LGBT organization*. We also serve the trans community. There are not a lot, about four now who use our services. We do provide services with health and networks in the Dominican Republic for trans people. With the women's organization, it's very new and so I don't have a lot of infor-

mation, but we are working with them for development. And they are learning from us.

(Nixon 2011, emphasis added)

Using the logic of the organization's executive director, SEROvie is now a *real* LGBT organization because it involves women, the previously missing "L" in LGBT. Non-transgender women, who had been peripheral to the life of SEROvie until the earthquake, are now imagined as part of its constituency. The women's organization referenced in this interview is Femme en Action contre la Stigmatisation et la Discrimination Sexuelle (FACSDIS), which was initiated in 2010 to work with lesbians, bisexual women, and transgender men and women. While Laguerre narrates that FACSDIS developed from the initiative of same-sex-desiring women with the assistance of SEROvie, a narrative that is consistent with FACSDIS's own origin story, the women's organization was purposefully cultivated by SEROvie staff after the earthquake. The SEROvie program manager, Reginald Dupont, told me that because SEROvie was working only with men (a comment that elides the participation of trans* women), they started looking for a leader to mobilize women after the earthquake. He and the other SEROvie staff perceived the lack of women's involvement in SEROvie to be a deficit. The reason that he, as well as other SEROvie staff and volunteers, provided for the development of this program was that having everyone—men and women—in the same place makes people more comfortable and, therefore, participants are more likely to return.[7] However, it is my impression that this was one of the effects of creating a women's organization rather than the impetus for doing so. SEROvie sought out a leader to mobilize women that resulted in the creation of its "sister" organization, FACSDIS, to manifest the "L" part of LGBT and therefore attract more grant funding from foundations outside of Haiti, though FACSDIS organizers ended up critically mobilizing beyond the "L" in generative and courageous ways that take up a more radical politics of alignment with marginalized Haitians.

INTRODUCING THE DISCOURSE OF LGBT COMMUNITY TO HAITI

The shift of discourses within Haiti from a plethora of terms to "LGBT community" at the same time as the earthquake was not coincidental. As Miranda Joseph writes in *Against the Romance of Community*, "communities are frequently said to emerge in times of crisis or tragedy, when people imagine themselves bound together by a common grief or joined through some extraordinary effort" (2002, vi). This is certainly true of the LGBT community in Haiti. The January 2010 earthquake and its aftermath exacted a heavy toll on burgeoning same-sex-desiring and gender-creative Haitians trying to enact social change. My three research sites experienced losses of leadership, membership, and infrastructure. The FOSAJ director who had provided resources for local masisi and madivin organizers to intervene in homophobic sexual politics—of which Lakou and its "Zonbi, Zonbi" performance is only one example—perished under the rubble of a hotel, while a few kilometers away walls of the FOSAJ warehouse came crashing down. Sixteen people were at a SEROvie support group meeting when the center collapsed in the earthquake; fourteen died. Many of these same people sought services or worked in a volunteer capacity at Promoteurs Objectif Zéro SIDA (POZ), whose buildings were also unusable after the earthquake. Survivors were pulled from under the ruins at each site, and although some required immediate medical attention, they were concerned about potential homophobic and transphobic discrimination from medical professionals.[8] All of this, however, was just the beginning of the devastation. In the Protestant Christian perspective that dominated public discourse at the time, the unnatural and therefore sinful acts of homosexual Haitians were said to have been the underlying cause for the devastation—God's punishment for the tolerance of homosexuality. Another flare-up of homophobic violence rippled across Haiti as a result.

While same-sex-desiring and gender-creative Haitians certainly had a sense of the ways that they were together differentially affected by the earthquake, and therefore a "community" framework might make sense, the period immediately after the earthquake marked an accelerated enmeshment with the global LGBTQI, specifically the IGLHRC and the Astraea Lesbian Foundation for Justice, known colloquially as Astraea. IGLHRC and Astraea initiated their formal connections with queer Haitian groups and organizations in 2009, but the 2010 earthquake intensified the degree of support they offered Haitians. The global LGBTQI introduced the discourse of "LGBT community" to Haiti in the course of offering support. Here I document how those shifts took place in the context of IGLHRC's partnership with SEROvie and Astraea's funding of FOSAJ.

THE INTERNATIONAL GAY AND LESBIAN HUMAN RIGHTS COMMISSION

After he was hired in 2009 as the executive director of the IGLHRC, Cary Alan Johnson brought Haiti into the scope of the organization's international mission. Johnson, who had previously served as IGLHRC's senior Africa specialist and manager of its office in Cape Town, is known not only for being a global crusader for LGBT rights, but for particular concern about "the HIV crisis in black men." Thus, his interest in Haiti was in some ways an extension of the work he had been doing for several decades in various countries in Africa. He says this about his initial trip to meet with the staff members of SEROvie: "In the fall of 2009, I traveled to Haiti to get a better understanding of emerging LGBT communities, the impact of HIV on men who have sex with men (MSM), and how LGBT were responding to the HIV crisis. At the time, I met some talented, committed individuals, who were mainly working in the context of the HIV prevention, treatment and care sector, but were also steadily carving out a space for the promotion and protection of a broad set of human rights for LGBT people" (Cary Alan Johnson 2010b). In this excerpt from Johnson's blog written after the earthquake, he characterizes the "LGBT communities" as emergent at a time when, as I indicated earlier in this chapter, this discourse was not being used in Haiti.[9] While he goes on to acknowledge that SEROvie's constituents are "gay and bisexual men and transgender women," this excerpt sets the stage to read these groups within a preexisting LGBT community framework. In the final sentence, Johnson also articulates the work of SEROvie—"HIV prevention, treatment and care"—with those of IGLHRC—"the promotion and protection of a broad set of human rights for LGBT people." A temporal trick is performed here that attributes those qualities taken on by SEROvie after the earthquake and its greater enmeshment with the global LGBTQI—that is, an LGBT community framework and understanding of its work in the service of human rights—to the organization before the earthquake. This passage erases that both of those qualities might have resulted from collaboration with IGLHRC.

IGLHRC intensified its partnership with SEROvie because of the earthquake. As stated in the spring/summer 2010 issue of IGLHRC's newsletter, "the January 2010 earthquake forced IGLHRC to move outside our normal areas of work and respond to the urgent needs of the Haitian LGBT community" (IGLHRC 2010, 3). Three days after the earthquake, the executive director of SEROvie, Steve Laguerre, sent a message to Cary Alan Johnson to apprise him of the disaster's immediate impact on the organization. Johnson posted his message as part of a fund-raising appeal to benefit relief work in Haiti—"Donate Directly to Relief and Support Efforts for the LGBT Community in Haiti" (Johnson 2010a). As early as this time, Johnson was hailing an LGBT community in order for same-sex-desiring and gender-creative

Haitians to be understood under the internationally intelligible yet hegemonic terms of the global LGBTQI. IGLHRC raised more than $10,000 for the organization in a matter of days and provided additional support to SEROvie by garnering much-needed supplies. Since SEROvie's office had collapsed, the staff was working from makeshift quarters to try and meet the needs of its constituents—including food, clean water, clothes, and medication. Even though IGLHRC's humanitarian support at this time enacted a minimalist biopolitics, or "the temporary administration of survival" (Redfield 2005, 344), their response certainly played a huge role in SEROvie's ability to carry out this work.

SEROvie was also being supported by the American Foundation for AIDS Research (amfAR). Before the earthquake, SEROvie had received two significant amfAR grants. In mid-2007, amfAR launched its MSM Initiative "to provide small, targeted grants to grass-roots groups in support of innovative HIV/AIDS services for MSM in resource-limited countries" because "as the HIV/AIDS pandemic enters its second quarter-century, HIV is spreading rapidly among men who have sex with men (MSM)" (amfAR 2007). SEROvie was among the first organizations funded as part of the MSM Initiative community awards; amfAR awarded their grant application project, "MSM and HIV in Haiti," $49,888 in 2008. The follow-up grant application for 2009 emphasized SEROvie's outreach work with "MSM communities." This grant application invoked community as did many of the other applications from Caribbean organizations, which is not surprising considering that amfAR prioritized funding for community-based organizations. SEROvie was awarded the $40,000 grant. Then, after the earthquake, they received another $15,000 grant from amfAR. Notably, around the same time that IGLHRC was hailing an LGBT community in Haiti, amfAR broadened its funding terms from "MSM" to "LGBT." amfAR provided institution-building support for its grant recipients, such as the *Fundraising Toolkit* (amfAR 2011). These materials, like the grant application processes, are also pedagogical in terms of teaching organizations the terminology to use when describing its work. The *Fundraising Toolkit*, for instance, uses "MSM" and "LGBT" together, as in "MSM/LGBT," whereas amfAR had previously used an MSM framework (amfAR 2012).

However, IGLHRC rather than amfAR brought SEROvie into the international spotlight in the wake of the tragedy by highlighting the plight of Haiti's LGBT community for international audiences interested in LGBTQI human rights. Thus their "minimalist biopolitics" were part of a larger biopolitical shift where same-sex-desiring and gender-creative Haitians were not only sometimes MSM (subjects of risk) but also LGBT (subjects of rescue) in a way that produced an "LGBT Haitian" population and reframed the "Haitian population" generally. I detail more about the IGLHRC-SEROvie partnership after providing a sense of the impact of foreign foundation funding on queer Haitian organizing in Jacmel.

THE ASTRAEA FOUNDATION FOR LESBIAN JUSTICE

Astraea describes itself as "the only philanthropic organization working exclusively to advance LGBTQI human rights around the globe," and as such can be considered the philanthropic counterpart to IGLHRC in the global LGBTQI (Astraea 2020). Astraea provided its first grant to a Haitian organization—FOSAJ—in 2009. I was living and working at FOSAJ during the time that the U.S. director of the arts center, Flores "Flo" McGarrell, was writing the grant application and visiting Astraea in New York. I assisted him in several ways, including editing the application for the $10,000 grant that Flo drafted, since I had formerly been a director of a nonprofit program and a successful grant writer. Because of my research, I also served as one of FOSAJ's references since I could speak to how the organization's programs supported masisi and madivin residents of Jacmel. The grant was intended to support FOSAJ's operational costs (and therefore the work it was already doing), the creation of new programs for women, and an antidiscrimination arts festival. After the earthquake, Astraea provided a $6,760 emergency grant to Lakou, the performance troupe that had been affiliated with FOSAJ. Lakou discontinued its association with FOSAJ for a period of time after the earthquake because the new director had an antagonistic relationship with almost all of the artists in the troupe. For that time, Lakou moved to a new arts center, initiated by Alison, a white U.S. American lesbian and best friend of Flo McGarrell who had been with him working on a FOSAJ program when the earthquake struck. Alison, Rebecca (a white queer independent film producer from the United States who had been intimately involved with Flo), and I connected with the International Program officer at Astraea, Rosa, who guided us to secure the emergency grant as advocates for Lakou.[10] Rosa facilitated post-disaster support in other ways as well. For example, she introduced Lakou members to a lesbian feminist collective in Santo Domingo, Tres Gatas, that was interested in expanding their solidarity work with Haitian feminists to same-sex-desiring and gender-creative Haitians.[11] The emergency grant covered limited-duration costs of housing and basic necessities—food, water filters, and transportation. In other words, it also enacted a minimalist biopolitics. When the grant expired, the members of Lakou (by then Gran Lakou) were interested in seeking more funds from Astraea to continue their work and finally plan the antidiscrimination arts festival, but they were ineligible because of problems with the administration of the emergency grant, a point I return to shortly. This is to say that the earthquake momentarily intensified Astraea's commitments to same-sex-desiring and gender-creative people in Haiti, just as it did for IGLHRC's partnership with SEROvie.

The seeds of this relationship were planted in 2008. When Flo became the director of FOSAJ in the fall of that year, he worked with the artists and board to devise a fund-raising plan for the arts center, which included seeking grants from foundations like Yèle Haiti as well as other strategies like art auctions, corporate partnerships, and individual asks through the center's social networks in the United States, Canada, and France. Flo's proposal to apply for an Astraea grant met with some resistance by a few board members and artists who thought that the application was a waste of time because FOSAJ, as a non-LGBTQI-specific organization, was a poor candidate for funding. Some of the FOSAJ artists who had been involved in the organization for the longest amount of time also objected to expanding the organization's support of same-sex-desiring and gender-creative Haitians. Only one artist expressed objections in explicitly antigay terms, while the other protests were implicitly homophobic. For instance, a few artists couched their objections in terms of personal problems with the same-sex-desiring and gender-creative artists at FOSAJ who started Lakou or worked in the women's shop. They contended that the artists were a magnet for drama that detracted from the center's purpose. More often, though, the older generation of artists indicated that they did not want FOSAJ to become known as affiliating with masisi and madivin because they believed it would harm the organization's reputation. The debates around these issues ensued even after Astraea awarded the grant.

However, Flo moved forward with the application once he reached a compromise with the majority of artists and board members, one in which the application emphasized that FOSAJ was made up of many marginalized groups in Haiti, not solely madivin and masisi. This was in fact more closely aligned with how the majority of those associated with the organization as staff, board members, and artists viewed FOSAJ—as a creative refuge for the undercommons. This compromise ultimately meshed well with Astraea's desire for the application to speak to the organization's diversity. For instance, Astraea requires applicants to provide information about diversity within the organization along certain lines of difference. Flo and another staff member translated Astraea's diversity survey into Kreyòl, to the greatest extent possible. Of the forty-one respondents who reflected the key stakeholders in the organization (board members, staff, volunteers, and artists), Flo reported to Astraea that "10 responses . . . do not conform to binary gender defini-tions; 26 LGBQ responses (5 people checked more than one box); 15 have ability differences; 17 religious minorities, likely to be Vodouists; 15 single parents; 9 with LGBT family members; 7 people living with HIV/ AIDS; We are 100% low income/poor here; 10 sex workers, both men and women."[12] While these categories reflected Astraea's interests, there are other places on the application that articulated diversity in FOSAJ's terms. As an example, here is the section of the grant application about FOSAJ's constituency:

> While FOSAJ was not founded as a queer organization—by the very fact that we welcome many people who don't "fit in" mainstream Haitian soci-ety—naturally a great percentage of us are queer. We have three Lesbian and Bisexual women, three gay and bisexual men on the board and directorship, our director is an out trans-man. In addition to the Madivin (Lesbian) and *masisi* (Gay) in our community, we are also artists, street youth, people who live with a disability, deportees, sex-workers, Haitian Rasta, Vodouists and other marginalized peoples. This diversity makes us stronger as we face similar challenges in discrimination from mainstream Haitian society—who often defines success through outward appearance of traditional family values, up-ward mobility, disregard for abnormality, and religious and cultural choices such as Vodou and Haitian Rasta lifestyles.

Flo's strategy was to foreground the involvement of same-sex-desiring and gender-creative people in FOSAJ in a way that was intelligible to Astraea, but also to highlight that the politics of the art center were such that criminalized groups in Haiti—street youths, sex workers (also one of Astraea's catego-ries), deportees, Rasta, and Vodouizan—were central to the organization, not just as "outreach groups." This attribute of FOSAJ actually informed the center's local reputation more than anything else. Jacmelians who knew that I lived there, including those who would come by and use FOSAJ's services, encouraged me to move to someplace "safer" and told me that the artists were drug dealers, thieves, criminals, and "bad boys." These men, especially the ones with dreadlocks, also regularly faced discrimination in their daily lives—verbal harassment, barred entry to certain establishments, and em-ployment and housing discrimination.[13] Like masisi and madivin, they also faced ostracism from their families. The vision of FOSAJ—as included in the application and described to me by Flo, the staff, and the board—was to form alliances between these criminalized groups of people and other people who were regularly discriminated against and marginalized, such as disabled people, single mothers, and masisi and madivin, through an arts-based support network. The queer vision of the organization was much more aligned with "more thorough resistance to regimes of the normal" than with LGBTQI (Warner 1993, 11). "Queer" holds a space for all kinds of nonnormativity, which includes LGBT (FOSAJ noted elsewhere in the application that it is primarily foreigners involved with the organization who used these terms), madivin, and masisi, as well as other cast out of Haitian mainstream society.

The process of applying for a grant forced FOSAJ to imagine itself for the first time in terms of an LGBTQI community, and yet throughout the application there is pushback against this framework. The grant application criteria overview stated that "Astraea's International Fund for Sexual Minorities supports groups, projects, or organizations working toward progressive social change which are led by lesbian, gay, bisexual, transgender, queer and intersex (LGBTQI) communities and directly address oppression based on sexual orientation and/or gender identity/expression." As I have already mentioned, "queer" in FOSAJ's vision was a set of radical politics rather than, as Astraea intends here, an identity category. Flo additionally indicates that the social categories of LGBTQI do not resonate for many same-sex-desiring people in Haiti, and he elaborates the multiple meanings of *masisi* and difficulties of accounting for its meaning in Astraea's terms.[14] This qualifier follows the first account of gender and sexual nonnormativity in Astraea's terms in the report of the survey results. Masisi and madivin are absent, subsumed under "LGBQ" and existing outside the gender binary. However, when FOSAJ staff had the opportunity to use their own terms to describe the work of the organization, "LGBTQI" is quite remarkably absent. The acronym is used half as frequently as "queer," *masisi*, and *madivin*, and, interestingly, mostly in terms of the organization's future work.[15] Only once in the entire thirty-page application is FOSAJ described as an LGBTQI organization, and that is in the context of asserting that Haiti has no other organizations for sexual minorities.[16]

These nuances were lacking from the second letter of intent and the emergency grant application that I helped submit after the earthquake. In the rush to secure much-needed resources for the members of Lakou, my collaborator and I were more than willing to constitute LGBTQI Haitians as a population with needs above and beyond those of other Haitians because of the flare-up of homophobic violence, as encouraged by the International Program officer at Astraea. The narrative in these documents also included a section to elaborate that the group, not to mention masisi and madivin in general, was essentially ousted from FOSAJ when the person who assumed the directorship after Flo's death was an artist unapologetically vocal about disliking homosexuality. While these narratives accurately reflected Lakou members' accounts of post-earthquake changes, the language of LGBTQI community mirrored Astraea's language rather than Lakou's. The coordinators gave us documents, for instance, with demographic information about the group that used the terms *masisi* and *madivin*, and these were rewritten into the narrative as "gay," "lesbian," and "LGBTQI." In a reversal of the original application, *masisi* and *madivin* appear only once in the main body of the document while "LGBTQI and other marginalized communities" is ubiquitous. My U.S. collaborator Alison, who spearheaded the extensive application process and drafted the documents, described the Kreyòl and English terms as commensurate. As the editor of the document I did not raise any issues with the framing because I understood the narrative to strategically align with Astraea's funding priorities.

I want to pause to reflect on why we—as white, middle-class queer U.S. Americans—were positioned as intermediaries in this process of seeking funding from foundations outside of Haiti. To begin with, one must have the resources to find out information about the foundations that offer grants and the knowledge to assess the "fit" of the mission and programs with the foundation's mission, an arduous task in and of itself. Then, navigating the grant application process requires regular access to technology (e.g., cell phones, computers, and Internet) as well as cultural capital that none of the ti masisi and ti madivin of Jacmel in these instances had the opportunity to accrue such as English-language proficiency, familiarity with bureaucratic procedures, and certain kinds of professionalization. Even the U.S. Americans who participated in the grant-writing processes in these instances found the procedures overwhelming despite having advanced degrees and working in positions that required detailed budgets. In all aspects the grant application process favors those in Haiti who not only are from the middle and upper classes but who have some connection to the United States. In the instance of the Astraea grant, queer U.S. Americans were the ones applying for the funding rather than queer Haitians and, in the instance of the SEROvie grants, they were Haitians who obtained advanced degrees in the United States. In these ways and others, the process of applying for a grant reproduces the same inequities that, at least in Astraea's instance, the foundations are funding organizations to remedy.

U.S. Americans and middle- and upper-class Haitians are also in better positions to administer the grants—within Haiti they are believed to have the "capacity to manage," as the director of another organization relayed to me during fieldwork. Lakou was ineligible to apply for subsequent grants from Astraea due to the absence of grant reports from the emergency grant. The Lakou coordinators did not have the cultural capital to undertake such a task, and the Astraea grants did not include any training components for such endeavors. The coordinators did not know which purchased items needed receipts, let alone how to keep a budget. They struggled with the professional protocols of communicating with Astraea, and importantly, each message between Lakou and the International Program officer needed to be translated, work that I and others performed for the group.[17] In the end, the grant administration issues ultimately led to a loss in the group's cohesion. Lakou grappled with serious internal conflicts about how the money was supposed to be spent, and eventually the coordinator most often in communication with Astraea was accused of stealing the grant money. The other members of Lakou were also suspicious of Alison, who they perceived as being "in charge" since she wrote the grant and was the codirector of the newly formed arts center where Lakou was based. Suffice it to say that, for reasons I have outlined, the group was set up to fail but then was treated as "bad subjects" of grant funding. Rather than acknowledging how structural inequalities informed every part of the process, Astraea decided not to give Lakou recommendations for future funding.

THE HARMS OF GLOBAL LGBTQI LIBERALISM

Despite their differences in approaches, then, both IGLHRC and Astraea performed a kind of selective recognition. Their identity politics framework informed how they supported Haitians who had been through the trauma of the earthquake—LGBTQI helping LGBT. The acute form of victimization at issue here is the experience of homophobia, and to a lesser extent, transphobia. In *Democratic Insecurities: Violence, Trauma, and Intervention in Haiti*, Erica Caple James draws on her grounded research and a range of theorists to argue that "selective recognition practices frequently generate 'triage' interventions that remedy immediate or acute suffering rather than transform the structural political, economic, and social conditions that contribute to chronic forms of insecurity" (2010, 90). She notes that these triage interventions are aimed at the level of "bare life" (Agamben 1998) because they are conducted under conditions—like the earthquake—that permit (or promote) enactments of minimalist biopolitics, which is the case in IGLHRC and Astraea's support of LGBT Haitians. They were offering funding for basic necessities such as food, water filters, tents and other forms of temporary shelter, hygiene kits, and condoms. The funding was not aimed to create lasting change in Haiti by addressing the structural conditions that shaped same-sex-desiring and gender-creative Haitians' lives, although by constituting an LGBT community or population, it had a long-term impact.

These changes were catalyzed by more than the humanitarian outreach—IGLHRC partnered with SEROvie on a research project about the effects of the earthquake on Haiti's LGBT community. Through this research, IGLHRC came to take on a central role in knowledge production about gender and sexuality in Haiti after the earthquake. They produced and circulated research briefings, press releases, and other media that narrated Haiti as a bad (failed) state that only exists in its repressive form in ways that promote violence and homophobia. The solution to these issues, IGLHRC posits in these documents and in their actions, can be found in intergovernmental organizations (IGOs) like the United Nations and NGOs that are working in the best interests of LGBT people.

In the description of the organization's work on its website, IGLHRC highlights its role in knowledge production for the global LGBTQI. "Together with our partners, we create visibility for human rights violations by monitoring and documenting abuses and by responding to human rights emergencies" (IGLHRC, 2014). As I learned from my interviews with staff and volunteers, IGLHRC research is often conducted from its New York office and only sometimes includes going to the places that it produces knowledge about in its efforts for "global advocacy." In this instance, IGLHRC sent a team of researchers to Haiti in April 2010 to work with SEROvie to assess the situation on the ground for the "LGBT community." Executive Director Cary Alan Johnson led the research team. His travel companions were two IGLHRC staff members—Marcelo Ernesto Ferreyra, the Latin American/Caribbean coordinator, and a researcher with French-language skills, Samara D. Fox, who was a last-minute substitute for an IGLHRC board member who was unable to go—neither of whom had been to Haiti before. Their one-week research trip included ten- to fifteen-person focus groups with approximately sixty people in SEROvie's networks and about ten in-depth individual interviews that allowed IGLHRC researchers to focus on voices underrepresented in the focus groups, such as those of women. Johnson, Ferreyra, and Fox additionally interviewed staff at SEROvie and employees with UN agencies in Haiti.

From this research with SEROvie, IGLHRC produced a briefing paper in English and French about LGBT life in Haiti after the earthquake. The fourteen-page document in English, available on the IGLHRC website, is titled *The Impact of the Earthquake, and Relief and Recovery Programs on Haitian LGBT People* (IGLHRC 2011). Samara Fox, who had experience writing IGLHRC action alerts, drafted the briefing, and the other IGLHRC staff members edited the document before its release in March 2011. The SEROvie executive director, Steve Laguerre, and program director, Reginald Dupont, are listed as principal authors with the IGLHRC research team members; although they did not write the report, they arranged the focus groups and individual interviews and provided feedback to Fox about the accuracy of the briefing. The briefing had extensive international circulation and its findings have been used by others—journalists, UN agencies, and academics—as an authoritative source on post-earthquake conditions for LGBT people.

In IGLHRC's terms, the briefing works against a narrative of equal suffering in the wake of natural disaster by highlighting the particular needs and vulnerabilities of the LGBT population of Haiti as a marginalized group. The narrative is one of decline, specifically that the earthquake "heightened pre-existing inequalities and prejudices" and the marginalization of LGBT individuals, families and communities (IGLHRC 2011, 2). There is a long explanation of what makes the LGBT community in Haiti different than other marginalized groups, namely their experiences with homophobia and transphobic gender violence. In a way, the briefing perpetuates the idea that Haiti is inherently homophobic. Even though the IGLHRC research team had never been to Haiti before 2010, the briefing references "pervasive" homophobia in Haiti before the earthquake (IGHRC 2011, 3). In this decontextualized mention, what does "pervasive" mean? Few insights are offered except, according to the briefing, the things that kept the LGBT population of Haiti safe before the earthquake were regular patterns of movement, developed social networks, and secure housing. These things were disrupted by the disaster, and the only LGBT organization (an inaccuracy in the briefing), SEROvie, was decimated. To say that friends, walls, and an organization kept the LGBT community safe missed a class-based analysis; there were many same-sex-desiring and gender-creative Haitians who lived comfortably before and after the earthquake and also that those who were affected by the earthquake were of those classes in Haiti who were just able to afford secure housing.

The IGLHRC briefing reports that new kinds of challenges were introduced in this context of "pervasive" discrimination, violence, and stigma such as models for distributing aid that only recognized female-headed households, no recognition of the special needs of LGBT persons in relief work, arbitrary arrests and detention, and significantly, blame for the earth-quake by "religious zealots" (IGLHRC 2011, 7). The briefing does not pro-pose solutions for all of these problems but rather advocates for rebuilding organizations in Haiti that serve the LGBT population. The briefing says that post-earthquake recovery is an opportunity for accountability, respect, equality, and, most of all, inclusion of LGBT people, such as bringing LGBT leadership to the table at inter-agency planning meetings. The final words of the briefing that encapsulate IGLHRC's agenda are "While earthquakes may occur naturally, homophobic discrimination does not. The time to end the impact of transphobia and homophobia in emergency response and preparedness is now" (10).

Many topics regarding post-earthquake conditions glossed in the IGLHRC briefing came up in the context of my research with same-sex-desiring and gender-creative Haitians in Jacmel.[18] However, the Jacmelians accused certain Protestant churches in town—particularly those of the Baptist denomina-tion—of fueling the hatred they faced in the wake of the earthquake rather than "religious zealots" writ large. It was reported to me that these church leaders and congregants blamed homosexuals, among others, for the earth-quake because their actions had brought God's punishment. This message was broadcast from the pulpit as well as on the radio. Legba, a gay artist in Lakou who was displaced by the disaster, reported this in his account of his post-earthquake trials and tribulations:

> Everywhere people were saying "Down with masisi, down with masisi! They caused this misery [mizè]." There were sermons on the radio that said the same thing. I don't understand haters [in English]. We didn't cause this misery. We are in it.
> *Did people say those things at your [Catholic] church, too?*
> The church broke in the earthquake. [. . .] But those people are not Catholic. I know they are not Catholic. They are angry, angry, angry. The homophobes [homofòb]! Wow!

I never heard the particular anti-homosexual sermons on the radio that Legba and other Haitians often mentioned. From what people in both Jacmel and Port-au-Prince reported to me, however, this fervor was concentrated in the weeks immediately following the earthquake, although the animos-ity toward masisi and madivin lingered far longer. The IGLHRC briefing mentions post-earthquake sermons to this effect but does not mention in what kinds of churches or that the religious-based movements that spread these homophobic sexual politics have their historical roots in the United

States. Pat Robertson makes an appearance in the report for his notorious "Haiti made a blood pact with the devil" comments, and the authors express concern that relief efforts might bring to Haiti more of his kind (IGLHRC 2011, 8). However, what is missing is an account of the long, slow Protestant encroachment in Haiti detailed in chapter 2, which began in earnest in the 1950s on the tail of the U.S. occupation; also absent are the transnational evangelical connections that explain those hateful sermons and place them in a historical context. The fact that the United States has been exporting homophobic sexual politics to Haiti for more than half a century does not figure in the global LGBTQI's representation of Haiti.

Among the tangible effects of scapegoating of same-sex-desiring and gender-creative Haitians were violent verbal and physical confrontations and forced relocation, especially in instances where people were in temporary shelter. Legba and Mirabo were the only same-sex-desiring and gender-creative Haitians I knew in Jacmel who lived for an extended period of time in the internally displaced persons (IDP) camps that sprung up in any available open space in Haiti—parks, sidewalks, dirt lots, medians between the two sides of a road. By the time I reconnected with them after the earthquake in mid-March, they had already moved twice because of negative experiences in the IDP camps. The first time, the tent they lived in had been robbed of all its belongings, and the second time Mirabo was confronted by a crowd in the camp. As Mirabo said:

> One day I went to the market to buy food, and when I arrived back on the plaza, someone called me a masisi. It was a young man—a difficult situation. He yelled, "masisi! masisi!" He was between me and the tent. He and his friends, they threw rocks at me. Other people came to see what was happening, and they did not tell him to stop. Things changed after the earthquake. People became angry at masisi because of the Baptists. I didn't want to fight with them, so I left the camp. We found a new place to live.

Legba and Mirabo, like many of my informants in Jacmel, had struggled to find regular housing even before the earthquake. They would sleep a couple of nights in one house, then a couple of nights in another. The IDP camps presented an opportunity for a semi-regular place to sleep, but both were anxious about the lack of security since—as unpartnered masisi—they had few allies where they lived. In the last camp where I visited them, however, a bunch of women adopted them into the network that they set up to share responsibilities for things like watching over the tents and collective cooking. Mirabo said that he won them over with his delicious food.

Almost everyone else made homeless by the earthquake moved in with family, often in the areas outside Jacmel proper. Most of these welcomed returning to their family home, and only one person, Charles, expressed discomfort living with his family in Lavale. Even though he does not come from a representative group, when we met up for a drink, what Charles—who self-described as gay and then later masisi—told me reflected some of the post-earthquake changes in sexual politics.

> My mother and father are Baptists. . . . They have become real church people because of [the earthquake]. This makes my life so hard. They used to say ignorant things. Bad things. "Masisi have sex for money. Masisi are rich." But now? Now they blame masisi for everything. "Masisi made the earthquake." They turned into slanderers.
> *How do you respond?*
> "It's not true! It's not true!" You know? They do not know that I am masisi. But my sisters do. [Our parents] infect them with that religious attitude/disposition that causes people to attack other people.

Charles had never before been subject to this kind of homophobic violence, which may be because of his performance of masculinity and also because he occasionally dates women. However, he told me in an interview before the earthquake that he was often in the position of sticking up for his effeminate friends when they were verbally harassed in the streets. As with most same-sex-desiring organizers I have worked with in Haiti, he has a strong stance against anti-masisi attitudes and actions, as well as an analysis of how these things are fomented by evangelical Christianity. Although he was raised Baptist, the second most common religious background among my informants after Catholicism, he started practicing Vodou as an adult because, as he said, "it is the true Haitian religion." He, of course, also would often recite the romantic narrative of Vodou as supporting all kinds of non-normative differences—mentioning homosexuality and disability specifically.

Protestant informants also reported shifts within their congregations. Same-sex-desiring Haitians were surprised by the intensity of antihomosexual fervor that became part of the daily life of their churches. Cassandre, a lesbian woman partnered with a man with whom she parents a young son in their home that was undamaged by the earthquake, recounted to me:

> After those first thirty seconds when the world was falling apart, everyone helped each other. Everyone, without exception. It was later that people said that homosexuals made the earth tremble. Why did they say that? I don't know.

What did they say?

You know. Masisi and madivin are sinners. We made Haiti sick.

Sick?

Yes, sick.

Like HIV/AIDS ?

No. Not AIDS. Sickness of the spirit. They say it is the fault of homosexuality, and they want to cure it. So they pray for the deliverance of
Haiti.

Who says this?

The pastor at my [Seventh-day Adventist] church. The other women in
my prayer group.

What do you think?

Thanks to God, I am still alive. Every day is hard, but it is no one's fault.

Faith is an important part of life in Haiti. Cassandre generally found a place
of belonging in her congregation, and her church was an important space
of healing for her after the trauma of the earthquake. Yet she disagreed with
the Seventh-day Adventist position about the earthquake's cause, as I am
sure many other congregants did as well. Her assertion that the earthquake
was "no one's fault" ran counter to the narrative of divine retribution that
circulated transnationally among some kinds of evangelicals.

Junior, one of the congregants of a large Baptist church in Jacmel with a
congregation that nearly doubled in January 2010 as people were "called to
become Disciples of Christ," shed some light on some other dimensions of
this narrative.

The situation [at the church] changed [after the earthquake]. The devoted members of the congregation, their hearts were not filled with
love for Jesus Christ. They said that God is punishing Haiti because
of sexual immorality. They not only fault *pederas* [pejorative term for
homosexuals], but prostitutes and adulterers. This eruption against
gays filled me with fear.

Why?

Because those same people were saying, "Death to masisi!"

Wait. They said that in the church?

Not in the church. They said it on the streets.

They? The same people in your church?

Yes. Well, they are the same thing.

Junior proceeded to tell me that the force with which people in his church
had started to condemn homosexuality seemed related to the name-calling

and other injurious speech against gays that he heard in his neighborhood, such as a man who lived around the corner from him waxing on about how people need to get rid of homosexuals in Haiti. When I inquired further about who had said, "Death to masisi!" Junior said that he never heard it himself, but that members of Lakou told him this story. I never found the original source, but because a similar story was reported in Port-au-Prince, it may have traveled by word of mouth through social networks. Whether or not someone actually said, "Death to masisi!," mortal fear was not unfounded. Many people knew of Avadra and Franck's story told in previous chapters. With the increased antihomosexual fervor immediately after the earthquake, who knew what was possible? But, as Junior also noted, homosexuality was not the only reason that his church cited for God's punishment: sexual immorality in many forms was faulted. The narrative of divine retribution, therefore, went beyond blaming homosexuals for the earthquake.

This point is important because if one were to take at face value the claims about homophobia in Haiti generated by the global LGBTQI and the international media, then homosexuals would seem to solely shoulder the burden of responsibility for the earthquake in these discourses.[19] This is not a purposeful bias to not discuss other kinds of people negatively impacted by the discourse of divine retribution, but instead it is a product of the transnational travels of identity politics that produce selective recognition of particular kinds of subjects and injuries—in this instance, LGBTIQ and homophobia.[20] I am equally certain from my interviews with IGLHRC researchers and many of the same people they interviewed at SEROvie that these reports about homophobia in Haiti accurately reflect how same-sex-desiring and gender-creative Haitians in these research settings narrate the disaster. A queer ethnographic lens takes these stories seriously: as I show throughout this book, homophobia has serious material consequences for Haitians, and same-sex-desiring and gender-creative Haitians understood themselves to be experiencing a crisis after the earthquake. Yet this lens must necessarily be attuned to the silences around the stories (Foucault 1990, Trouillot 1995).

The global LGBTQI in post-earthquake Haiti effectively authorized a discourse that (only) homosexuals were scapegoated in narratives of divine retribution, resulting in high incidents of homophobic violence. One of the most noticeable silences is the lack of attention to the way that vodouizan were scapegoated for the earthquake in these narratives of divine retribution.[21] Without the kind of cultural capital of identity politics that same-sex-desiring and gender-creative Haitians have in the global LGBTQI, the violences suffered by vodouizan received very little attention outside the country.[22] These transnational identity politics cleaved homosexuals from Vodou, although the two travel together, as previous chapters explore. The resulting effects were that vodouizan became the queer Other to the LGBT community in Haiti and that the global LGBTQI missed an opportunity for a broader analysis of the ways that Vodou is a way to talk about queers of all kinds, including homosexuals.

The way that IGLHRC framed the briefing, moreover, had the effect of continuing certain legacies of U.S. imperialism in Haiti. The most flagrant issue of the 2011 report is that it represents the Haitian state as negligent at best and perpetuating homophobic violence at worst—solely in its repressive capacities—without contextualizing the histories of imperialist interventions that created that situation. It opens with a woeful gesture in that direction: "While Haiti has known more than its share of international exploitation, bad governance, political unrest, and natural catastrophes, the impact of the January 12, 2010 earthquake deserves special consideration" (IGLHRC 2011, 1). Just what this international exploitation consists of is missing from the briefing.

Moreover, the mention of bad governance and political unrest would seem to locate Haiti's problems solely within its existing apparatus of governance, which mirrors the primary justification for each of the U.S. military occupations of Haiti over the last century. This problematic framing also arises in the context of the briefing's mention of a report about Haiti by MADRE—an international women's human rights organization—that cast the lack of government response to reports of abuse and discrimination as being both problems of "political will and the capacity to respond" (MADRE quoted in IGLHRC 2011, 2–3). Capacity could be a veiled reference to the way that the Haitian state has been constantly undermined since its creation in 1804, both as a product of what we have come to recognize as the postcolonial condition and as retribution specifically aimed at the way that the Haitian Revolution and the successful formation of the Black republic upset white supremacist colonial regimes. As Dubois contends in *Haiti: The Aftershocks of History*, after all, "Haiti's present is the product of its history: of the nation's founding by enslaved people who overthrew their masters and freed themselves; of the hostility that this revolution generated among the colonial powers surrounding the country; and of the intense struggle within Haiti itself to define that freedom and realize its promise" (2012, 4). In his book, Dubois traces the many ways in which Haiti was undermined and reoccupied by imperial powers after its 1804 independence and how these events underwrote the outcomes of the earthquake and the capacity of Haitians to respond and rebuild on a large scale. Paul Farmer's account of the earthquake similarly begins with the "transnational social and economic forces with deep roots in the colonial enterprise" that caused Haiti's "chronic disabilities" when faced with a large-scale disaster, including nearly a century of U.S. intervention (2011, 3). Disembedded from its context in the MADRE report, however, the IGLHRC briefing reference to the Haitian state's lack of capacity seems to refer to the devastation of the earthquake; there are no mentions of the histories of imperialism.

There are other ways that the briefing rendered the Haitian state as impotent and in need of intervention. IGLHRC turns to the United Nations as an authoritative source on the broad impact of the earthquake on Haitians, although the briefing faults UN agencies and private volunteer organizations (PVOs) conducting humanitarian assistance after the earthquake for not including LGBT people in relief and recovery efforts (IGLHRC 2011, 10). SEROvie and IGLHRC moreover circulated the briefing at interagency meetings and among different segments of the United Nations and presented the findings to the Inter-American Commission on Human Rights. They also adapted the findings of the report to recommendations for the UN Human Rights Committee. In the ways the briefing was produced and circulated, then, the global LGBTQI made the argument that the problems with homophobia in Haiti and their potential solutions are to be found in PVOs, NGOs, and IGOs, such as the United Nations, which just need to be more inclusive of LGBT people. IGLHRC does not question why there is an overabundance of aid and relief organizations in Haiti.

In terms of the United Nations, it is noticeable that the 2011 IGLHRC brief does not mention that Haiti has been under continuous occupation by multinational UN "peacekeepers"—whose armed soldiers, white trucks, and armored tanks have become integrated into the Haitian landscape—since the early 1990s. The briefing was written and circulated before the outbreak of the cholera epidemic introduced to Haiti by UN soldiers that killed close to ten thousand people and affected hundreds of thousands more, and before the international media picked up stories of the soldiers using rape as a tool of biopolitical power.[23] It was a moment when it was still possible for outsiders to defend the MINUSTAH, before it had come under global scrutiny. Yet as the previous chapter details, Lakou and other same-sex-desiring and gender-creative Haitians had a queer critique of this occupation as connected to other kinds of imperialist interventions throughout Haiti's history. IGLHRC missed an opportunity to use the briefing as a platform to make an argument for the demilitarization of aid in Haiti as a beneficial action for same-sex-desiring and gender-creative Haitians. Instead, its liberal narrative that Haiti is a bad (failed) state disavows the effects of colonialism, imperialism, and ongoing militarization and posits solutions in precisely the detrimental neoliberal processes—"rescues" staged by PVOs, NGOs, and IGOs—that have devastated postcolonial Haiti.

So it is true that IGLHRC and the briefing garnered resources for "Haiti's LGBT" at a time when other channels, including the American Red Cross's LGBT Relief Fund, were not reaching same-sex-desiring and gender-creative Haitians. But at what cost, and with what consequences? First of all, even though the global LGBTQI met the short-term needs of these Haitians, they did nothing to address long-terms needs. As my discussion of Astraea indicates—and as I detail further in the next chapter about the social movement in Haiti against homophobia after 2012—these grants created conflict among Haitian organizational leadership and diverted the groups' mission and goals to put them in the cycles of seeking out more funding. The global LGBTQI, most importantly, did not address the root causes of the structural inequalities. Second, same-sex-desiring and gender-creative Haitians were wrested into international intelligibility as LGBT. This is true of the many promotional materials used by Astraea, IGLHRC, and the international media outlets plugged into the global LGBTQI as well as in the terms used within Haiti.[24] Not only did the global LGBTQI constitute "LGBT Haitians" as a population, but their purpose for doing so was to rescue them from the devastation of a country riddled with homophobia. This move both obscures that contemporary homophobic sexual politics in Haiti are largely a product of U.S. imperialism in Haiti and, of concern for future politics, invites future rescue missions from other NGOs and the United Nations.

2013

6

THE EMERGENCE OF A
SOCIAL MOVEMENT
AGAINST HOMOPHOBIA

This chapter further explores the interplay between two transnational social movements in Haiti—evangelical Christianity and LGBTQI rights—in relationship to postcolonial homophobia. I begin by analyzing the emergent social movement by and for same-sex-desiring and gender-creative Haitians that coalesced around a shared commitment to challenging homophobia. While the performance troupe Lakou and the health organization SEROvie had independently conducted antihomophobic work for years, the global LGBTQI and those of us who traveled through Haitian social networks brought people, groups, and established organizations into greater contact after the earthquake. These connections laid the foundation for new groups and organizations to form and for generative collaborative work to take place toward a similar goal. This network culminated in a Haitian social movement, the emergence of which I mark at the International Day Against Homophobia (IDAHO) events in 2012, when Haitians representing various established and burgeoning institutions focused on health, advocacy, activism, and the arts collaborated on events. Though the collaborators adopted a stance against "homophobia" as the framework for the IDAHO events, their interpretations of the term and therefore preferred strategies to uproot it varied. These differences clarified during a flare-up, or intensified period of postcolonial homophobia, in summer 2013. The catalyst in this instance was a coalition of evangelical Christian organizations that staged marches in the capital of Port-au-Prince and other cities to oppose same-sex marriage, regardless of the fact that it was not—nor was it likely to be—legal. As with the Pierre-Louis controversy in 2008 and the evangelical Christian response to the earthquake in 2010, postcolonial homophobia shaped the demonstrations against same-sex marriage as well as responses to them. Here I document the 2013 marches and their effects on same-sex-desiring and gender-creative Haitians, especially their impact on the relationships among the IDAHO collaborators.

Lakou performed at the IDAHO events, though with the new moniker "Gran Lakou [big or better lakou] Folklorik" directed by Mirabo and Legba with an almost entirely different roster of performers. After the conflicts described in the previous chapter, Lakou transformed into Gran Lakou, an "LGBT inclusive" dance group without the anti-imperialist political mission envisioned by Avadra and other performers from the original configuration. Its performances and self-promotion materials on social media—particularly Facebook—regularly featured the rainbow flag. As Gran Lakou increasingly focused on LGBT and then LGBTI-specific work, the dance group developed a relationship with Fondasyon SEROvie. Fondasyon SEROvie booked Gran Lakou to perform at its events when funds were available to pay the performers, their transportation costs from Jacmel, and occasionally lodging costs in Port-au-Prince (at least until SEROvie had on-site emergency housing available to the performers). Gran Lakou members additionally acted as an extension of SEROvie in Jacmel by conducting sexual health trainings and distributing condoms and lubricants from UNAIDS. By this time, even though I maintained a relationship with (Gran) Lakou and sent financial support to its members—including for Mirabo to open a "Peace House" for homeless and near homeless same-sex-desiring Haitians—the balance shifted to spending more of my time in the field in Port-au-Prince and surrounding areas rather than Jacmel.[1] The groups and organizations conducting work by and/or for same-sex-desiring and gender-creative Haitians in the capital city changed dramatically from when I initiated fieldwork (and have again in the time since), and so I proceed with a description of the ones featured in this chapter as they were in 2012 to 2014 to trace debates about homophobia in Haiti—SEROvie, renamed Fondasyon SEROvie, and an activist group called Kouraj.

Fondasyon SEROvie has existed in some form since the 1990s. As chapter 5 discusses in greater detail in, SEROvie was a product of development projects for MSM that—since the earthquake and its collaborations with the IGLHRC and other representatives of the global LGBTQI—defined itself as working for the LGBT community in Haiti. SEROvie started providing small grants during this time, but its primary function was still health and advocacy. It had a nationwide network of peer educators—like the members of Gran Lakou—who conducted safe-sex education and continued its long-term HIV/AIDS outreach mission to MSM, hence the name that combines the words "seropositive" and "life." SEROvie hosted support groups for the LGBT community at its office in Port-au-Prince and provided services to its "beneficiaries," including crisis support, medical treatment, legal counsel or advocacy, and shelter. SEROvie's advocacy additionally included public education to teach people about homophobia and the LGBTI community in Haiti.

Kouraj, whose name means courage, was an activist organization developed after the earthquake by a group of friends interested in organizing politically to defend the rights of same-sex-desiring and gender-creative people. They hailed these Haitians as the M community—*masisi, madivin, makomer, miks*—instead of as the LGBT community (at least situationally). The organization was briefly associated with the social enterprise Yanvalou (named after a rhythm and dance in Vodou), started by *blan* (foreigners) who directed the proceeds to Kouraj for their political work on behalf of the M community. Kouraj's work resembled that of SEROvie, albeit on a lesser scale, in that they distributed sexual health materials and hosted social events. They also increasingly liaised between same-sex-desiring and gender-creative Haitians and anyone interested in this "population"—state officials, global LGBTQI rights organizations, academics, lawyers, public health workers, and same-sex-desiring and gender-creative blan living and working in Haiti—as experienced "native informants." This final aspect of Kouraj's work was facilitated by their divergence from SEROvie's strategy of quiet advocacy; as an activist organization, Kouraj intentionally increased the visibility of the "M Community" and loudly decried the problem of homophobia in Haitian and international media.

While Fondasyon SEROvie and Kouraj's shared commitment to human rights for same-sex-desiring and gender-creative Haitians led to a series of collaborations after the IDAHO events, their different frameworks for interpreting homophobia, and therefore the strategies they used to intervene in violence, resulted in a falling-out between the two organizations. Their conflict arose out of the context of widespread Protestant homophobia in Haiti, as well as the influence of global LGBTQI human rights organizations. The negative impact of evangelical Christian homophobia on same-sex-desiring and gender-creative people—the legacy of a century of U.S. imperialism in Haiti—is perhaps intuitive. It is less straightforward to consider the way that the interactions *between* evangelical Christians and antihomophobic advocates for LGBTQI human rights—whose comparatively recent work in Haiti was enabled by U.S. imperialism as well—exacerbate the deteriorating material conditions for same-sex-desiring Haitians. This chapter builds on the previous one to offer another example of postcolonial homophobia emergent from the confluence of these two dominant social forces in post-2010 Haiti. I track how the underlying logic of these two seemingly opposed transnational movements colludes to support greater foreign intervention in ways that continually impact the landscape of Haitian sexual politics and the efficacy of antihomophobic organizing.

INTERNATIONAL DAY AGAINST HOMOPHOBIA AND TRANSPHOBIA

On May 17, 2012, for the Congrès National de la Population LGBT, more than three hundred people from Haiti and the United States gathered at the newly rebuilt Hôtel Montana in Pétion-Ville, a wealthy suburb of Port-au-Prince referred to by some as the Haitian Beverly Hills. The one-day national conference was an historical occurrence, the first time same-sex-desiring and gender-creative Haitians from different organizations—including Housing Works Inc., Fondasyon SEROvie, Femme en Action Contre la Stigmatization et la Discrimination Sexuelle (FACSDIS), Promoteurs Objectif Zéro SIDA (POZ), Kouraj, and others—converged publicly under the sign of "LGBT."[2] Almost two and a half years after the earthquake, they joined together with a message for Haiti: *OMOSEKSYALITE se pa yon mal, se OMOFOBI ki fè mal.* This phrase, displayed on a rainbow banner behind the stage in the conference hall, translates in English as "HOMOSEXUALITY isn't wrong or sinful, it is HOMOPHOBIA that hurts."[3] Excited participants sat around large tables with rainbow-flag centerpieces to listen to the program. The lineup of speakers included representatives from the UN, SEROvie, Kouraj, and other organizations. Each speaker offered a different perspective about discrimination against same-sex-desiring, gender-creative, and/or HIV-positive people in Haiti.

The conference coincided with the International Day Against Homophobia, described on the campaign's website as a day of events around the world to "draw attention to violence and discrimination experienced by LGBTI people internationally." IDAHO was created in 2004 when global LGBTQI human rights organizations—the International Lesbian Gay Bisexual Trans and Intersex Association (ILGA), the International Gay and Lesbian Human Rights Commission (IGLHRC), the World Congress of LGBT Jews, and the Coalition of African Lesbians—signed onto the initiative; the first IDAHO events took place in 2005. As a project, IDAHO—now known as the International Day Against Homophobia, Transphobia & Biphobia—attempted to balance the universal and the particular. The campaign lacked central-ized coordination to the extent that individuals, groups, and organizations around the world planned their own events and register them on the "May 17" website—a date that commemorates the World Health Organization's decision in 1990 to declassify homosexuality as a mental disorder.[4] How-ever, the IDAHO Committee—whose members were neither mentioned on the website nor listed in the annual reports—determines themes for the events each year. Event planners incorporated "Fighting Homophobia In and Through Education," the 2012 theme, into the Congrès National de la Population LGBT through the mission to educate attendees as well as the general public about homophobia and same-sex sexuality and, to a lesser extent, issues facing gender-creative Haitians.[5]

The Congrès National de la Population LGBT was the first event in Haiti associated with the IDAHO campaign. New York–based Housing Works Inc., whose CEO had taken a special interest in Haiti, assumed primary respon-sibility for planning the event. The organization received a grant from the Levi Strauss Foundation "to address HIV/AIDS stigma and discrimination by creating a network to strengthen human rights protection and access to treat-ment among vulnerable populations in Haiti," and the Congrès National de la Population LGBT was their solution to create this network, or—as Housing Works reported in their online publicity materials—"spearhead grassroots advocacy." Housing Works staff determined the location of the event as well as the keynote speaker, heterosexual Canadian diplomat M. Nigel Fischer, the United Nations resident coordinator and humanitarian coordinator in Haiti as well as the acting head of MINUSTAH. Several UN agencies with established relationships to Housing Works cosponsored the conference. Housing Works staff asked SEROvie to mobilize people through their peer educator networks to attend the conference. The newly founded organization Kouraj eventually assumed a place at the planning table because its presi-dent, Charlot Jeudy, worked with Housing Works staff. Kouraj organized the conference after-party. Each of the organizations represented on the plan-ning committee—including SEROvie's sister organization, FACSDIS—was allocated time on the program.

The conference message—"OMOSEKSYALITE se pa yon mal, se OMOFOBI ki fè mal"—was decided jointly by the collaborators. This phrase seems not to indicate what particular struggles same-sex-desiring and gender-creative people in Haiti contend with in the sense that IDAHO events did in other places—for example, "stop bullying in our schools" and "decriminalize homo-sexuality." Yet the conference planners and participants expressed to me that the message was a much-needed response to the ways that same-sex-desiring and gender-creative Haitians had been treated since the earthquake. Kouraj, which made the banner with this message, sponsored a radio advertisement in Kreyòl in the style of a public service announcement to coincide with the Congrès National de la Population LGBT. The advertisement contextualizes this phrase:

> Have you ever been walking down the road and come across a man or a woman who is choosing a sexual life with another man or another woman? And you think you should insult them, hit them, or even worse, you want them to die? That is called homophobia. It means that you do not accept people who are different than you because they do not have the same sexuality as you. Your liberty stops where another's begins. *Homosexuality doesn't hurt, homophobia does.* Respect and tolerate people who are different than you sexually. It is better than hating them.

Since same-sex sexuality was not illegal as it was and continues to be in other countries, the conference organizers identified day-to-day interactions as the site of their intervention. As a peer educator at SEROvie noted at the conference, "this is where homophobia is felt most strongly." The conference presentations by SEROvie members, moreover, included testimonies about the pervasiveness and escalation of verbal and physical violence directed at same-sex-desiring and gender-creative Haitians after the earthquake. The message of the conference shifted the locus of the "problem of homosexuality in Haiti" from homosexuals to the perpetrators of discrimination and violence.

The 2012 IDAHO Annual Report features a photo of the Congrès National de la Population LGBT banner with the description underneath: "Haiti celebrated its first IDAHO in 2012 with a groundbreaking conference in Port-au-Prince that brought together more than 300 people to discuss discrimination based on sexual orientation and gender identity in Haitian society. Also held were LGBT movie screenings, among which was a documentary about Haitian homosexuals, and a party for the LGBT community"(IDAHO 2012, 14). The event received a fair amount of publicity in Haiti, and Kouraj engaged a broader audience by posting photos and video on social media. Even SEROvie on its Facebook page circulated photos from the conference of speakers and the backs of participants' T-shirts declaring "N'ayons pas peur de la différence c'est ce qui donne un sens a la vie" (do not be afraid of the difference that gives meaning to life)—the organization's privacy policy to protect the identities of its beneficiaries was temporarily abandoned in the excitement.

After this initial IDAHO event, Kouraj and SEROvie continued to collaborate. Kouraj was a signatory to a 2012 report filed to the UN Human Rights Committee that built on the research SEROvie and IGLHRC compiled in 2010 and previously distributed to UN agencies.[6] The report, "Supplementary Information on Haiti Regarding the Treatment of Lesbian, Gay, Bisexual, and Transgender Individuals (LGBT)," cites the IGLHRC/SEROvie research briefing discussed in the previous chapter and reasserts many of its key points, including the increase of violence against LGBT Haitians after the earthquake. The report includes additional evidence to argue that this homophobic violence had become normalized—testimonials from Kouraj about negative interactions with law enforcement who did not pursue perpetrators of interpersonal violence, reports from FACSDIS about sexual abuse perpetrated against members of the LGBT community (with the note that they are likely engaged in survival sex work because of lack of economic opportunities), and research conducted earlier in the year by the Hastings to Haiti Partnership (HHP) that illuminated that rural Haitians in Jérémie faced similar problems to their urban counterparts.[7] The report emphasized that these problems violate international law, specifically the UN International Covenant on Civil and Political Rights (ICCPR), ratified by Haiti in 1991. The report maintains that "Haiti lacks legal protections for LGBT individuals" and encourages the United Nations to ask questions of the Haitian government about which rights they would enact for the LGBT community.

SEROvie and Kouraj collaborated again with Housing Works to plan the second Congrès National de la Population LGBT for IDAHO 2013. The event, convened again at the Hôtel Montana, was headlined by a similar cast of organizational representatives and boasted two hundred participants. The director of Housing Works announced that, with the grant from the Levi Strauss Foundation and additional funding from the Elton John Foundation, the organization intended to launch trainings for LGBT organizations in Haiti to use Martus software to document human rights abuses. The Martus Project was intended to collect information in systematic and quantifiable ways amenable to policy makers, including accounts of discrimination and violence already well-known and documented qualitatively by these organizations, public health advocates, and academic researchers like myself.

The day's events included a screening at the U.S. embassy of *Des hommes et dieux* (Lescot and Magloire 2002), an ethnographic documentary about masisi in Haiti. The SEROvie report about IDAHO 2013 describes the documentary this way:

This film highlights the place that homosexual men occupy in Haitian Vodou; *it's known that Vodou is the only religious worldview that embraces homosexuality without discrimination.* It's the only place where they can express themselves freely without feeling excluded. Some male homosexual Vodou initiates believe that the spirits have turned them gay, because even when they're not effeminate in daily life, they are when the spirits mounts [*sic*] them. Other initiates hold the contrary opinions that they are born homosexual but those with the opposing view are finding an excuse to explain their homosexuality. ("Haiti IDAHO Report 2013"; emphasis added)

The connections between Vodou and same-sex sexuality and gender creativity are reinstated here, in a way that emphasizes Haiti's progressiveness in a regime of global LGBTQI human rights that measures places by their treatment of LGBT people on a scale of homophobic to homo-friendly. However, the film had mixed reviews in the crowd at the IDAHO events. Gay SEROvie participants—including the peer educator who submitted this report—considered the film outdated and only pertaining to a minority of same-sex-desiring and gender-creative Haitians. They are the "other initiates" reflected in the last sentence who dislike the term *masisi* and are embarrassed by what they consider to be premodern ideas, namely that the lwa makes one have same-sex desires. *Masisi* is perceived as not conforming to appropriately modern sexual subjectivities that, as I mention below, SEROvie inculcates in its participants.

The second Congrès National de la Population LGBT for the International Day Against Homophobia in 2013 was the last collaboration between the two organizations before a chain of events related to antigay demonstrations in the summer generated major conflicts between Fondasyon SEROvie and Kouraj. The source of these conflicts—differing frameworks for what homophobia means and therefore the tactics to intervene in it—came into play throughout these early collaborations, but they were superseded by the shared goal of enacting legal protections for same-sex-desiring and gender-creative people in Haiti. After the conflicts, the two organizations collaborated on events with each other as well as with other organizations, but they additionally positioned against each other as recipients of funding through their activities and interpersonally, since institutional conflicts often become individualized.

THE UNDERLYING TENSIONS

While both SEROvie and Kouraj supported the framing of homophobia in "OMOSEKSYALITE se pa yon mal, se OMOFOBI ki fè mal," the way these two groups theorize homophobia differentially mark them: SEROvie, the Haitian instantiation of a *global* movement for LGBTQI rights, and Kouraj a *Haitian* movement for same-sex-desiring and gender-creative people. SE-ROvie has assimilated a universal definition of homophobia from the global LGBTQI, performed by a peer educator in a meeting that I attended where the participants were tasked with creating a magazine about homophobia in Haiti for SEROvie's outreach efforts. He asked the group: "What is homophobia?" After several people chimed in with answers focusing on specific instances or kinds of discrimination and violence, he told the group: "there are two parts to the word—homo and phobia. The first refers to homosexuals, and the second means a fear of something. When you put them together, it means a fear of homosexuals. This fear plays a role in all the situations that people mentioned, and it comes from ignorance." This definition is a close recitation of the liberal definition of homophobia that comes from U.S. psychotherapist George H. Weinberg's *Society and the Healthy Homosexual* (1972). When I asked where he learned it, the peer educator told me that it was at a training in the United States for LGBT organizations, which he attended after the earthquake. This definition carries over into the advocacy work of SEROvie that perceives homophobia in Haiti as a product of generalized religious ignorance about and fear of the LGBT community.

Kouraj, on the other hand, attributes the frequency of homophobia in Haiti to European ideas of sexual dimorphism that undergird the speciation of homosexuals and heterosexuals, the queering of Haiti in U.S. representations of "voodoo," as well as the more immediate importation of U.S. evangelical Christian homophobia that I discussed in previous chapters. In their tract about the M community, Kouraj cites theses influences for turning *masisi, madivin*, and *makomer* into words associated with negativity: "notably prostitution, HIV/AIDS, sin, possession, and pedophilia." Thus, their political project begins by reclaiming these Kreyòl terms as exemplified by the founding document of their organization, "Deklarasyon Masisi" (Kouraj 2012a; translated on their website as "*masisi* manifesto"). Kouraj's declarations situate masisi as a Haitian sexual subjectivity that was not invented in the United States of America. Masisi are those who live in Haiti and have given their lives to Haiti. They are the children of revolutionary Jean-Jacques Dessalines who secured Haiti's independence.[8] Dessalines, the creator of the first constitution of a free Haiti, is mentioned twice, and the manifesto invokes his revolutionary spirit in its references to liberty in the final lines: "Yè nou te nwa, jodi a nou se masisi, demen nap Moun" (Yesterday we were Black, today we are masisi, tomorrow we will be people).[9]

One of the first documents that the activist organization released is called "On the Notion of 'LGBT' versus 'M' (Masisi, Madivin, Makomer, Mix): A Haitian Movement for Rights" (Kouraj 2012b).[10] This document responds to inquiries asking "why KOURAJ chooses to speak of the M Community (Masisi, Madivin, Makomer, Mix) when the acronym LGBT (Lesbian, Gay, Bisexual, Transgender) is used around the world with 'universal' meaning." The tract has two short sections—"What Words Tell Us" and "The Necessity to Make a Choice." The first one begins thus: "The 'LGBT' notion does not correspond to the Haitian reality. The majority of persons who self-identify as not subscribing to the identity norm are Masisi, Madivin, Makomer, or Mix. The strong acculturation Haiti has undergone through a strong presence of organizations, international institutions, and its relationship with the United States has left those concerned with the false assumption that 'Masisi, Madivin, Makomer, and Mix' were simply pejorative equivalents in Kreyòl for gay, lesbian, transgender, and bisexual" (Kouraj 2012b). This stance on LGBT quite obviously differs from SEROvie's, implicated as it is in its strong relationship to the United States. This statement is not just about SEROvie, however, but about the proliferation of NGOs in general and how they have contributed to the LGBT-ification of same-sex-desiring and gender-creative sexual politics in Haiti. Before starting Kouraj with his friends, Charlot Jeudy worked in the NGO sector for the international development organization Oxfam and then Housing Works, where he learned the language of LGBT. The declaration of the "false assumption" underlying the way that LGBT and its component parts are considered "value-free" equivalents for Kreyòl configurations of gender and sexual diversity makes the important point that how these terms circulate matter, and that the way that they are circulating currently—within social movements in Haiti and, I would add, in the limited scholarship in queer Haitian studies—are troubling because of their connections to U.S. imperialism.

The remainder of that section of the Kouraj publication briefly outlines the meaning of each of the "M" terms, while the second section provides the reasoning for reclaiming these terms instead of adopting LGBT.

> Due to the strong dysphoria amongst the notions of LGBT, those of heterosexuality and homosexuality, and the Haitian reality, we find ourselves in the necessity to make a choice. Either we accept the acculturation that would transform the M Community and reorganize it into the LGBT community over the long term, or we refuse it. KOURAJ, due to its strong independence and critic role it plays in Haitian society, has decided to reject the importation of terminology because KOURAJ engages to change Haitian society such that not a single other person will be deprived of his or her full joy of human rights due to his or her sexual orientation or gender identity. (Kouraj 2012b)

The terminology that Kouraj rejects, as they proceed to mention, is connected to a "Americano-European movement" that has a long history that cannot be erased when LGBT travels to different contexts. "The most effective strategy is not to recuperate the heritage of the Americano-European movement while trying to jump stages by passing directly from the inexistence of a LGBT community to its creation, but rather to work with Haitian reality and impose a terminology in the service of the M community" (Kouraj 2012b).

Kouraj members mobilized this queer cultural nationalism in their practice of using the language of *masisi*, *madivin*, *makomer*, and *miks* in their advocacy efforts in the Haitian public sphere. While the tract would seem to imply that Kouraj rejects LGBT outright and insists on the counter-identification of Kominote M, I offer instead that they initially *disidentified* with the term "LGBT." Elaborated by queer theorist José Esteban Muñoz in *Disidentifications: Queers of Color and the Performance of Politics*, "disidentification is the third mode of dealing with dominant ideology, one that neither opts to assimilate within such a structure nor strictly opposes it; rather, disidentification is a strategy that works on and against dominant ideology" (1999, 11). Disidentification is a survival tool for minoritarian subjects that "recycles" and "rethinks" encoded meanings and "looks into the past to critique the present and helps imagine the future" (25). Muñoz contends that disidentification is a key strategy for U.S. queers of color to perform politics, and the term also beautifully articulates with the Black strategies of survival and resistance under white imperialism in Saint Domingue and Haiti—Kreyòl and Vodou being the best examples.

Kouraj could not get away from the term LGBT that saturated Haiti, but it is an organization of queers who intentionally turned around to the "Hey, you there!" interpellation of the global LGBTQI in their beginning years—or deployed what Ana-Maurine Lara calls "strategic universalisms" (2018). They used the term in the French and English versions of their websites, ostensibly written for foreigners, *only to mark its failures in this tract and others.* They used this term in their communications with blan in person, too. During my initial conversations with Kouraj officers on the phone and over dinners, for instance, they would say "LGBT" with its Kreyòl pronunciation. Charlot told me that it is not because they are using an assumed shared language, but because blan like me do not know about Haiti. Each such interview or exchange involved a component in which Kouraj members expose the limits of LGBT. But there is something more subtle that is difficult to represent about how Kouraj members *performed* LGBT. It would perhaps be more accurate to say that LGBT was wielded playfully, with an excess of sentiment—not sarcastic, but almost—and a twinkle in the eye that signaled that there is much more to the meaning of LGBT in their usage of the term. They, therefore, not only articulated gender and sexuality in a way that had international intelligibility, Kouraj activists *worked on and against LGBT* in a variety of ways that foregrounded the importance of place, history, and power. Kouraj officers and members organized the Kominote M between the opposing constraints of the global LGBTQI and the religious homophobia of evangelical Christianity.

ANTI-GAY PROTESTS IN HAITI

"Nou pa dakò! Nou pa dakò! Nou pa dakò!" (We don't agree!) Thousands of passionate protestors filled the Avenue de la République in front of the Palais National d'Haiti in Port-au-Prince on July 19, 2013. As they chanted, the demonstrators fervently waved in the air Bibles and church pamphlets, Haitian flags, palm branches, and handwritten signs that read "Viv La Fanmi" (long live the family), "ABA Maryaj Homosexiel" (down with homosexual marriage), and "Maryaj Gason ak Gason Fanm ak Fanm Se Malediksyon" (marriage between a man and a man or a woman and a woman is a malediction). The public protest wound through the streets of the capital city on that scorching summer day, gathering momentum as it reached Champs de Mars, the location of many government buildings and the largest public park in the city that had recently—at the order of President Michel Martelly—been cleared of camps filled with people displaced by the 2010 earthquake.

A former government commissioner, Jean Renal Senatus, described his participation in the event during a televised interview for a major news outlet: "We are marching today to say 'no' to this affair of immorality. The struggle that we started fighting long ago continues. Today many inquiries, many proposals are being made so there will be homosexual marriage in the country. We came to join our forces with the forces of the Evangelical church, Vodou practitioners, and Freemasons in the country that declare marriage between a man and a man is unacceptable, marriage between a woman and a woman is unacceptable" (*Le nouvelliste* 2013). While some participants expressed the virulent anger that one might expect to be integral to this struggle over sexual politics, the overall tone of the demonstration was joyous. The public performance invited participation from passersby who would join in the revelry as trucks and vans rigged with speaker systems blasted popular Christian songs in Haitian Kreyòl. Evangelical pastors facilitated engagement through the Black religious tradition of call and response. One of these men, for instance, made an impassioned street sermon on a megaphone about the gospel supporting monogamous, heterosexual marriage. He invited those around to come in closer and started the chant, "One woman!," to which the crowd would respond, "One man!" After every third or fourth response, he would declare, "That is what God wants!" Another orchestrated a variation on "Nou pa dakò!" ("We disagree!") where he would shout the statement, and the crowd would alternate with the response "Masisi!" and "Madivin!" Then they would all end with the spirited rolling chant, "Nou pa dakò!"

A group of men in suits and ties led an altered adoration in Haitian church music for the occasion as they danced down the street in the midst of the crowd. They sang: "This masisi who is lagging [trennen] behind, this masisi who is lagging behind, who is lagging behind, he lags so much, he lags, he lags, this masisi who is lagging behind. This madivin who is lagging behind, this madivin who is lagging behind, who is lagging behind, she lags so much, she lags, this madivin who is lagging behind. He leads [mennen] forth, He leads forth, He leads forth, Jesus leads forth; He leads forth, he leads forth, he leads forth, Jesus leads forth." The parallel structure of the verses set up masisi/madivin and Jesus in opposition. The rhyming Kreyòl verbs trennen and mennen in the song have temporal connotations that provide insight into how the protestors consider each of these figures. Trennen generally means lagging, dragging, lingering, or dawdling. It is associated with being underdeveloped, whether by choice in the form of parès (laziness/sloth) or through an unchangeable condition that disables one's cognitive functions. Trennen, therefore, signals an outlier to chrononormativity (Freeman 2010), someone who is slow or behind. By contrast, mennen signals an action in the present that gestures toward a better future. The song can be interpreted to mean that masisi/madivin are dragging Haiti backward in time and that they are partially—if not solely—to blame for the nation's underdevelopment that can only be transcended through the future promised by Jesus.

These verbs undoubtedly project moral connotations. Those who trennen by choice are perceived to be immoral and often engaging in nefarious or illicit activities. The vakabon (vagabond, scoundrel, or delinquent) is a social figure whose activities are described with this verb. He is a "bad boy" who rejects domestic arrangements in favor of wandering the street. The use of trennen associates masisi/madivin with this figure and conjures up images of men (primarily) and women (to a lesser degree) who reject their families to slink through the shadows to find opportunities for sex. Their threat to the family is also encapsulated in another term sometimes used interchangeably in Haiti with masisi, pederas, as people imagine grown men preying on male children.

The queerness of the position of masisi/madivin in this performance is also evident in the politics of verticality in the staging and movement. In front of the singers, a smaller group of men in jeans and T-shirts ambled on all fours, like animals, playing the role of masisi/madivin. Considering the lyrics, their actions could even be described as *trennen sou vant-yo* (creeping or slithering). In the great chain of being that undergirds contemporary Christianity, this closeness to the earth signals a kind of animality placed in further distance from God than the human. This performance of creeping confirms what the self-identified gay men and masisi from the majority poor have told me over the years: society considers ti masisi the lowest of the low. The singers, by contrast, embodied humanity by remaining upright. Their contradistinction was further emphasized by the way that they reached upward toward heaven while exalting Jesus.

The public performance created a clear sense of "us" and "them," and invited onlookers to identify with the sturdy men who stood for Haiti's progress. Their creative display drew people of all ages from the sidewalks who clapped along with the song and joined in its later verses. Another stretch of marchers sang, "Masisi pap pase. Ane a m' deside pou m' sèvi Bondye. Madivin pap pase. Nou pote viktwa, madivin pap pase." (Masisi will not come through/win. This year I am decided that I will serve the Lord. Madivin will not win. We have the victory, madivin will not win.) The *nou* in this verse reinforces the we/us who are marching toward victory, producing a sense of affinity and affiliation across different segments of the Haitian population. It aligned with the chant "Nou pa dakò!" (We disagree!) to unite a symphony of sound—clapping, cheering, preaching, chanting, singing—on the streets of the capital city to voice opposition to same-sex marriage in Haiti.

Yet same-sex marriage has never been allowed in Haiti, and while the threat seemed real to Haitian politicians, there was no formal proposal in place to legalize it at the time of the protest. Haitian and international media included many references to a proposed or impending bill for state consideration, which prompted many official discussions of such an event. But obtaining the ability to legally marry was not a priority nor serious political strategy for LGBT or Kominote M advocacy or activist organizations in Haiti. These organizations were more focused on expanding the constitutional protections guaranteeing the freedom of expression to specifically provide protections against homophobic and transphobic discrimination. Same-sex-desiring and gender-creative Haitian organizers—including some from SEROvie—speculated that the march was a response to comments that Kouraj president Charlot Jeudy had made on a popular radio program in late May. He responded to a question from the host about whether he thought Haiti was close to accepting same-sex marriage: "Marriage is love, the love of two human beings. Marriage is a right. How do you deprive people of that right? On what basis? I think that this hypocrisy must end!" ("Interview" 2013). The interview was recirculated online with the bold headline in French "Haitian homosexuals want to get married," to which Kouraj posted a link on their social media sites ("Les homosexuels" 2013). Other Kouraj posts included news about the legalization of same-sex marriage in France on May 18, 2013, and information about the first wedding held a few weeks later. Could these provocations have catalyzed the protest in Port-au-Prince and another large public performance against same-sex marriage that took place on the main boulevard of the southern coastal city of Jacmel on July 28? It is certainly possible, but I offer another explanation for the demonstrations connected to the legacies of U.S. imperialism in Haiti.

In Haiti, same-sex-desiring and gender-creative people were not the only ones with eyes toward the global contests over same-sex marriage in early 2013; Christian religious leaders watched in anticipation as well. On the day before the announcement of the U.S. Supreme Court decisions in two cases pertaining to legal recognition of same-sex marriages, the recently formed Coalition Haïtienne des organisations religieuses et morales (CHO, Haitian Coalition of Religious and Moral Organizations) held a press conference denouncing the widespread acceptance of homosexuality in France and the United States and declaring its intentions to hold a march against same-sex marriage in Haiti on July 19. As the CHO president Pentecostal Pastor Gérard Forge explained, their opposition to same-sex marriage in particular and homosexuality in general stemmed from religious conviction and conservative interpretations of the Bible: "Fundamentally speaking, God does not agree [with the practice of homosexuality] . . . because of the misery he brought to Sodom and Gomorrah. Thus, because we do not want to know the same misfortunes, we are obliged to take a position."[11] The story of the fall of Sodom and Gomorrah has had particular traction in the wake of the earthquake in Haiti. Evangelical networks in Haiti—out of which CHO was formed—have leveraged the story in various campaigns against what they perceive to be social ills affecting the moral fabric of Haitian society, including sex work, rèstavèk (indentured child labor), and the practice of homosexuality. The public declaration of "Nou pa dakò!" and march against same-sex marriage with signs proclaiming "ABA Sodòm ak Gomò Viv La Famille" (down with Sodom and Gomorrah, long live the family) was such an endeavor.

I posit that the marches against same-sex marriage in Port-au-Prince and Jacmel in summer 2013 were more than just instances of local cultural politics or religious homophobia with devastating consequences for same-sex-desiring and gender-creative Haitians. As a beginning line of inquiry, we can ask why the CHO positioned themselves against the more libertine attitudes toward homosexuality in France and the United States in particular. Certainly, these two countries happen to be places where highly publicized contests over same-sex marriage were taking place in 2013, but so were many others where same-sex marriage was legalized around the same time—including Brazil, Uruguay, and New Zealand. Yet the CHO representatives mentioned only France and the United States in their press conference, which has more to do with Haiti's enduring historical relationships with those countries as a former French colony and as a laboratory for U.S. imperialism for the last century. As much as the CHO was donning a postcolonial nationalist position against the supposed widespread acceptance of homosexuality in France and the United States—and perhaps against the ways that rights for homosexuals in the limited form of legalized same-sex marriage had "gone global" and reached its tendrils into Haiti—consider for a moment the ways that their manifestations resembled public demonstrations against same-sex marriage in those countries earlier in 2013.

The most impressive displays against same-sex marriage took place in France. In anticipation of a political move by President François Hollande and his Socialist Party for "le mariage pour tous" (marriage for all), a coalition with unofficial ties to the Roman Catholic Church formed in early fall 2012 under the sign "La Manif Pour Tous" (Protest for Everyone). Their platform stood against same-sex marriage, parenting by same-sex couples (including access to joint adoption, certain reproductive technologies, and surrogacy), and any instruction in gender studies in schools to combat sexism and harmful stereotypes. When the Socialist Party finally introduced a bill to the National Assembly in November 2012 that would allow same-sex couples to marry and adopt children, La Manif Pour Tous organized public opposition to the bill. Their first demonstration on January 13, 2013, converged at the Eiffel Tower in the Parisian Champ des Mars and drew an estimated half million people, an unusually high turnout even in a country like France, where protests are a national pastime. Protesters carried banners, signs, flags, and balloons—many with an outline of an ostensibly heterosexually parented nuclear family—in what has become the movement's trademark colors of white, pink, and blue. The sanctioned slogans for La Manif Pour Tous included: "One Father + One Mother, It's Elementary!"; "No to the Legal Project 'Marriage for All'"; "Marriage-o-phile, Not Homophobe"; and "Paternity, Maternity, Equality." One of the few signs that incorporated English, "Made in Papa + Maman," appeared on babies along the route (I am quite sure that the organizers did not think of the ironically queer implications of this message). Two weeks later, the

100,000-person march with celebrities and state representatives in support of the bill barely garnered any media attention compared to the colorful, critical mass at La Manif Pour Tous. The La Manif Pour Tous coalition had sparked a wide-reaching social movement around the issues of same-sex marriage and queer reproduction that mobilized more people than had been out in the streets since the debates around education reforms three decades before.

The initial demonstration's popularity led to subsequent La Manif Pour Tous marches on March 24, April 21, and May 26, the last of which the co-alition staged on Mother's Day, a week after the law went into effect, making France the fourteenth country where same-sex marriage is legal at a federal level. These demonstrations made international headlines as tensions mounted and protestors used more extreme measures to display their opposition to same-sex marriage. While La Manif Pour Tous maintained a significant public presence and created opportunities for people with a variety of perspectives and creative inclinations to express opposition to the bill, its spokespeople distanced themselves from right-wing extremists, protestors who embraced more radical tactics that prompted police responses—such as the use of water hoses, tear gas, and mass arrests—as well as from those who physically and verbally assaulted people perceived to be LGBTQ. They strategically drew a firm distinction between themselves as people who are for traditional marriage and families, but not antigay per se, and those "homophobes" who commit acts of violence.

In the United States, conservative movements similarly converged around a "pro-family" and "pro-marriage" platform leading up to the Supreme Court decisions. The National Organization for Marriage (NOM)—a nonprofit organization founded in 2007 with the purpose of introducing the Proposition 8 ballot measure in California to oppose same-sex marriages—spearheaded a coalition of religious and religiously affiliated "pro-family" organizations to demonstrate in front of the Supreme Court Building while the justices heard oral arguments in *Hollingsworth v. Perry*, the case to decide the fate of Proposition 8. The demonstrations included a March for Marriage on March 26, 2013, an event that drew several thousand people and that NOM organizers hoped to be an annual occurrence like the March for Life against the practice of abortion. Many of the speakers at the March for Marriage rally, including the cofounder and president of NOM, actually placed their actions in a lineage of resistance to state mandates allowing for any form of access to abortion services. Opposition to abortion is a notable difference between the U.S. movement and La Manif Pour Tous.

The event started with a rally on the National Mall and went past the Capi-tol on the way to the Supreme Court Building, where it rubbed up against an equally large gathering of marriage equality supporters. The March for Marriage had striking similarities with La Manif Pour Tous, whose Washington, D.C., chapter cosponsored the event. Marchers carried large banners and signs that read, "Every Child Deserves a Mom and Dad" and "A Los Niños Les Va Mejor Con Una Mamá y Un Papa" (kids do best with a mom and a dad). A representation of the heterosexually parented nuclear family with a mom and dad holding hands, with a child—one girl and one boy—on either side of the couple, appeared prominently on the signs in white. The pastel sea of pink and blue in France, however, was replaced with the bolder, patriotic colors of red (for women), white (for children), and blue (for men) to accompany the U.S. flags.

The citational practices at work are difficult to miss, yet at least in one way, the March for Marriage had more in common with the July 19 demonstration in Port-au-Prince. Whereas La Manif Pour Tous purposefully underplayed its connections to the Roman Catholic Church and cast its actions in secular terms because of the hegemony of *laicité* (separation of church and state) in France, Christian religiosity was excessively apparent at the March for Marriage—from the lineup of sponsors, the religious rhetoric of the speakers, the number of people wearing clerical clothing, and the backdrop of contemporary Christian music. Segments of the march sung hymns, and as they approached the Supreme Court Building, they knelt on the ground to pray. However, the activists they met there were not just those prancing gleefully around in rainbow booty shorts blasting disco and electronica greeting the new arrivals with "Hey, hey! Ho, ho! Homophobia has got to go!" They also came face-to-face with a large crowd with members of the same Christian religions—Catholic, Protestant, and Mormon—represented in the March for Marriage as well as people from other faith communities who had just come from a marriage equality event called "A Prayer for Love and Justice." This kind of counterdemonstration was not present in Port-au-Prince or Jacmel, although queer Haitians and their allies—most of whom are also Christians—were organizing in other ways.

While the March for Marriage in Washington did not garner much media attention outside of Christian networks and LGBTQ rights watchdog sites, the French and Haitian protests made headlines internationally. What emerges from the archive of media representations is the use of coded civilizational discourse in descriptions of the events. The French manifestations were unexpected because French culture is perceived to have liberal—that it, "civilized"—attitudes toward sexuality in general, and homosexuality in particular. The manifestations in Haiti, while noted to be a rare if not unprecedented occurrence, were less surprising than the ones in France. They were attributed to a general antagonism of Haitian culture toward homosexuality, which compared to France would be considered "uncivilized," although that specific term was never used.[12] Civilizational discourses have an implied racial meaning; in this case where representations of former colonizer and colony are situated side by side, French tolerance is associated with whiteness and Haitian intolerance with Blackness. Homophobia, then, was operating as a racializing discourse.

These racialized civilizational discourses emerge particularly in representations of instances of violence connected to the demonstrations. In both France and Haiti, a rash of violent incidents targeting people perceived to be homosexual, LGBT, or otherwise queer followed in the wake of the public demonstrations, as documented by human rights groups in both places. As much as French culture might be perceived to be sympathetic to the struggles of homosexuals, however, these particular instances of violence were slow to emerge in mainstream reporting about the clashes over same-sex marriage. This temporal lag is indicative of the ways that France is constructed as a space where homophobia does not exist. While the first La Manif Pour Tous demonstration took place just after the New Year, coverage of the incidents did not come into prominence until early April. The impetus for this coverage was a self-portrait of a seemingly well-to-do white man, Wilfred de Bruijn, taken after he was assaulted in Paris while walking arm and arm with his boyfriend. The photo of his bruised and bloodied face went viral after he posted it on Facebook with the caption, "Sorry to show you this. It's the face of Homophobia" (de Bruijn 2013). This representation of social violence was very individualized—de Bruijn embodying the effects of homophobia as a singular event. In interviews, de Bruijn simultaneously mentions that violence of this kind happens with some regularity, yet that it seems inimical to the values of France. He struggled with reconciling his experiences with homophobic violence with the general feeling that France is not homophobic.

This was not the case in Haiti, where news of the violence spread even more rapidly than information about the "rare" demonstration in Port-au-Prince. Haitian and international media sources reported with gruesome detail that, after leaving the march against same-sex marriage, protestors had killed two assumed-to-be homosexual men (e.g., "Death Threats" 2013; "Two Accused Homosexuals" 2013), and the news spread like wildfire on social media. In the week following the demonstration, I received emails and text messages from people in the Dominican Republic, the United States, Canada, the Netherlands, Jamaica, and Germany anxious to know what happened because they had heard that gay Haitians were being slaughtered in the streets. A Dominican American scholar sent me a press release signed by nearly twenty Haitian and Dominican organizations condemning the violence. I frantically emailed and called the key Haitian organizers with whom I had been working for five years by that point. Everyone with whom I talked was unharmed, and no one knew any details about the specific incident that had been picked up in the media, although they remarked on its believability since there had been an increasingly hostile climate toward masisi, madivin, and other same-sex-desiring and gender-creative people in Haiti since CHO had announced its intentions to hold an event. Then, a week after the march, the *Miami Herald* reported that the spokesman for the Haitian National Police said that, although men perceived to be homosexual had been harassed, no one had been killed (Charles 2013). While some media sources like the *Washington Post* deleted their articles from the online archive, many stories about the imagined event remain as of this writing (e.g., Littauer 2013, Walters 2013).

Why did this story have so much currency? Why were international audiences so eager to spread news that two "gay" men had been brutally murdered in Haiti? As one answer to those questions, global LGBTQI human rights organizations have marked homophobia as one of the greatest social problems of our time, and they use stories such as this one to garner support for their mission of promoting rights for their designated key population of gender and sexual minorities. News about the "hate crimes" were circulated by the global LGBTQI with partnering programs in Haiti: Housing Works (Boyuan 2013) and the Astraea Lesbian Foundation for Justice ("Heightened LGBT Violence" 2013). The latter included the story in a briefing about recent murders of homosexual men in Cameroon and Jamaica, which are—like Haiti—postcolonial states with predominantly Black populations.

Many appreciate the zeal with which global human rights organizations work to address homophobia whenever and wherever it occurs. However, the ways that their work ultimately produces postcolonial spaces—particularly those in Africa, the Caribbean, and the Middle East—as having exceptional problems with homophobia that are somehow unrelated to the legacies of imperialism is cause for serious concern. Although their intentions may be altruistic—like the work of IGLHRC, done with the hopes of making a more socially just world—the organizations' work colludes with the imperialist imperatives of erasing knowledge of colonial histories and their legacies and portraying Black and brown populations as inherently and excessively violent. The popularity of the story from Haiti, then, stems from the fact that it aligned with these imperatives and produced Haiti, the Black republic, as a site of unbridled violence, in this instance targeting homosexual men.

This was not the first time that the so-called problem of Haitian homophobia had been identified as a crisis vis-à-vis its imagined racial proximity to Jamaica, and it will certainly not be the last. Racial proximity takes precedence over geographic proximity in this instance because, while the Caribbean countries are only separated by a strait of approximately 190 kilometers, Haiti shares an island with the Dominican Republic and is geographically closer to Cuba. All these geographically proximate Caribbean nations have significant populations of African decedents with a lighter-skinned elite, but Jamaica and Haiti are popularly considered to be Black nations rather than Creole/mestizo (racially mixed) as the Dominican Republic and Cuba are constructed. The history of *mestizáje* (miscegenation) is particularly important in terms of how the latter imagine their nations. As anthropologist Jafari S. Allen contends in the context of Cuba, mestizáje is a racial project that recenters white European heritage in Latin America and celebrates the destruction of Blackness (2011, 48). Anti-Black racism is likewise part of the Dominican Republic's national history that celebrates its independence from Haiti, the Black republic, rather than Spain. The Dominican Republic is also infamous for its history of state-sponsored projects to "whiten" the population, whether by encouraging immigration from Europe or expunging Haitian immigrants and their descendants.

The slippage between Jamaica and Haiti is more about reproducing Euro-U.S. imaginaries of Black violence. Anthropologist Deborah A. Thomas (2011) has brilliantly unpacked the notion of exceptional violence in postcolonial Jamaica, and here I want to extend the analysis to the realm of sexual politics. Jamaica has come to signify "Black homophobia" transnationally based on existing laws that criminalize same-sex sexuality as well as its antigay dance hall scene. There are certainly queer postcolonial publications reworking this narrative (e.g., Chin 1997, Ellis 2011), but this scholarship has far less impact than the wide-reaching machinery of the global LGBTQI. Thus, accounts of homophobia in Haiti often hinge on references to Jamaica. For instance, the graphic mini documentary "Haiti's Scapegoats: Homophobia in the Aftermath of the 2010 Earthquake" (Dijckmeester-Bins 2012) introduces viewers to Haitian homophobia through Jamaica. While viewers look at an illustrated map of the region, the film narrates: "The Caribbean has a long history of homophobia. In Jamaica, being gay is a criminal offense. In Haiti, this is not the case. The law is, in fact, quite progressive" (Dijckmeester-Bins 2012). The narrator here is referencing the fact that, unlike Jamaica and many other former British colonies, Haiti does not have laws against sodomy or "buggery." This narration seemingly sets up a contrast between Haiti and Jamaica, but it is quickly followed by a videotaped interview—the only one in the whole film—with an U.S. staff member of SEROvie saying that even if the laws are progressive, the "society as a whole" might not accept homosexuality or end discrimination against homosexuals (Dijckmeester-Bins 2012). This leaves viewers with the impression that the law (and the ways that it signals specific colonial inheritances) does not matter and that the two countries are more alike than different in terms of their (Black) homophobic cultures.

To critically contend with these representations is not to say that antigay violence is not a problem in Haiti. Over the years of my research, I have witnessed many homophobic incidents and been told of many more, ranging from small slights to put people in their place to brutal murders. The problem is very real and creates a climate of fear that—for some same-sex-desiring and gender-creative Haitians—makes life in Haiti miserable, dangerous, or impossible. But it is imperative to understand the structural forces that shape these lives and provide a historical context for the large demonstrations against same-sex marriage in 2013. This allows for a different story about "Haitian homophobia" *as postcolonial homophobia*—one with immediate ties to a century of U.S. military, political, economic, religious, and social interventions in Haiti.

FALLOUT

On the ground, same-sex-desiring and gender-creative Haitians and their allies were not necessarily reading the demonstrations in the same way that I was based on my previous years of research—namely as part of the transnational travels of religion that followed particular paths in Haiti because of prior evangelical Christian missions after the U.S. occupation almost a century ago. They were contending with the immediate aftereffects of the demonstrations: another spike in homophobic violence in Haiti similar to what happened after the Michèle Pierre-Louis controversy and the immediate aftermath of the earthquake. Instead of attributing these acts of violence to broader social forces that collude to oppress same-sex-desiring and gender-creative Haitians, SEROvie blamed Kouraj, or as a former SEROvie peer educator told me succinctly, by going on the radio and increasing the visibility of LGBT Haitian organizing, "Charlot Jeudy started a war between the straights and the gays." This sentiment was echoed by then current SEROvie staff and participants, as well as a U.S. American who had worked for SEROvie and conducted research with them after the earthquake and had been featured in the "Haiti's Scapegoats" video. The biggest point of contention is that Charlot and members of Kouraj did not know how to work within the long-established religious systems of sexuality in Haiti that demanded discretion. Kouraj regularly appeared in the Haitian media and used social networking sites to organize, and they prided themselves on having the courage to put their faces behind their words when so many people before them had shied away from such publicity. This visibility, moreover, was coupled with an insistence on articulating sexual politics using the Kreyòl terms *masisi, madivin, makomer,* and *miks.* In general, those associated with SEROvie told me that these campaigns indicated either that Kouraj "does not know how things work in Haiti" or that they do but still "selfishly caused trouble for everyone."

The charge that Kouraj "does not know how things work in Haiti" is loaded with connotations that are necessary to unpack, ones related to two common criticisms about Kouraj by SEROvie affiliates and other same-sex-desiring and gender-creative Haitians. The first is that Kouraj officers, and by extension its members, "lack class." They are what Lakou members would have called *ti masisi;* they are masisi of Haiti's majority poor who came from and often still lived in downtown Port-au-Prince—a city structured by what Achille Mbembe calls a politics of verticality, rich at the top and poor at the bottom (Mbembe 2003, 18–19). This class difference is also signaled in racist references to color, namely the comparative darkness of Kouraj members' skin tones. To say that they "do not know how things work in Haiti" is a way for the Haitian elite and aspiring *boujwa* (bourgeoisie) to police the boundaries of work for gender and sexual minorities in Haiti through a sexual politics of respectability and discretion. It is also a way of mitigating the fear that poor and Black Haitians might make some changes.

The second charge is that Kouraj is a front for *blan* interests in Haiti. There were certainly signals that was the case, including early English media accounts about Kouraj that highlighted the pivotal role of David, a white U.S. American, in forming the group. In David's and my email exchanges, he noted that this narrative of the group was used to launch the social enterprise Yanvalou—described in fund-raising materials as the first LGBT bar and cultural center in Haiti—to fund Kouraj's political work. In retrospect, he regrets putting himself so much in the public eye, "given the public misconception in Haiti of homosexuality as a foreign import (hence, our public communications campaign that homophobia, and not homosexuality, is an import)."[13] David and the other Kouraj members characterize his and his boyfriend's involvement with the organization as solidarity work—much of it being focused on publicizing Kouraj's campaigns on its website and social media sites like YouTube. Based on my interviews with Kouraj members and less on my brief email interactions with David, my assessment is that David had a passion for activism that aligned for a time with the group of friends who founded Kouraj, and that this helped galvanize the work that they were committed to doing anyway.

In the very least, the accusation that Kouraj "does not know how things work in Haiti" references that the organization was relatively new to the scene, which may have contributed to the unfolding of events. By contrast, SEROvie had a long track record of working without incident. SEROvie staff told me that they worked deliberately to build connections with other agencies and institutions—including the U.S. embassy and many different facets of the United Nations that publicize their pro-LGBT politics—in a way that would maintain its reputation. The foundation's work was not explicitly activist-oriented or political like Kouraj's, but instead was couched in terms of health, advocacy, and human rights. The staff made strategic choices in terms of SEROvie's public profile: very little information about the foundation was posted on its website; the Facebook pages were managed in a way that highlighted respectable activities such as fund-raisers, conferences, and educational programs; and the director and public representative of SEROvie had been a heterosexual ally with a wife and children. SEROvie staff also cultivated a women's program (FACSDIS) in part to be properly LGBT (see chapter 5), but also to decrease speculations that the office space was for masisi.

The staff and peer educators, in fact, rarely used this term—masisi—or any of the others that Kouraj attempted to reclaim in the context of their work. As I learned from interviews, focus groups, and particularly participant observation, they used "homosexual" when necessary, as its meaning is widely understood and translates easily between Kreyòl, French, and English. However, they preferred the less-pejorative and discrete terms of "LGBT" and its individual components, learned through interactions with the global LGBTQI. These terms are taught to beneficiaries through outreach work, support meetings, and one-on-one interactions. The pedagogy of LGBT at SEROvie included modeling the use of "LGBT community" in these interactions and substituting "LGBT" or one of its parts when responding to someone who has used a different term such as masisi. Sometimes SEROvie staff explicitly corrected other people's use of language. The few times I used the "M Community" in person or emails—influenced by Kouraj's manifesto and working with Lakou—they told me I should say "LGBT community." Several staff members and those associated with SEROvie expressed that they prefer the English terms—similar to other same-sex-desiring and gender-creative Haitians—because of the pejorative connotations of the Kreyòl terms that have often been used against them. They perceived "gay," "lesbian," and "LGBT" as lacking the negative affective punch of *masisi* and *madivin*.

But there was another level to SEROvie's pedagogy focused on correcting people's self-descriptions or asserting to participants or other staff members that someone was really "X," even if they thought they were "Y". There were a few genres of this frequent self-correction: Women who self-identified as lesbians would be told that they were "really bisexual" if they ever had sex with men. Feminine men who self-identified as "gay" or "homosexual" would be told that they were transgender women, especially if they ever wore makeup and/or feminine clothing or performed in drag. Likewise, masculine women with extra piercings or who wore men's-style clothing who self-identified as "lesbians" were told they were transgender men or—later, after SEROvie staff accumulated more knowledge about U.S. gender configurations—"butches" or "tomboys." It seemed a few times that SEROvie staff members wanted me to witness the interactions and authorize the correction, when they would turn to me in front of the person (and usually others), and say "right?" These moments created extreme unease for me as someone coming from U.S. queer settings that place a great deal of importance on *self*-identifications as well as decolonial/leftist social movements and related academic fields animated by concerns with the politics of naming and epistemological violence.

It became clear through years of interactions with SEROvie peer educator Daniel that he considered his personal use of the terms "gay" and "LGBT community," and generally communicating in English (in addition to Kreyòl and French), as cultural capital that contributed to his relatively modest class ascent. Daniel learned English without formal training by watching U.S. music videos and television (in the same way he learned all the choreography in Beyoncé videos), and this skill helped secure him a stable job in low rungs of the NGO-sector hierarchy. The job with SEROvie provided opportunities to accrue more cultural capital by being invited to an ambassador program with access to a U.S. visa and by traveling outside the country—often to the United States—for trainings and conferences. English—including terminology and conceptions of sex, gender, and sexuality, and U.S. "queer" and "trans" pop cultural knowledge—was therefore associated with possibilities for social and economic mobility. I understood that SEROvie's pedagogical approaches—enacted by Daniel and others—were perhaps not intended to divide through "I-know-better-because-I-am-an-expert" conceit (to maintain a position slightly above the rest) or solely uphold a politically correct stance. It could also be interpreted as affective labor to share cultural capital with beneficiaries in a similar social and economic position, opening new ways to imagine oneself in relationship to others.

However, while ill intention did not guide these pedagogical practices, they nonetheless had harmful effects beyond privileging the imperialist language of English in Haiti or a supposedly more universal and modern sexual subjectivity. They are the perfect example of what scholars of Black radical traditions Stefano Harney and Fred Moten theorize as *governance* (2013). Governance extends Foucauldian theories of governmentality as a way to refer to "the management of self-management" and self-representation, as well as the "generation of interests . . . [such] as wealth, plentitude, potential" (Harney and Moten 2013, 55). Harney and Moten call NGOs the laboratory of governance, meant to infuse Blackness—its laziness and unwillingness to capitulate to the demands of now-late capitalism—with vitality and, therefore, with harnessable labor power. By creating interests in the world as it is, the NGO through governance generally subverts any chance of creating different kinds of relations and prefiguring the world as it could be.

Another way of saying this is that these practices generate interests that are what queer theorist Lauren Berlant refers to as cruel optimism, "a relation [that] exists when something you desire is actually an obstacle to your flourishing" and "a relation of attachment to compromised conditions of possibility whose realization is discovered to be *im*possible, sheer fantasy, or *too* possible, and toxic" (2011, 1 and 22). Berlant's formulation is generous; we are all to varying extents engaged in relations of cruel optimism. In the case of same-sex-desiring and gender-creative Haitians, especially those among the majority poor, the compromised conditions of possibility include postcolonial homophobia, other manifestations of U.S. imperialism and ongoing foreign militarization in Haiti, the necropolitical conditions of grinding poverty, and accelerated death. The promise of "LGBT community" was that it offers a way out of both poverty and homophobia. However, the social and economic mobility of LGBT workers in the NGO sector like Daniel was only *contingently* available to a handful of people, not to same-sex-desiring and gender-creative Haitians in general.

Finally, and perhaps most importantly, "LGBT community" offers a space of belonging extended by the global LGBTQI who offer specific strategies of contending with homophobia and transphobia. Yet the global LGBTQI, as the previous chapter discusses, has posed obstacles to the flourishing of Haitians in general. This includes IGLHRC's failure to recognize militarization—of aid after the earthquake and in Haiti in general—as a threat to the safety, health, and general well-being of same-sex-desiring and gender-creative Haitians. In collaborating with UN agencies, MINUSTAH, and the U.S. embassy, the global LGBTQI seemingly justifies the occupation. In addition to the other examples of this collaboration offered throughout this book, the Astraea Lesbian Fund for Justice that provided assistance to FOSAJ and Lakou's work in the past and to FACSDIS in recent years was taking part in a USAID initiative to advance LGBTI-inclusive development launched in 2013. USAID is one of the many tools that the United States has used to undermine the effectiveness of the Haitian state. In general, these collaborations that bypass the Haitian state or discipline it through international governmental organizations have the circular effect of portraying a bad/failed Haitian state in need of intervention.

CONCLUSION

Competing with the transnational imperialist discourse of Haiti as the premodern land of voodoo that perverts the Black republic is an emergent imperialist discourse that Haiti is inherently homophobic. These conflicting discourses work together to disavow the effects of European colonialism, U.S. imperialism, and ongoing military occupation by the United Nations, thereby constructing Haiti as an autonomous nation of its own creation. One thing that I cannot emphasize enough is that to speak of Haiti—the Black republic—one is always in a conversation about race. The implied assumption of these transnational discourses transmitted in the register of sexual politics is that these problems—either that Haiti is premodern or "failing" at being modern—are a product of Blackness that cannot be resuscitated by whiteness, though there is apparently no reason to stop trying to do so. The results of these interventions are overall deteriorating conditions for same-sex-desiring and gender-creative Haitians.

Despite the fallout, SEROvie and Kouraj united in at least one respect: they shared the sense that the discrimination and violence after the well-publicized manifestations was worse than it had been in 2010. They—along with the other groups and organizations mentioned in this chapter—sought to address it in many different ways along with their respective missions: tracking the prevalence of violent incidents, reporting cases to local authorities when they had the permission of victims (which was not typical), publicizing major events such as a mob attack on a British-Haitian gay couple's engagement party and an armed break-in to the Kouraj office, and providing much-needed services for same-sex-desiring and gender-creative Haitians as things worsened—mental health support and transitional housing.

Yet queer anti-imperialist activism toward something like Lakou's vision for revolutionary change came to seem impossible in the NGO laboratories of governance. As Haiti's history teaches us, though, resistance teems just beneath the surface (even within the NGO plantations), beyond capture by (neo)colonial capitalism. Going beyond and integral to the necessary work to improve the daily lives and material conditions of same-sex-desiring and gender-creative Haitians, the creative revolutionary work of transforming social relations for *all* Haitians is kept alive through Vodou, fugitive intimacies, popular uprisings, and fleeting performances that sustain resistance and generate new relationalities.

EPILOGUE

The Transnational #BlackLivesMatter Movement
and the Serialization of Black (Queer) Death

The final years of my research about postcolonial homophobia in Haiti coincided with the emergence of the Black Lives Matter movement in the United States. The movement mobilized under the hashtag #BlackLivesMatter—initiated in 2013 by Alicia Garza, Patrisse Cullors, and Opal Tometi—to respond to murders of African American youths and adults and the criminalization of Black life. The Black Lives Matter movement made household names of many whose breath was violently stolen, rescuing them from the fate of quickly forgotten stories on the evening news. Trayvon Martin. Michael Brown. Eric Garner. Tamir Rice. Sandra Bland. Breonna Taylor. Paying necessary attention to the details of unfolding events, the Black lives lost at the hands of police and neighbors, and the injustices stacked one on top of another ruptured any remaining illusion that the election of President Barack Obama had ushered in a post-racial U.S. society. There is no more escaping the fact that racism, as "the state-sanctioned and/or extralegal production and exploitation of group-differentiated vulnerability to premature death" (Gilmore 2007, 247), shapes the places where we work and live. Police killed Philando Castile less than a half mile from my home on the University of Minnesota–Twin Cities campus. Officers of the Minneapolis Police Department killed Thurman Belvins, Jamar Clark, George Floyd, and Amir Locke in the city where I teach. Their deaths galvanized widespread collective action that shifted popular narratives from focusing on individual circumstances—"a few bad apples"—to systematic thinking about anti-Black racism and white supremacy.

While rooted in the particular geopolitics of the United States, Black Lives Matter is a worldwide movement that contends with abuses in policing and militarization, illuminates global ideologies of anti-Blackness, and honors and revalues Black lives and world building. Haitian people have been integral to this movement and have expressed in various ways what Marlene Daut so succinctly declared: "The Haitian Revolution is the original Black Lives Matter movement" (quoted in Bojarski 2021). I conclude this book by thinking about the Black Lives Matter movement's politicization of Black deaths in relationship to postcolonial homophobia in Haiti and the forms of action same-sex-desiring and gender-creative Haitians have had to invent in the face of intensified vulnerability to premature death.

The Black Lives Matter movement's politicization of Black deaths has precedents in past African American social movements. One well-known example due to its contemporary relevance to extrajudicial killings of Black people is the campaign against lynching led by the National Association for the Advancement of Colored People (NAACP) in the early twentieth century. Each time a Black person was killed anywhere in the United States from 1920 to 1938, the NAACP suspended a flag that read "A MAN WAS LYNCHED YESTERDAY" from a window outside their national headquarters building in New York City. Disrupting the comfortable illusion of physical and ideological distance from lynching, the flag reminded New Yorkers going about their daily lives in a country that sanctioned the brutalization and dehumanization of anyone with brown or Black skin that they were complicit in this violence. NAACP removed the flag under the threat of eviction, but it was revived for the Black Lives Matter movement by the artist Dread Scott following the murder of Walter Scott with the altered text, "A MAN WAS LYNCHED BY POLICE YESTERDAY."

"Man" in this updated political statement insists on the humanity of the dead, including by marking their gender—namely the overrepresentation of African American, Latino, and Indigenous *boys* and *men* who do not survive encounters with the police. Building on the activist scholarship of U.S. women of color and Indigenous feminists, particularly the intersectional framework offered by Kimberlé Williams Crenshaw (1991), the Black Lives Matter movement has illuminated that police also kill Black women and girls with horrifying regularity.[1] The African American Policy Forum report *Say Her Name: Resisting Police Brutality against Black Women* (AAPF, Crenshaw, and Ritchie 2015) utilizes a "gender inclusive" framework to approaching the issue of police violence in the United States, one that centers the "cases" of Black women and girls. *Say Her Name* highlights that while their cases can fit already-developed narratives from the targeting of boys and men, shifting the focus to Black women and girls provides a fuller picture of anti-Black state violence—such as, criminalizing survivors of violence, gender and sexuality policing, sexual assault, and use of excessive force against mothers and their children. The report and the #SayHerName movement work to bring these issues to popular attention, as have the high-profile police murders of Sandra Bland and Breonna Taylor.

Black feminist scholars contribute to Say Her Name and Black Lives Matter by theorizing antiracism broadly in relationship to and beyond the realms of policing and the prison industrial complex. In "Why Did They Die? On Combahee and the Serialization of Black Death" (2017), Terrion L. Williamson contends with the murders of Black women and girls where racist policing may not be immediately responsible but is nonetheless part of the geopolitical conditions of anti-Black racism that renders vulnerability and value in life and death. She inverts the law enforcement definition of serial murder as "the unlawful killing of two or more victims by the same offenders in separate events" to "the intentional killing of three or more [similarly situated] persons in separate events within a designated geographic area . . . to privilege the victims rather than the perpetrators" (332). While Williamson's research is ongoing, by the time her article had gone to press, she had counted more than five hundred similarly situated Black women and girls in the United States since the early 1970s whose deaths fit this definition of serial murder.

Terrion L. Williamson's theorization of the serialization of Black death draws on the activism of the Combahee River Collective (CRC), best known for their essay "A Black Feminist Statement" (1983). In her article, Williamson draws on another publication in the collective's archives: a pamphlet originally titled "Six Black Women: Why Did They Die?" written and distributed as part of a mobilized response to the deaths of Black women and girls in Boston in 1979. By May of that year, twelve Black women and girls between the ages of fifteen and fifty-three had been murdered. As Williamson details, the official state logics about these serial murders (by her definition) were premised on the underlying assumption that "violence experienced by black women in black communities was a mundane fact of black life that mandated no real cause for alarm" (2017, 330). All of the CRC's organizing efforts, including the ~~Six Seven Eight Nine Ten Eleven~~ Twelve Black Women: Why Did They Die? pamphlet contradicted this naturalization of the murders by expressing anger at the devaluation of these women's lives and enacting care for other Black women and girls with advice for protecting themselves.

Key to the CRC and Williamson's theoretical work is that the police claimed that these were "individual 'crimes of passion' in which the victims personally knew their perpetrators" rather than a "maniacal white serial killer preying on black women" (Williamson 2017, 330). Representing the cases in this way supposedly justified the lack of urgency in police response compared to their investigation of a serial rapist targeting white women around the same time. Williamson points out the "curious logic: a single perpetrator (in a white neighborhood) requires a more intense police response than multiple perpetrators (in a black neighborhood), and victims who know their victimizers personally are owed less protection than those who do not" (330). It also disconnected the cases in a way that Williamson's redefinition of serial murder repairs. She illuminates, following the CRC, that the deaths of Black women may not be connected through perpetrators but rather through the material conditions that led to their devaluation: "The CRC recognized that the violence that so often conditions the lives of black women is not simply a byproduct of black life or black kinship, but a socially and politically constructed outcome of the various intersecting modalities of oppression endured by black women—including sexism, heterosexism, classism [capitalism], and racism—that everyone, including people who do not identify as black or as women, have a stake in doing something about, not only because it will save black women's lives, but because it will save their own lives as well" (Williamson 2017, 331). Thus her work on the serialization of Black death focuses on these conditions and others (e.g., deindustrialization in the Midwest) that shape the lives and deaths of similarly situated Black women in specific times and places.

The Black Lives Matter movement—and Williamson's Black feminist activist scholarship in particular—informs my thinking on a legacy of postcolonial homophobia that reached a crisis point in the years of widespread mobilization against police violence and the loss of Black lives in the United States: the violent deaths of same-sex-desiring and gender-creative Haitians. When I started my fieldwork in 2008, the threat of fatal homophobic violence was rarely expressed as a concern by my interlocutors. Even the nearly fatal attack on Avadra's boyfriend (chapter 3) did not create the specter of this threat for other same-sex-desiring and gender-creative Haitians who knew them, though people were well aware of how much violence one can endure while remaining alive. In the years since the 2013 antigay protests, however, this specter has loomed large.

Some homophobic incidents have been covered in international media, including some of those briefly mentioned in the last chapter. In August 2013, a male gay couple's engagement party was attacked by a group of people hurling rocks, glass bottles, and Molotov cocktails.[2] In November 2013, men broke into the office of the human rights advocacy organization Kouraj, tied up Kouraj members and threatened them with guns and machetes, and stole their files and equipment (Amnesty International 2013). Kouraj officers decided to close and continue their operations elsewhere because of death threats. In September 2016, the organizers of what was going to be the first LGBT film festival in Haiti, Massimadi, also received death threats and were ordered by police to cancel the event.[3] But the ongoing and persistent violence against same-sex-desiring and gender-nonconforming people is rarely mentioned in the mainstream media outside of these big incidents, though Haitian and international human rights organizations have documented it to some extent.[4]

In October 2014, I was contacted by Daniel, a peer educator at SEROvie who was a key informant for this project. SEROvie had received a letter threatening to kill a dozen prominent people associated with Haitian organizations serving same-sex-desiring and gender-creative people. Daniel told me in response: "So I tell a lot of the LGBT people to be careful. To watch where they are going. Know who you are around and who you will befriend because it's not safe. I am afraid for my life. They can kill me and there will be no justice. So that's the way it is in Haiti." Daniel, whose name circulated on a death list, made the difficult decision to leave his family, friends, and the country he loves because the day-to-day conditions were too unbearable. He said, "Because of this violence, you can't think about your future anymore. You wonder, will it be me next? Will today be the day that I die?"

One of the people named on the list who has since been murdered is Charlot Jeudy from Kouraj, whom I had not seen since we attended a memorial for the Orlando Pulse Nightclub shooting victims in summer 2016. He was found dead in his home on November 25, 2019. The media reported that he said shortly before his death that: "It does appear that the [homophobic] incidents are escalating. . . . In fact, there are many members of these organizations and activists on the ground who are now trying to leave Haiti and trying to get international attention with regards to what's happening in Haiti at this time" (CBC Radio 2019). Jeudy's friends encouraged him to leave, as someone who had been targeted for violence before and often received death threats. But he refused to leave the difficult work of changing hearts and minds in Haiti.

There are many more people who have been murdered since 2013—often those with male embodiment from the majority poor—though they are not activists in the public eye and therefore their deaths are deemed not newsworthy. Graphic messages about these deaths, often containing photographs of bodies, circulate among same-sex-desiring and gender-creative Haitians. Sharing this information—holding on to the evidence—as well as grieving the dead is part of a political process to give meaning to the lives and deaths of fellow same-sex-desiring and gender-creative Haitians. These circulations are unlike warnings in the public sphere meant to scare people out of Haiti, like graffiti declaring "ABA Masisi" ("Down with masisi!"). In 2015, I received a slew of emails about a video circulating in the Haitian social media sphere: "Angry Mob Beat and Burn Alive Two Men Accused of Homosexuality."[5] While some comments decried the sickening actions in the video, many more supported this kind of violence with comments like "ABA Masisi!" or "Burn all the homosexuals."

What can be done in the face of these nightmarish scenes and foreclosed futures—so close and yet so far away from the simultaneous queer world-building practices of Haitians? Following the lead of same-sex-desiring and gender-creative change makers in Haiti who recognize and mourn these deaths, as well as the Black feminist work of the Combahee River Collective and Terrion Williamson, I conclude this book with the serialization of Black queer death in Haiti as a political act aligning with the Black Lives Matter movement. As with the Black women in Boston or in the Midwest, most of these deaths can be—and have been—attributed to individual circumstances. Wrong place, wrong time. Bad hookup. Attempted robbery. Jealous (ex-) lovers. Separately they can be explained away, but when put together using Williamson's reframing of serial murder, then we are compelled to "name the conditions that had produced the . . . deaths and the . . . subsequent failure to acknowledge or contend with their deaths in any meaningful way" (Williamson 2017, 328).

Instead of naming the dead—a complicated political practice with an international readership outside of Haiti—I offer this book as an answer to the question, "Why did they die?" As I hope I have imparted, "homophobia" or "Haitian homophobia" is not only an insufficient answer, but rather it compounds the conditions that resulted in the premature deaths of these same-sex-desiring and gender-creative Haitians. The story of "Why did they die?" is a long one that reaches back before recent homophobic incidents, before the 2013 protests, before the 2010 earthquake and the new wave of missionaries, and before the 2008 Michèle Pierre-Louis controversy. It is about European colonialism, U.S. imperialism, anti-Blackness, heteropatriarchy, foreign militarization, the humanitarian NGOs that lean into imperial zones of abandonment and neglect, the complex interplay of transnational social movements, and how the conditions for life and death are shaped by these histories and various forces. Naming and confronting these conditions is essential work against postcolonial homophobia on the way to creating futures where same-sex-desiring and gender-creative Haitians can flourish.

NOTES

DEDICATIONS

1. At the conclusion of the "Interrogating Anti-Black Racism and Disablement" symposium, Alexis Pauline Gumbs (a self-described "queer black troublemaker, a black feminist love evangelist and a prayer poet priestess") invited attendees to activate new energy in the room by offering dedications. Who led us on a path so that we wound up at the symposium? Who was integral to the conversation but not physically in the room? Who else needed the insights of our conversations, our work together?

2. Howard describes twice-told stories (2001, 5) as one of his queer history methodologies for "men like that" in the U.S. South.

3. The names throughout this book are pseudonyms, with few exceptions for public figures and/or those who are deceased.

INTRODUCTION

1. See Delva 2012, "First Do No Harm" 2012, "UN Police in Haiti" 2012, Weisbrot 2011.

2. Desmangles 2012 and KOSANBA 2012 contain brief statements describing the resonances of these terms.

3. Queer postcolonial scholarship illuminates how these racialized discourses of homophobia are a product of contemporary imperialisms. See Hawley 2001, Massad 2002, Puar 2007, Salih 2007, Wahab 2012.

4. This emphasis on the state in global LGBTQI human rights organizations is discussed extensively in Thoreson 2014. It is also the subject of many essays in Weiss and Bosia 2013.

5. Gill cites Wekker 2006, Tinsley 2010, Allen 2011, King 2014, Nixon 2015, Ellis 2015, and Walcott 2016. One might also include Glave 2008, Agard-Jones 2012, Lara 2012 and 2020, as well as work in queer Haiti studies cited below.

6. This scholarship includes progressive works in the humanities and social sciences that explicitly center homophobia, such as King et al. 2012 as well as works that broadly addresses the naturalization of heteropatriarchy and denigrations of same-sex sexuality and "deviant" gender and sexuality. See, for example, Afi Quinn 2018; Agard-Jones 2009; Alexander 1994, 1997, and 2005; Gosine 2013; Kempadoo 2004; Lara 2020; Murray 2012; Wahab 2012 and 2020.

7. Since the publication of the "Nou Mache Ansanm" special issue, the field of queer Haitian studies has continued to emerge with new monographs (Hammond 2018, Tinsley 2018, Strongman 2019) and articles (Tift 2018, Albanese 2019, Chapman 2019, Nowkocha 2019, Cariani 2020, LaMothe 2020, Azor and Estimphil 2021, Durban 2021). Another article out of the Haitian Studies Association "Rights to Live Creatively" initiative, "The Rights to Live Creatively: Queering the *Moun* and Contesting "Rights" through Contemporary Haitian Arts Praxis" by Dasha A. Chapman and Mamyrah A. Dougé-Prosper, is forthcoming.

8. As the only popular ethnographic representation of same-sex desire and gender creativity in Haiti in its time, *Of Men and Gods* has been written about and theorized by several Haitian and Caribbean studies scholars, including Dubois 2008, Tinsley 2011 and 2018, and King 2014. Read also Lescot and Magloire 2017.

CHAPTER 1. PERVERTING HAITI

1. As a starting place, Trouillot 1995, Ulysse 2015, Casimir 2020, and Dash 1997 provide necessary context for thinking about history and imperialist representations of Haiti. To learn about Haiti's history, read Bellegarde 1938, C. L. R. James 1938, Fick 1990, Daut 2015, Dubois 2004 and 2012, Gaffield 2015, Garrigus 2006, Geggus 2002 and 2014, Polyné 2010.

2. For more on the connotations of these terms, see Desmangles 2012 and KO-SANBA 2012.

3. See Kempadoo 2004 for a broad analysis of how the Caribbean region has been constructed via racialized hypersexuality and heteropatriarchy.

4. Laurent Dubois notes that "the term seems to have been used in this way before he came along—he perhaps chose it, or was given it, for this reason—though his life and death imbued it with new significance" (2004, 51). For more, see Geggus 1991 and Mobley 2015.

5. Gaffield 2015 refreshingly complicates this narrative of international recognition of the new republic.

6. Lacking from the speech at the World's Fair: Columbian Exhibition—an event to celebrate four hundred years of European colonization in the Americas—is the coincidental detail that Christopher Columbus's ships anchored in the bay of Môle-Saint-Nicolas during his first voyage to the new world.

7. For extensive documentation of these laws, see Ramsey 2011.

8. Strings 2019 provides an extended analysis of the Hottentot Venus.

9. This story was fictionalized in Toni Morrison's award-winning novel, *Beloved* (1987).

10. On a related note, Lydon K. Gill mentions that Frances and Melville Herskovits make what is "perhaps the earliest ethnographic mention of homosexuality on the island [of Trinidad]" as well (2018, 2–3). Their brief comments appear in *Trinidad Village* (1947). Kamala Kempadoo notes that, with their research across the Caribbean, "the Herskovits produced a body of work that affirmed the uniqueness and particularity of Afro-Caribbean culture that was seen to derive from West African customs and heritages, termed Africanisms" (2004, 16).

11. The phenomenon of heterosexual transmission is helpfully unpacked in Patton 1985 and Geary 2014.

CHAPTER 2. THE MISSIONARY POSITION

1. My transcription.

2. Among U.S. evangelicals for whom Haiti had become the place d'jour of missionary work in the 1990s was a far-right movement called Spiritual Mapping, or Third Wave, connected to the Church Growth Movement. McAlister traces the transnational travels of Spiritual Mapping, whose "flow of information and people . . . ran from the U.S. to Haiti to the U.S. and back again" (2012, 203). According to McAlister, the Spiritual Mapping movement believes that God and the devil are waging a war, so the movement needs to concentrate their spiritual efforts as evangelicals in places that have been devastated by colonialism and that continue to be sites of what they call demonic entrenchment. McAlister documents that disciples of Spiritual Mapping proponents Charles Kraft and C. Peter Wagner, Haitian and U.S. Protestant intellectuals at U.S. seminaries, wrote books about Haiti throughout the 1990s, constructing it as a prime example of places plagued by demonic entrenchment. By 1997, movement members had kicked off a "large-scale, public crusade" to wage spiritual warfare in Haiti at the site of Bwa Kayiman where, as they contend, Haitians "made a pact with the devil" in return for liberation (McAlister 2012, 205). McAlister's work effectively traces the production and dissemination of the "blood pact with the devil" story—the evangelical history of the Haitian Revolution—later popularized by Pat Robertson.

3. Brooks unsurprisingly also cites Samuel P. Huntington among his influences.

4. This quotation pertains to the representation of Islam in U.S. "religious" and "secular" discourses in particular, but it has broader application to postcolonial studies.

5. This highly controversial mission that militarized U.S. emergency aid to Haiti drew criticism from people all along the political spectrum—leftist leaders throughout Latin America as well as conservative leaders in France and Canada who were livid that the United States assumed military control of the airport and therefore impacted a significant amount of relief efforts.

6. For more of this history connected to broader considerations about race, religion, and U.S. empire, see Wenger 2017.

7. These demographic changes are traced in scholarship about Protestantism in Haiti: Melvin Lloyd Butler 2005, Conway 1978, Jeanty 1989, Lain 1998, Andrea Jeantil Louis 1998, Bertin M. Louis 2011, Payne 2012, Ménard-Saint Clair 2012, Romain 1986.

8. For more context about the songs and dance of the Gede related to queer life, see chapter 4 of Dasha Chapman's book manuscript, "Grounding Practice: Dancing Haiti on Tè Glise."

9. The method is described in Boyd 2008 and Boyd and Ramírez 2012.

10. In translated excerpts from interviews, I retain the terms used by interviewees to describe gender and sexuality in their original language.

11. McCune 2014 elaborates the complexity of discretion for Black men in the United States, with different histories, pressures, pleasures, and constraints than the discretion that I describe here.

12. For more about Appolon's work, visit https://jeanappolonexpressions.org and read Chapman 2016.

CHAPTER 3. EVANGELICAL CHRISTIAN HOMOPHOBIA AND THE MICHÈLE PIERRE-LOUIS CONTROVERSY

1. The subtle but important differences between these two texts arise from the contexts in which they were written rather than intellectual disagreements. Pharr was writing in the context of the U.S. women's movement, including lesbian of color feminisms articulated in texts such as the Combahee River Collective Statement (1983), Lorde 1982 and 1984, Moraga and Anzaldúa 1984, and Anzaldúa 1987. The U.S. women's liberation movement was riddled with conflicts about sexuality, both in terms of homophobia and lesbian involvement in the movement, but also in terms of a long-raging debate within lesbian feminisms about whether sex was a site of pleasure or danger, or both—known as the sex wars (for more information, see Rubin 1984 and Vance 1984). Queer theory, the context of Pellegrini's piece, was shaped by these concerns within feminism, the pathbreaking work of Michel Foucault's *History of Sexuality*, as well as the devastation of the AIDS epidemic and, therefore, the specific material conditions of homosexual life and death. Pellegrini 1992 was published just after Sedgwick 1990 and another seminal text whose influence can be seen in her analysis, Judith Butler 1990.

CHAPTER 4. "ZONBI, ZONBI" AT THE GHETTO BIENNALE

1. For more about the group, visit their website (www.atis-rezistans.com) or watch the documentaries Gordon 2009 and Denis 2002.

2. This story is told in greater detail in Gordon 2017.

3. Kathy Acker papers, 1948–1997, Duke University Rubenstein Rare Book and Manuscript Library. My travel to the collection was enabled by a Mary Lily Research Grant from the Sallie Bingham Center for Women's History and Culture.

4. I had recently helped Flo with a piece of performance art about U.S. overconsumption, food waste, and culinary tourism in the project "I Wanna Jam It with You" at FOSAJ. It was described in Kotretsos 2009.

5. The examples in her book are mostly about masisi and madivin. However, one of the characters in rara songs that McAlister mentions in relationship to female sexuality (2002, 74)—Suzèt—has been described to me as *èrmafrodit* (hermaphrodite) or using the more explicit terms of *ti koko anba grenn* (little vagina under testicles).

6. Sedgwick is referring to Foucault 1990, in which Foucault traces the historical consideration of sexuality in terms of acts to the specification of individuals beginning with the homosexual, a term that was coined in 1870 (42–43). Heterosexual, as a definition, came later, but the terms did not come into popular use until the early twentieth century. For more about this history, see Katz 2006.

7. See Kate Ramsey 1995 about the development of *fòklò* in the mid-twentieth century in connection to ethnology and tourism in Haiti.

8. *Dézafi* has four translations in the Valdman's *Haitian Creole–English Bilingual Dictionary* (2007): 1) cockfight, 2) challenge in a cockfight, 3) challenge, and 4) disturbance. Frankétienne is notorious for his use of language with multiple layers of meaning, and dézafi seems to simultaneously refer to all of these. The title of the published French translation—*Les affres d'un défi* (1979)—highlights the "challenge" meaning of dézafi. An English version of the novel was published in 2018, but the title remained untranslated.

9. Kaiama L. Glover recounts that the spiralists offered no manifesto and purposefully few definitions of the movement (2010, 21). In an interview, Frankétienne described Spiralism as "a movement from the bottom to the top, from the simple to the complex. And in each spiral structure, each new turn is deeper and richer than the last one. the spiral defines the perpetual movement of life and of all evolving things; it is the characteristic of dialectic" (Rowell 1992, 390).

10. See Aponte 2010, Farmer 1994, Laguerre 1993, Trouillot 1990a. Carolle Charles (1995) offers a feminist analysis of the effects of the Tonton Macoutes on gender politics in Haiti.

11. The documentary by Gordon and Parisio (1997) offers more insight into the far-reaching consequences of these actions to eradicate swine fever.

CHAPTER 5. THE SEXUAL POLITICS OF RESCUE

1. The global LGBTQI did not conduct outreach specifically to Haitians who are intersex, hermaphrodite, or *ti koko anba grenn* (little vagina under testicles). The "I" traveled with the package of LGBT and LGBTQ, with a slight lag. Thanks to David Rubin for thoughtful comments about this development in Haiti in relationship to the transnational travels of "intersex" and intersex imperialism (2015).

2. See Manalansan 2003, Cantú 2005, Shah 2005, Massad 2007, and Puar 2007.

3. See Edmonds 2013, Jobe 2011, Katz 2013, Francois Pierre-Louis 2011, Schuller 2012, Wagner 2014, Zanotti 2010.

4. As with many HIV/AIDS prevention organizations that define who they direct their outreach and services to through "risk groups," the staff of SEROvie used the term "MSM," or the French equivalent, *hommes ayant des relations sexuelles avec d'autres hommes* (HSH), to describe their target population.

5. From the SEROVie website (accessed 2013), which is no longer active.

6. "Bisexual" and "bisexuality" were terms rarely used in Haiti, except by the bourgeoisie and former diaspora, despite the fact that many people expressed that they have sexual attraction and intimate relationships with both men and women. As Avadra, a Jacmelian masisi, told me in an interview: "The common people do not know the term 'bisexual.' This is intellectual stuff. I learned it from books and friends. In Haiti, if you are a [queer] man, you are masisi. If you are a [queer] woman, you are madivin." When I was in the field, the people who used the term "bisexual" who had not lived abroad were affiliated with NGOs in the years after the earthquake.

7. When I asked why people are more comfortable, I was told by one of the former peer educators that it was important for optics: having women in the SEROvie space meant that people who might be watching the organization from outside would be less likely to perceive it as gay.

8. In one extreme case, a transgender woman who was at SEROvie during the earthquake and suffered a concussion and several broken bones obtained transportation to Santo Domingo, the Dominican Republic—more than a five-hour drive on a good day—for care at a hospital. Her story is the focus of Durban 2017b.

9. Our paths did not cross during his visit, but I heard through the grapevine that an "international gay" had visited the organization. This description peaked my interest because "international" was a term that in a queer Haitian context usually referred to men who were both *aktif* (active/top) and *pasif* (passive/bottom). When I figured out that "international" indicated that Johnson was a foreigner, I found it interesting that people did not use the term *blan* ("white"/foreigner). While *blan* can be used for foreigners who are Black, like Johnson, he also speaks French fluently. The "international," I assume, came in part from the description of his organization.

10. The reason for highlighting my involvement in these different grant-writing processes is twofold. The first is to position myself as someone who had an interest in securing international philanthropic funding for the activist and artistic visions of queer Haitians. I supported this kind of hustling because, as a former nonprofit director of a youth social justice program, I knew the difference large grants make in the people's everyday lives. Nonprofits and NGOs are seductive not only because they "do good" in a general sense but because, as Miranda Joseph asserts, "projects . . . are often important to the very survival of the people served by the organization, precisely because nonprofits are useful to capitalism" (2002, 74). This was always true in resource-poor Haiti, also known as "NGO capital of the world," but it was especially the case after earthquake. My critique of this system of philanthropy, therefore, comes from experiences being on the inside and having a stake in the outcomes of this funding, albeit not in the same way as those the grants immediately served. The

second reason is that my involvement provided intimate insight into the ways that FOSAJ, and then Lakou, articulated itself to the global LGBTQI. I was privy to many of the conversations about how to frame the grants and have access to the grant applications, which is not true of the other organizations mentioned here that do not release their grant application documents.

11. In March 2010, Tres Gatas hosted one of the organizers of Lakou who had business at the U.S. consulate in Santo Domingo at the same time that they hosted me and my partner for a couple nights while we were making our way back to Haiti.

12. Flores McGarrell and Maïlé Alphonse, "Astraea Lesbian Fund for Justice for Sexual Minorities: Application for Fanal Otentik Sant D'A Jakmel," grant application, 2008, 3. The authors shared this application with me.

13. McAlister 2002 includes a more extensive discussion of Dreds and the Haitian Rasta community.

14. McGarrell and Alphonse, 8.

15. Here are examples from the application about the use of these terms: "As we begin to build our network through outreach to 'LGBTIQ' people, we look forward to the discoveries of new identities and Kreyòl words that lay waiting ahead of us." Under evaluation and indicators of success: "We empower even more people through art and culture than we did before, especially women and LGBTI people." And "Attract 5–10 new women and LGBT FOSAJ artist members."

16. McGarrell and Alphonse, 7.

17. Because of this experience, when I was asked to serve as a translator for Astraea several years later to communicate with the directors of another organization in Haiti with whom I was working as a researcher, I instead recommended a queer-friendly colleague.

18. During this time, I worked from a collective house that had survived the earthquake since the FOSAJ building had considerable damage.

19. For examples of media coverage, see Armstrong 2010 and 2013, Bins 2012, Cavna 2012, Dijckmeester-Bins 2012, Lambertson 2010.

20. This is related to the anthropological imaginary in queer research contexts, articulated so eloquently by Valentine 2007.

21. McAlister traces the responses of a conservative Pentecostal congregation in Port-au-Prince that, like U.S. evangelicals, "develop[ed] a punitive theodicy of the quake as God's punishment of a sinful nation" (2012, 11), what I have been calling divine retribution. The sin of homosexuality is never mentioned, but McAlister does mention the blame of Vodou. However, she gives the impression that divides within Christianity are perceived by the congregation to be as much at fault for the earthquake as "devil worshipping" (14–24).

22. Other than McAlister's article, the scapegoating of Vodou within Haiti is largely neglected in academic literature about the earthquake. The one scholar I heard speak publicly about how the earthquake "engineered a new era of religion in Haiti" that legitimized Protestant intolerance of Vodou is Haiti studies scholar Claudine Michel, a

founding member of KOSANBA: The Scholarly Association for the Studies of Haitian Vodou and Culture. There is nothing about the specific churches that incited violence against vodouizan. As with the reports about homophobia after the earthquake, anecdotes about what was being said in the pulpits of Jacmel and Port-au-Prince about vodouizan came to me secondhand. The effects of the scapegoating—widespread violence directed toward individuals as well as religious spaces, such as the desecration of *perestil* (Vodou temples)—garnered some attention in English-language media (Dodds 2010, Pierre-Pierre 2010). The stories tend to concentrate on one incident in Cité Soleil, where an angry crowd of evangelical Haitians interrupted a three-day Vodou ceremony to honor the lives claimed in the earthquake, throwing stones at the people in attendance. Yet there was far less concern with extent of the impact of the "religious war" waged on vodouizan, as a friend in Jacmel characterized the attacks.

23. For more information, see Snyder 2017.

24. The discourse of LGBT community may have also traveled through other paths such as individuals conducting relief work, journalists, and the proliferation of LGBT funding sources (e.g., the American Red Cross LGBT Relief Fund, Rainbow World Fund, and Rainbow Relief-Houston). These, however, would not necessarily have made as much of a difference as Astraea and IGLHRC in terms of how queer Haitian groups and organizations described themselves.

CHAPTER 6. THE EMERGENCE OF A SOCIAL MOVEMENT AGAINST HOMOPHOBIA

1. A fuller description of the Peace House project appears in Chapman 2015.

2. In years prior, some organizations had collaborated on public events for MSM.

3. "OMOSEKSYALITE se pa yon mal, se OMOFOBI ki fè mal" can be translated into English in various ways. "Mal" denotes something negative, such as a sin as well as something wrong or that causes problems. Homosexuality here is being defined against these things.

4. The website is at https://may17.org.

5. Non-trans* organizers and participants related that this event was the first time that they had ever heard the term "transphobia." For the subsequent IDAHO event, Housing Works Inc. made T-shirts for the event planners that read "Ann konbat omophobi and transfobi tout kote" (Let's combat homophobia and transphobia everywhere), which they displayed prominently in the SEROvie meeting room.

6. Beyond SEROvie, IGLHRC, and Kouraj, the other signatories included MADRE, the International Women's Human Rights Clinic at CUNY, the Center for Gender and Refugee Studies, the Hastings to Haiti Partnership, and the Institute for Justice and Democracy in Haiti.

7. This research has not yet been published. It was shared with me by the partnering organizations.

8. The lack of connecting "masisi" to a Vodou genealogy in this declaration and

other documents is conspicuous. However, I believe that it is assumed when the word is invoked, since Kouraj's audience is first and foremost Haitians. I also maintain that it is the way that they practice discretion, unlike Lakou who mobilized these connections for queer critique.

9. This line, read by Charlot at the IDAHO event, was remembered by the white, U.S. Housing Works founder only as "today we are masisi, tomorrow we are people," thereby erasing the way that Kouraj situated itself in a historical lineage of Black revolutionary resistance and rewriting their meaning to make them compatible with the mission of the global LGBTQI.

10. The original, French-language version of this document might be better translated as "the elaboration of a Haitian movement." Here I use the title provided on the English version of Kouraj's website.

11. Press conference with Coalition Haïtenne des organisations religieuses et morales, broadcast June 25, 2013, on MetroNews Haiti.

12. For another example of this colonial dynamic of comparing the sexual politics of metropole/colony regarding homophobia, see Agard-Jones 2009.

13. Email to the author, September 12, 2013.

EPILOGUE

1. For more on intersectionality, see Crenshaw 2022. Intersectionality studies has developed into a large interdisciplinary field that exceeds Crenshaw's original concept.

2. In the news, Brady 2013; in queer Haiti scholarship, LaMothe 2017 and 2020.

3. In the news, Brice 2016.

4. For instance, Haitian organizations and the IACHR noted the increase in attacks against individuals after the 2013 marches against same-sex sexuality (see IACHR 2013). Their documentation of homophobia and transphobia in Haiti was also included in IACHR 2015.

5. The link to the posted video is no longer active.

BIBLIOGRAPHY

Afi Quinn, Rachel. 2018. "Dominican Pride and Shame: Gender, Race, and LGBT Activism in Santo Domingo." *Small Axe* 22 (2): 128–43.

African American Policy Forum, Kimberlé Williams Crenshaw, and Andrea J. Ritchie. 2015. *Say Her Name: Resisting Police Brutality against Black Women.* New York: African American Policy Forum and the Center for Intersectionality and Social Policy Studies, July 2015. https://static1.squarespace.com/static/53f20d90e4b0b80451158d8c/t/560c068ee4b0af26f72741df/1443628686535/AAPF_SMN_Brief_Full_singles-min.pdf.

Agamben, Giorgio. 1998. *Homo Sacer: Sovereign Power and Bare Life.* Redwood City, CA: Stanford University Press.

Agard-Jones, Vanessa. 2009. "Le jeu de qui?: Sexual Politics at Play in the French Caribbean." *Caribbean Review of Gender Studies* 3 (1): 1–18.

———. 2012. "What the Sands Remember." *GLQ: A Journal of Lesbian and Gay Studies* 18 (2–3): 325–46.

Albanese, Mary Grace. 2019. "Unraveling the Blood Line: Pauline Hopkins's Haitian Genealogies." *J19: The Journal of Nineteenth-Century Americanists* 7 (2): 227–48.

Alexander, M. Jacqui. 1994. "Not Just (Any) Body Can Be a Citizen: The Politics of Law, Sexuality and Postcoloniality in Trinidad and Tobago and the Bahamas." *Feminist Review* (48): 5–23.

———. 1997. "Erotic Autonomy as a Politics of Decolonization: An Anatomy of Feminist and State Practices in the Bahamas Tourist Economy." In *Feminist Genealogies, Colonial Legacies, Democratic Futures*, edited by Chandra T. Mohanty and Jacqui M. Alexander, 105–42. New York: Taylor & Francis.

———. 2005. *Pedagogies of Crossing: Meditations on Feminism, Sexual Politics, Memory, and the Sacred.* Durham, NC: Duke University Press.

Allen, Jafari S. 2011. *¡Venceremos?: The Erotics of Black Self-Making in Cuba.* Durham, NC: Duke University Press.

Allman, James. 1980. "Sexual Unions in Rural Haiti." *International Journal of Sociology of the Family* 10 (1): 15–39.

———. 1985. "Conjugal Unions in Rural and Urban Haiti." *Social and Economic Studies* 34 (1): 27–57.

AmfAR. 2007. "AmfAR Launches MSM Initiative." AmfAR: Making AIDS History, June 26, 2007. www.amfar.org/content.aspx?id=126.

———. 2011. *Fundraising Toolkit: A Resource for HIV-Related Community-Based Projects Serving Gay, Bisexual, and Other Men Who Have Sex with Men (MSM) and Transgender Individuals in Low- and Middle-Income Countries.* AmfAR AIDS Research and the MSM Initiative. www.amfar.org/uploadedFiles/_amfarorg/Around_the_World/MSMToolkit.pdf.

———. 2012. "A Fundraising Resource for HIV-Related Community-Based Projects Serving MSM." April 2012. www.amfar.org/content.aspx?id=10456.

Amnesty International. 2013. "Urgent Action: LGBTI Organization's Office Attacked in Haiti." Amnesty International, November 26, 2013. www.ijdh.org/wp-content/uploads/2013/11/UA-AMR-36.021.2013-LGBTI-organizations-office-attacked-in-Haiti.pdf.

———. 2014. "Homophobia Still Tolerated by Governments around the World." Amnesty .eu, May 16, 2014. www.amnesty.org/en/latest/news/2014/05/homophobia-still-tolerated-governments-around-world/.

Anzaldúa, Gloria. 1987. *Borderlands/La Frontera: The New Mestiza.* 1st ed. San Francisco: Aunt Lute Books.

Aponte, David. 2010. "The Tonton Macoutes: The Central Nervous System of Haiti's Reign of Terror." Council on Hemispheric Affairs, March 11, 2010. www.coha.org/tonton-macoutes.

Armstrong, Lisa. 2010. "Being Gay and HIV-Positive in Haiti (Video)." *Atlantic,* September 26, 2010.

———. 2013. "Haiti After the Earthquake: Homosexuals Find Acceptance in Voodoo." Outer Voices podcast, February 21, 2013. http://outervoices.org/wp/?p=873. Accessed February 26, 2013.

Astraea Lesbian Foundation for Justice. 2014. "About Us." www.astraeafoundation.org/who-we-are/about. Accessed June 2014.

———. 2020. "Call for New Advisory Board—Intersex Human Rights Fund." January 27, 2020. www.astraeafoundation.org/stories/intersex-fund-advisory-board-application-2020/.

Azor, Josué, and Hetera Estimphil. 2021. "The Rights to Live Creatively." *NACLA Report on the Americas* 53 (1): 94–97. https://doi.org/10.1080/10714839.2021.1891650.

Bastien, Remy. 1961. "Haitian Rural Family Organization." *Social and Economic Studies* 10 (4): 478–510.

Bellegarde, Dantès. 1938. *La Nation Haïtienne.* Paris: J. de Gigord.

Bellegarde-Smith, Patrick. 2006. "Resisting Freedom: Cultural Factors in Democracy-The Case for Haiti." In *Vodou in Haitian Life and Culture: Invisible Powers*, edited by Claudine Michel and Patrick Bellegarde-Smith, 101–16. New York: Palgrave Macmillan.

Berlant, Lauren. 1997. *The Queen of America Goes to Washington City: Essays on Sex and Citizenship*. Durham, NC: Duke University Press.

———. 2011. *Cruel Optimism*. Durham, NC: Duke University Press.

Berlant, Lauren, and Michael Warner. 1998. "Sex in Public." *Critical Inquiry* 24 (2): 547–66.

Bins, Caroline. 2012. "Haiti's Scapegoats—Homophobia Spikes After the Earthquake." *Cartoon Movement* (blog), January 12, 2012. http://blog.cartoonmovement .com/2012/01/haitis-scapegoats-homophobia-spikes-after-the-earthquake.html.

Bojarski, Sam. 2021. "Exploring Haitian Independence, the Original 'Black Lives Matter' Movement." Institute of the Black World 21st Century (IBW21), February 2, 2021. https://ibw21.org/news/exploring-haitian-independence-the-original -black-lives-matter-movement/.

Boyaun. 2013. "Two Gay Men Killed in a Rally in Haiti." Housing Works, July 23, 2013. www. housingworks.org/advocate/detail/two-gay-men-killed-in-a-rally-in-haiti.

Boyd, Nan Alamilla. 2008. "Who Is the Subject? Queer Theory Meets Oral History." *Journal of the History of Sexuality* 17 (2): 177–89. https://doi.org/10.1353/sex.0.0009.

Boyd, Nan Alamilla, and Horacio N. Roque Ramírez, eds. 2012. *Bodies of Evidence: The Practice of Queer Oral History*. New York: Oxford University Press.

Brady, Tara. 2013. "British Red Cross Worker and His Gay Partner Attacked and Their Engagement Party Petrol-Bombed in Haiti Homophobic Attack." *Daily Mail*, August 12, 2013.

Brice, Makini. 2016. "Haiti's First LGBT Film Festival Postponed After Threats, Police Ban." *Reuters*, September 28, 2016, Emerging Markets sec. www.reuters.com.

Brooks, David. 2010. "The Underlying Tragedy." *New York Times*, January 14, 2010, New York edition, Opinion sec.

Butler, Judith. 1990. *Gender Trouble: Feminism and the Subversion of Identity*. New York: Routledge.

———. 1993. *Bodies That Matter: On the Discursive Limits of "Sex."* New York: Routledge.

———. 1997. *Excitable Speech: A Politics of the Performative*. New York: Routledge.

Butler, Melvin Lloyd. 2005. "Songs of Pentecost: Experiencing Music, Transcendence, and Identity in Jamaica and Haiti." PhD diss., New York University. ProQuest 305464549.

Cantú, Lionel. 2005. "Well-Founded Fear: Political Asylum and the Boundaries of Sexual Identity in the U.S.-Mexico Borderlands." In *Queer Migrations: Sexuality, U.S. Citizenship, and Border Crossings*, edited by Eithne Luibhéid, 61–74. Minneapolis: University of Minnesota Press.

Cariani, Tesla. 2020. "Glimpsing Shadows: Affective Witnessing in Noctambules and 'Of Ghosts and Shadows.'" *Parallax* 26 (3): 303–17.

Casimir, Jean. 2020. *The Haitians: A Decolonial History*. Chapel Hill: University of North Carolina Press.

Cavna, Michael. 2012. "Haiti's Scapegoats: Cartoon Movement's Compelling Video Tells of LGBT Abuse." *Washington Post: PostTV* (blog), January 14, 2012. www .washingtonpost.com.

CBC/Radio Canada. 2019. "Death of 'Fierce Activist' Jeudy Charlot Has Haiti's LGBTQ Community on Edge." Canadian Broadcasting Corporation, November 27, 2019. www.cbc.ca/radio/asithappens/as-it-happens-wednesday-edition-1.5375300/death -of-fierce-activist-jeudy-charlot-has-haiti-s-lgbtq-community-on-edge-1.5375658.

Chapman, Dasha A. 2015. "Dancing Haiti in the Break: The Labors and the Grounds of Dance in Haiti and Its Diasporas." PhD diss., New York University.

———. 2016. "The Diasporic Re-Membering Space of Jean Appolon's Afro-Haitian Dance Classes." *Black Scholar* 46 (1): 54–65.

———. 2019. "Embodying Dantò, Performing Freda, Dancing Lasirenn: Yonel Charles's Choreographic Elaborations of Ezili." *Journal of Haitian Studies* 25 (2): 4–40.

Chapman, Dasha A., Erin L. Durban, and Mario LaMothe. 2017. "Nou Mache Ansanm (We Walk Together): Queer Haitian Performance and Affiliation." *Women and Performance: A Journal of Feminist Theory* 27 (2): 143–59. https://doi.org/10.1080/ 0740770X.2017.1315227.

Charles, Carolle. 1994. "Sexual Politics and the Mediation of Class, Gender, and Race in Former Slave Plantation Societies: The Case of Haiti." In *Social Construction of the Past: Representation as Power*, edited by George Clement Bond and Angela Gilliam, 44–58. New York: Routledge.

———. 1995. "Gender and Politics in Contemporary Haiti: The Duvalierist State, Transnationalism, and the Emergence of a New Feminism (1980–1990)." *Feminist Studies* 21 (1): 135–64.

Charles, Jacqueline. 2013. "Haiti Police Deny Reports of Killing During Anti-Gay Protest." *Miami Herald*, July 26, 2013. www.miamiherald.com.

Chauncey, George. 1994. *Gay New York: Gender, Urban Culture, and the Making of the Gay Male World, 1890–1940*. New York: Basic Books.

Chidester, David. 1996. *Savage Systems: Colonialism and Comparative Religion in Southern Africa*. Charlottesville: University Press of Virginia.

Chin, Timothy S. 1997. "'Bullers' and 'Battymen': Contesting Homophobia in Black Popular Culture and Contemporary Caribbean Literature." *Callaloo* 20 (1): 127–41.

Cohen, Cathy J. 1997. "Punks, Bulldaggers, and Welfare Queens: The Radical Potential of Queer Politics?" *GLQ: Journal of Lesbian and Gay Studies* 3 (1): 437–65.

Collins, Patricia Hill. 1991. "The Sexual Politics of Black Womanhood." Chapter 6 in *Black Feminist Thought: Knowledge, Consciousness, and the Politics of Empowerment*. New York: Routledge.

Combahee River Collective. 1983. "The Combahee River Collective: A Black Feminist Statement (1978)." In *Home Girls: A Black Feminist Anthology*, edited by Barbara Smith, 264–75. New York: Kitchen Table—Women of Color Press.

Comhaire-Sylvain, Suzanne. 1958. "Courtship, Marriage and Plasaj at Kenscoff, Haiti." *Social and Economic Studies* 7 (4): 210–33.

Conner, Randy, with David Hatfield Sparks. 2004. *Queering Creole Spiritual Traditions: Lesbian, Gay, Bisexual, and Transgender Participation in African-Inspired Traditions in the Americas*. New York: Harrington Park Press.

Conway, Frederick James. 1978. "Pentecostalism in the Context of Haitian Religion and Health Practice." PhD diss., American University. ProQuest 302878481.

Crenshaw, Kimberlé Williams. 1991. "Mapping the Margins: Intersectionality, Identity Politics, and Violence against Women of Color." *Stanford Law Review* 43 (6): 1241–99.

———. 2022. *On Intersectionality: Essential Writings*. New York: New Press.

Currier, Ashley. 2010. "Political Homophobia in Postcolonial Namibia." *Gender and Society* 24 (1): 110–29.

———. 2012. "The Aftermath of Decolonization: Gender and Sexual Dissidence in Postindependence Namibia." *Signs: Journal of Women in Culture and Society* 37 (2): 1–27.

Dash, J. Michael. 1988. *Haiti and the United States: National Stereotypes and the Literary Imagination*. London: Macmillan.

Daut, Marlene L. 2015. *Tropics of Haiti: Race and the Literary History of the Haitian Revolution in the Atlantic World, 1789–1865*. New York: Oxford University Press.

Davis, Wade. 1985. *The Serpent and the Rainbow*. New York: Simon and Schuster.

———. 1988. *Passage of Darkness: The Ethnobiology of the Haitian Zombie*. Chapel Hill: University of North Carolina Press Books.

Dayan, Colin. 1995. *Haiti, History, and the Gods*. Berkeley: University of California Press.

"Death Threats Captured on Video at Haiti Anti-gay Demonstration: Two Presumed Homosexual Men Were Beaten to Death in Haiti by Hundreds of Protestors Demonstrating against Proposed Marriage Equality Legislation." 2013. GayStarNews. com, July 20, 2013. http://scl.io/ ORHvDJuw#gs.a49yvoI. Accessed July 26, 2013.

de Bruijn, Wilfred. 2013. "Wilfred de Bruijn's Facebook Page." Facebook, last modified April 7, 2013. www.facebook.com/photo.php?fbid=10151552317384433&set=a .10150119035019433.291272.795204432&type=1&theater. Accessed August 18, 2013.

Decena, Carlos Ulises. 2011. *Tacit Subjects: Belonging and Same-Sex Desire among Dominican Immigrant Men*. Durham, NC: Duke University Press.

Delva, Joseph Guyler. 2012. "Pakistani U.N. Peacekeepers Sentenced in Haiti Rape Case." Reuters, March 12, 2012. www.reuters.com.

Denis, Maksaens. 2002. *E Pluribus Unum*. Documentary, 22 min. Paris: Collectif 2004.

Deren, Maya. 1953. *Divine Horsemen: The Living Gods of Haiti*. New York: Thames and Hudson.

Desmangles, Leslie G. 2012. "Replacing the Term 'Voodoo' with 'Vodou': A Proposal." *Journal of Haitian Studies* 18 (2): 26–33.

DeTemple, Jill. 2006. "'Haiti Appeared at My Church': Faith-Based Organizations, Transnational Activism, And Tourism In Sustainable Development." *Urban An-*

thropology and Studies of Cultural Systems and World Economic Development 35 (2/3): 155–81.

Dijckmeester-Bins, Caroline. 2012. "Haiti's Scapegoats: Homophobia in the Aftermath of the 2010 Earthquake." Vimeo, 6:43 min. http://vimeo.com/37122552.

Dodds, Paisley. 2010. "Voodoo Practitioners Attacked at Ceremony for Haiti Earthquake Victims." *New Orleans Times-Picayune*, February 23, 2010. www.nola.com/religion/index.ssf/2010/02/voodooists_attacked_at_ceremony_for_haiti_earthquake_victims.html. Accessed February 24, 2010.

Douglass, Frederick. 1893. "Frederick Douglass Lecture on Haiti (1893)." Oratory given at the Dedication of the Haitian Pavilion at the 1893 World's Fair, Jackson Park, Chicago, January 2. Accessed at http://thelouvertureproject.org/index.php?title=Frederick_Douglass_lecture_on_Haiti_(1893).

Dubois, Laurent. 1996. "A Spoonful of Blood: Haitians, Racism and AIDS." *Science as Culture* 6 (1): 7–43.

———. 2004. *Avengers of the New World*. Cambridge, MA: Harvard University Press.

———. 2008. "Filming the Lwa in Haiti." *Caribbean Studies* 36 (1): 215–19.

———. 2012. *Haiti: The Aftershocks of History*. New York: Henry Holt.

Durban, Erin L. 2013. "The Legacy of Assotto Saint: Tracing Transnational History from the Gay Haitian Diaspora." *Journal of Haitian Studies* 19 (1): 235–56.

———. 2017a. "Performing Postcolonial Homophobia: A Decolonial Analysis of the 2013 Public Demonstrations against Same-Sex Marriage in Haiti." *Women and Performance: A Journal of Feminist Theory* 27 (2): 160–75. https://doi.org/10.1080/0740770X.2017.1315229.

———. 2017b. "Postcolonial Disablement and/as Transition: Trans* Haitian Narratives of Breaking Open and Stitching Together." *TSQ: Transgender Studies Quarterly* 4 (2): 195–207. https://doi.org/10.1215/23289252-3814997.

———. 2021. "Whither Homophobia? Rethinking a Bad Object for Queer Studies from the Black Global South." *QED: A Journal in GLBTQ Worldmaking* 8 (1): 49–78.

Edelman, Lee. 2004. *No Future: Queer Theory and the Death Drive*. Durham, NC: Duke University Press.

Edmonds, Kevin. 2013. "Beyond Good Intentions: The Structural Limitations of NGOs in Haiti." *Critical Sociology* 39 (3): 439–52.

Ellis, Nadia. 2011. "Out and Bad: Toward a Queer Performance Hermeneutic in Jamaican Dancehall." *Small Axe* 15 (2): 7–23.

———. 2015. *Territories of the Soul: Queered Belonging in the Black Diaspora*. Durham, NC: Duke University Press.

Eng, David L., Jack Halberstam, and José Esteban Muñoz. 2005. "Introduction: What's Queer about Queer Studies Now?" *Social Text* 23 (3–4): 1–17.

Evans, L. Ton. 1922. "An Urgent Appeal in Behalf of Haiti, West Indies." In *Hearings Before a Select Committee on Haiti and Santo Domingo*, by U.S. Senate, Select Committee on Haiti and Santo Domingo, 1:227. Washington, DC: Government Printing Office. Accessed at Google Books, www.google.com/books/edition/Hearings

_Before_a_Select_Committee_on_Ha/frBmAAAAMAAJ?hl=en&gbpv=1, March 4, 2022.

Farmer, Paul. 1992. *AIDS and Accusation: Haiti and the Geography of Blame*. Berkeley: University of California Press.

———. 1994. *The Uses of Haiti*. Monroe, ME: Common Courage.

———. 2006. *AIDS and Accusation: Haiti and the Geography of Blame*. Updated ed. Berkeley: University of California Press.

———. 2011. *Haiti After the Earthquake*. New York: Public Affairs.

Fatton, Robert. 2014. *Haiti: Trapped in the Outer Periphery*. Boulder, CO: Lynne Rienner.

Ferguson, Roderick A. 2015. "Queer of Color Critique and the Question of the Global South." In "The Global Trajectories of Queerness: Re-Thinking Same-Sex Politics in the Global South." Special issue, *Thamyris/Intersecting: Place, Sex and Race Online* 30 (1): 49–56.

Fick, Carolyn E. 1990. *The Making of Haiti: The Saint Domingue Revolution from Below*. Knoxville: University of Tennessee Press.

Findlay, Eileen J. Suárez. 1999. *Imposing Decency: The Politics of Sexuality and Race in Puerto Rico, 1870–1920*. Durham, NC: Duke University Press.

"First Do No Harm: The UN in Haiti." 2012. *Economist*, April 28, 2012. www.economist.com/the-americas/2012/04/28/first-do-no-harm.

Fischer, Sibylle. 2004. *Modernity Disavowed: Haiti and the Cultures of Slavery in the Age of Revolution*. Durham, NC: Duke University Press.

Foucault, Michel. 1978. *The History of Sexuality*. Vol. 1. Translated by Robert Hurley. New York: Pantheon Books.

Frankétienne. 1975. *Dézafi (roman)*. Port-au-Prince: Editions Fardin.

———. 1979. *Les affres d'un défi*. Port-au-Prince: Imprimerie Henri Deschamps.

Frankétienne, Wynnie Lamour, and Kaiama L Glover. 2013. "From *Dezafi* and *Les affres d'un défi*." *Transition: An International Review* 111: 59–73.

Freeman, Elizabeth. 2010. *Time Binds: Queer Temporalities, Queer Histories*. Durham, NC: Duke University Press.

Froude, James Anthony. 1888. *The English in the West Indies: Or, The Bow of Ulysses*. London: Longmans, Green, and Co.

Gaffield, Julia. 2015. *Haitian Connections in the Atlantic World: Recognition after Revolution*. Chapel Hill: University of North Carolina Press.

Garfield, Richard. 2002. "Economic Sanctions, Humanitarianism, and Conflict after the Cold War." *Social Justice* 29 (3): 94–107.

Garrigus, John D. 2006. *Before Haiti: Race and Citizenship in French Saint-Domingue*. New York: Palgrave Macmillan.

Geary, Adam M. 2014. *Antiblack Racism and the AIDS Epidemic: State Intimacies*. New York: Palgrave Macmillan.

Geggus, David Patrick. 1991. "Haitian Voodoo in the Eighteenth Century: Language, Culture, Resistance." *Jahrbuch Für Geschichte Lateinamerikas* 28 (1): 21–52.

———. 2002. *Haitian Revolutionary Studies*. Bloomington: Indiana University Press.

———, ed. and transl. 2014. *The Haitian Revolution: A Documentary History*. Indianapolis: Hackett.

Gibbons, Elizabeth, and Richard Garfield. 1999. "The Impact of Economic Sanctions on Health and Human Rights in Haiti, 1991–1994." *American Journal of Public Health* 89 (10): 1499–504.

Gill, Lyndon K. 2018. *Erotic Islands: Art and Activism in the Queer Caribbean*. Durham, NC: Duke University Press.

Gilles, Claude. 2008. "Michèle Pierre-Louis saute un premier écueil . . ." *Le nouvelliste*, July 17, 2008.

Gilles, Jean-Élie. 1995. *Sur les pas de Diogène*. [USA]: J. E. Gilles.

Gilmore, Ruth Wilson. 2007. *Golden Gulag: Prisons, Surplus, Crisis, and Opposition in Globalizing California*. Berkeley: University of California Press.

Glave, Thomas. 2008. *Our Caribbean: A Gathering of Lesbian and Gay Writing from the Antilles*. Durham, NC: Duke University Press.

Glover, Kaiama L. 2010. *Haiti Unbound: A Spiralist Challenge to the Postcolonial Canon*. Liverpool: Liverpool University Press.

Gordon, Leah. 2009. *Atis-Rezistans: The Sculptors of Grand Rue*. Documentary, 32 min. Film London, London Development Agency.

———, ed. 2017. *Ghetto Biennale/Geto Byenal: 2009–2015*. Exhibition catalog. London: No Eraser Publishing.

Gordon, Leah, and Anne Parisio. 1997. *A Pig's Tale*. New York: Crowing Rooster Arts.

Gosine, Andil. 2013. "Murderous Men: MSM and Risk Rights in the Caribbean." *International Feminist Journal of Politics* 15 (4): 477–93.

Grewal, Inderpal. 2005. *Transnational America: Feminisms, Diasporas, Neoliberalisms*. Durham, NC: Duke University Press.

Günel, Gökçe, Saiba Varma, and Chika Watanabe. 2020. "A Manifesto for Patchwork Ethnography." *Cultural Anthropology*, June 9, 2020. Member Voices edition, Fieldsights sec.

"Haiti IDAHO Report 2013." 2013. International Day Against Homophobia & Transphobia/May 17th. https://may17.org/haiti-idaho-report-2013/.

Halberstam, Jack. 2005. *In a Queer Time and Place Transgender Bodies, Subcultural Lives*. New York: New York University Press.

Halperin, Victor, dir. 1932. *White Zombie*. Drama, 67 min. Halperin Productions.

Hammond, Charlotte. 2018. *Entangled Otherness: Cross-Gender Fabrications in the Francophone Caribbean*. Liverpool: Liverpool University Press.

Harney, Stefano, and Fred Moten. 2013. *The Undercommons: Fugitive Planning and Black Study*. Brooklyn, NY: Autonomedia.

Hart, Lynda S. 1994. *Fatal Women: Lesbian Sexuality and the Mark of Aggression*. Princeton, NJ: Princeton University Press.

Hartman, Saidiya. 2008a. *Lose Your Mother: A Journey Along the Atlantic Slave Route*. New York: Macmillan.

———. 2008b. "Venus in Two Acts." *Small Axe* 12 (2): 1–14.

Hawley, John C. 2001. *Postcolonial, Queer: Theoretical Intersections*. Albany: State University of New York Press.

"Heightened LGBT Violence in the Caribbean and Cameroon." 2013. Astraea Lesbian Foundation for Justice, July 31, 2013. www.astraeafoundation.org. Accessed June 5, 2014.

Herskovits, Melville J. 1937. *Life in a Haitian Valley*. New York: A. A. Knopf.

Herskovits, Melville J., and Frances S. Herskovits. 1938. *Dahomey, an Ancient West African Kingdom*. Vol. 2. New York: J. J. Augustin.

Hoad, Neville. 2007. *African Intimacies: Race, Homosexuality, and Globalization*. Minneapolis: University of Minnesota Press.

Howard, John. 2001. *Men Like That: A Southern Queer History*. Chicago: University of Chicago Press.

Hughes, Langston. 1932. "White Shadows in a Black Land." *Crisis* 39 (May): 157.

Hurbon, Laënnec. 1995. "American Fantasy and Haitian Voodoo." In *Sacred Arts of Haitian Vodou*, edited by Donald J. Cosentino, 181–97. Los Angeles: UCLA Fowler Museum of Cultural History.

Hurston, Zora Neale. 1938. *Tell My Horse: Voodoo and Life in Haiti and Jamaica*. Philadelphia: J. B. Lippincott.

IACHR: (Organization of American States) Inter-American Commission on Human Rights. 2013. "IACHR Condemns Recent Wave of Violence against LGBTI Persons in Haiti." Press release 54/13, July 30, 2013. www.oas.org/en/iachr/media_center/preleases/2013/054.asp.

———. 2015. *Violence against Lesbian, Gay, Bisexual, Trans and Intersex Persons in the Americas*. Document 36, November 12, 2015. www.oas.org/en/iachr/reports/pdfs/violencelgbtipersons.pdf.

IDAHO Committee. 2012. *The International Day Against Homophobia and Transphobia: "IDAHO–May 17th": Annual Report 2012*. https://may17.org/wp-content/uploads/2019/04/2012AnnualReport.pdf.

IGLHRC: International Gay and Lesbian Human Rights Commission. 2010. "Outspoken." Newsletter. International Gay and Lesbian Human Rights Commission. Spring/Summer 2010. http://iglhrc.org/content/outspoken-newsletter-springsummer-2010.

———. 2011. *The Impact of the Earthquake, and Relief and Recovery Programs on Haitian LGBT People*. International Gay and Lesbian Human Rights Commission. March 28, 2011. https://outrightinternational.org/sites/default/files/504–1.pdf.

———. 2014. "What We Do." IGLHRC: International Gay and Lesbian Human Rights Commission. https://iglhrc.org/content/what-we-do. Accessed July 13, 2014.

"Interview with Charlot Jeudy." 2013. Vision 2000 à l'écoute. Radio Vision 2000. Port-au-Prince, May 29, 2013.

Jakobsen, Janet R., and Ann Pellegrini, eds. 2008. *Secularisms*. Durham, NC: Duke University Press.

James, C. L. R. 1938. *The Black Jacobins; Toussaint L'Ouverture and the San Domingo Revolution.* New York: Vintage Books.

James, Erica Caple. 2010. *Democratic Insecurities: Violence, Trauma, and Intervention in Haiti.* Berkeley: University of California Press.

Jeanty, Edner. 1989. *Le Christianisme en Haiti.* Port-au-Prince: La Presse Evangelique.

Jensen, Jane. 2008. "Temporaries, Tokens, and Ceremonial Leaders." In *Women Political Leaders: Breaking the Highest Glass Ceiling*, 63–78. New York: Palgrave Macmillan.

Jobe, Kathleen. 2011. "Disaster Relief in Post-Earthquake Haiti: Unintended Consequences of Humanitarian Volunteerism." *Travel Medicine and Infectious Disease* 9 (1): 1–5.

Johnson, Cary Alan. 2010a. "Donate Directly to Relief and Support Efforts for the LGBT Community in Haiti." International Gay and Lesbian Human Rights Commission, January 15, 2010. https://iglhrc.org/content/donate-directly-relief-and-support-efforts-lgbt-community-haiti.

———. 2010b. "LGBT in Haiti, Three Months After the Quake." International Gay and Lesbian Human Rights Commission, April 13, 2010. http://iglhrc.wordpress.com/2010/04/13/lgbt-in-haiti-three-months-after-the-quake/.

Johnson, James Weldon. 1920. *Self-Determining Haiti.* New York: The *Nation Inc.* and the NAACP.

Joseph, Miranda. 2002. *Against the Romance of Community.* Minneapolis: University of Minnesota Press.

Kaoma, Kapya J. 2013. "The Marriage of Convenience: The U.S. Christian Right, African Christianity, and Postcolonial Politics of Sexual Identity." In Weiss and Bosia 2013, 75–102.

Katz, Jonathan Ned. 2006. *The Invention of Heterosexuality.* Chicago: University of Chicago Press.

———. 2013. *The Big Truck That Went By: How the World Came to Save Haiti and Left Behind a Disaster.* New York: Palgrave Macmillan.

Keating, Christine. 2013. "Conclusion: On the Interplay of State Homophobia and Homoprotectionism." In Weiss and Bosia 2013, 246–54.

Kempadoo, Kamala. 2004. *Sexing the Caribbean: Gender, Race, and Sexual Labor.* New York: Routledge.

Kennedy, Elizabeth Lapovsky. 1996. "'But We Would Never Talk about It': The Structures of Lesbian Discretion in South Dakota, 1928–1933." In *Inventing Lesbian Cultures in America*, edited by Ellen Lewin, 15–39. Boston: Beacon.

Kennedy, Elizabeth Lapovsky, and Madeline D. Davis. 2014. *Boots of Leather, Slippers of Gold : The History of a Lesbian Community.* New York: Routledge.

King, Rosamond S. 2014. *Island Bodies: Transgressive Sexualities in the Caribbean Imagination.* Gainesville: University Press of Florida.

King, Rosamond S., Angelique V. Nixon, Colin Robinson, Natalie Bennett, and Vidyaratha Kissoon, eds. 2012. "Theorizing Homophobias in the Caribbean—

Complexities of Place, Desire, and Belonging." *International Resource Network— Caribbean Region*, June. www.caribbeanhomophobias.org.

KOSANBA: The Scholarly Association for the Study of Haitian Vodou. 2012. "Media Alert: US Library of Congress Changes Subject Heading from 'Voodooism' to 'Vodou.'" Media Alert.

Kotretsos, Georgia. 2009. "Inside the Artist's Studio: Flo McGarrell." *Art21 Magazine*, August 28, 2009. http://magazine.art21.org/2009/08/28/inside-the-artists-studio-flo -mcgarrell/#.YQCWpi2caLg.

Kouraj. 2012a. "Deklarasyon masisi." https://kourajdotorg.files.wordpress.com/ 2012/02/deklarasyon-masisi.pdf.

———. 2012b. "From LGBT to M Community." www.kouraj.org/from-lgbt-to-m -community.

Kuser, John Dryden. 1921. *Haiti: Its Dawn of Progress after Years in a Night of Revolution*. Boston: R. G. Badger.

Laguerre, Michel S. 1993. *The Military and Society in Haiti*. New York: Macmillan.

Lain, Clinton Eugene. 1998. "Church Growth and Evangelism in Haiti: Needs, Problems, and Methods." DMin, Asbury Theological Seminary. ProQuest 304479893.

Lambertson, Andre. 2010. "Being Gay and HIV-Positive in Haiti." *Atlantic*, September 26, 2010. www.theatlantic.com.

LaMothe, Mario. 2017. "Our Love on Fire: Gay Men's Stories of Violence and Hope in Haiti." *Women and Performance: A Journal of Feminist Theory* 27 (2): 259–70. https://doi.org/10.1080/0740770X.2017.1315231.

———. 2020. "Witnessing Queer Flights: Josué Azor's Lougawou Images and Anti-homosexual Unrest in Haiti." In *Race and Performance After Repetition*, edited by Soyica Diggs Colbert, Douglas A. Jones Jr., and Shane Vogel, 242–69. Durham, NC: Duke University Press.

Lara, Ana-Maurine. 2012. "Of Unexplained Presences, Flying Ife Heads, Vampires, Sweat, Zombies, and Legbas: A Meditation on Black Queer Aesthetics." *GLQ: A Journal of Lesbian and Gay Studies* 18 (2–3): 347–59.

———. 2018. "Strategic Universalisms and Dominican LGBT Activist Struggles for Civil and Human Rights." *Small Axe: A Caribbean Journal of Criticism* 22 (2): 99–114.

———. 2020. *Streetwalking: LGBTQ Lives and Protest in the Dominican Republic*. New Brunswick, NJ: Rutgers University Press.

Le nouvelliste (by Abélard, Jean Marc Hervé, Jeanty Junior Augustin, Natacha Bazelais). 2013. "NON au mariage homosexuel, vive la famille." YouTube, 6:27 min. Posted July 22, 2013. www.youtube.com/watch?v=TmLR_an_zOU.

Lescot, Anne, and Laurence Magloire, dirs. 2002. *Des hommes et des dieux (Of Men and Gods)*. Documentary. Watertown, MA: Documentary Educational Resources.

Lescot, Anne, and Laurence Magloire. 2017. "Reflections on the 15th Anniversary of the Documentary Film *Of Men and Gods/Des hommes et [des] dieux*, 2002, Interview with Anne Lescot and Laurence Magloire, Introduced by Katherine Smith."

Women and Performance: A Journal of Feminist Theory 27 (2). www.womenand
performance.org/ampersand/lescot-magloire-smith-27-2.

"Les homosexuels Haitiens veulent se marier." 2013. Plongaye, May 30, 2013. www
.plongaye.com/2013/05/30/les-homosexuels-haitiens-veulent-se-marier/. Accessed
June 9, 2014.

Leyburn, James Graham. 2004 [1941]. *The Haitian People.* 4th ed. New Haven, CT:
Yale University Press.

Littauer, Dan. 2013. "Two Men Beaten to Death during Haiti Anti-Gay Demonstration." LGBTQ Nation, July 20, 2013. www.lgbtqnation.com/2013/07/two-men
-beaten-to-death-during-haiti-anti-gay-demonstration/.

Lorde, Audre. 1982. *Zami: A New Spelling of My Name.* Watertown, MA: Persephone.

———. 1984. *Sister/Outsider: Essays and Speeches.* Berkeley, CA: Crossing Press.

Louis, Andre Jeantil. 1988. "Catholicism, Protestantism and a Model of Effective
Ministry in the Context of Voodoo in Haiti." DMin, Fuller Theological Seminary.
ProQuest 304481173.

Louis, Bertin M., Jr. 2011. "Haitian Protestant Views of Vodou and the Importance
of Karacte within a Transnational Social Field." *Journal of Haitian Studies* 17
(1): 211–27.

Lowenthal, Ira P. 1976. "Haiti: Behind Mountains, More Mountains." *Reviews in Anthropology* 3 (6): 656–69.

Luibhéid, Eithne. 2008. "Queer/Migration: An Unruly Body of Scholarship." *GLQ:
A Journal of Lesbian and Gay Studies* 14 (2): 169–90.

Manalansan, Martin F., IV. 2003. *Global Divas: Filipino Gay Men in the Diaspora.*
Durham, NC: Duke University Press.

Marcus, George E. 1995. "Ethnography In/Of the World System: The Emergence of
Multi-Sited Ethnography." *Annual Review of Anthropology* 24 (1): 95–117.

Massad, Joseph Andoni. 2002. "Re-Orienting Desire: The Gay International and the
Arab World." *Public Culture* 14 (2): 361–85.

———. 2007. *Desiring Arabs.* Chicago: University of Chicago Press.

Mbembe, Achille. 2003. "Necropolitics." *Public Culture* 15 (1): 11–40.

McAlister, Elizabeth. 2000. "Love, Sex, and Gender Embodied: The Spirits of Haitian
Vodou." In *Love, Sex, and Gender in the World Religions*, edited by Joseph Runzo
and Nancy M Martin, 128–45. Oxford: One World.

———. 2002. *Rara! Vodou, Power, and Performance in Haiti and Its Diaspora.* Berkeley: University of California Press.

———. 2012. "From Slave Revolt to a Blood Pact with Satan: The Evangelical Rewriting of Haitian History." *Studies in Religion/Sciences Religieuses* 41 (2): 187–215.

———. 2014. "The Color of Christ in Haiti." *Journal of Africana Religions* 2 (3): 409–18.

McCune, Jeffrey Q., Jr. 2014. *Sexual Discretion: Black Masculinity and the Politics of
Passing.* Chicago: University of Chicago Press.

McGranahan, Carole, and John F. Collins, eds. 2018. *Ethnographies of U.S. Empire.*
Durham, NC: Duke University Press.

Melamed, Jodi. 2011. *Represent and Destroy: Rationalizing Violence in the New Racial Capitalism*. Minneapolis: University of Minnesota Press.

Ménard-Saint Clair, Yola. 2012. "Causes of Conversion from Catholicism to Protestantism in Haiti and the Role of Vodou after Conversion." MA thesis, Florida International University.

Métraux, Alfred. 1959. *Voodoo in Haiti*. Translated by Hugo Charteris. New York: Schocken Books.

Michel, Claudine, Patrick Bellegarde-Smith, and Marlène Racine-Toussaint. 2006. "From the Horses' Mouths: Women's Words/Women's Worlds." In *Haitian Vodou: Spirit, Myth, and Reality*, edited by Patrick Bellegarde-Smith and Claudine Michel, 70–84. Bloomington: Indiana University Press.

Mintz, Sidney Wilfred. 1985. *Sweetness and Power: The Place of Sugar in Modern History*. New York: Viking.

Mobley, Christina Frances. 2015. "The Kongolese Atlantic: Central African Slavery and Culture from Mayombe to Haiti." PhD diss., Duke University.

Moraga, Cherríe, and Gloria Anzaldúa, eds. 1981. *This Bridge Called My Back: Writings by Radical Women of Color*. 1st ed. Watertown, MA: Persephone.

Moreau de Saint-Méry, Médéric Louis Elie. 1789. *Description Topographique, Physique, Civile, Politique et Historique de La Partie Francaise de L'isle Saint Domingue*. Vol. 1. A. Philadelphie.

Morrison, Toni. 1987. *Beloved*. New York: Knopf.

Muñoz, José Esteban. 1996. "Ephemera as Evidence: Introductory Notes to Queer Acts." *Women and Performance: A Journal of Feminist Theory* 8 (2): 5–16.

———. 1999. *Disidentifications: Queers of Color and the Performance of Politics*. Minneapolis: University of Minnesota Press.

Murray, David A. B. 2012. *Flaming Souls: Homosexuality, Homophobia, and Social Change in Barbados*. Toronto: University of Toronto Press.

———, ed. 2009. *Homophobias: Lust and Loathing across Time and Space*. Durham, NC: Duke University Press.

Nixon, Angelique V. 2011. "Steve Leguerre—'LGBT Activism in Haiti through SEROvie'—Interview with Angelique V. Nixon." Theorizing Homophobias in the Caribbean: Complexities of Place, Desire and Belonging." Caribbean IRN Collection on the Digital Library of the Caribbean. www.caribbeanhomophobias.org/steevelaguerre.

———. 2015. *Resisting Paradise: Tourism, Diaspora, and Sexuality in Caribbean Culture*. Jackson: University of Mississippi Press.

Nwokocha, Eziaku. 2019. "The 'Queerness' of Ceremony: Possession and Sacred Space in Haitian Religion." *Journal of Haitian Studies* 25 (3): 71–90.

Olsen, Scott H. 1993. "Reverend L. Ton Evans and the United States Occupation of Haiti." *Caribbean Studies* 26 (1/2): 23–48.

Padgett, Tim. 2006. "The Most Homophobic Place on Earth?" *Time*, April 12, 2006. http://content.time.com/time/world/article/0,8599,1182991,00.html.

Patterson, Orlando. 1982. *Slavery and Social Death: A Comparative Study*. Cambridge, MA: Harvard University Press.

Patton, Cindy. 1985. "Heterosexual AIDS Panic: A Queer Paradigm." *Gay Community News*, February 9, 1985.

Payne, Nicole Carelock. 2012. "A Leaky House: Haiti in the Religious Aftershock of the 2010 Earthquake." PhD diss., Rice University. ProQuest 1272368309.

Pellegrini, Ann. 1992. "S(h)ifting the Terms of Hetero/Sexism: Gender, Power, and Homophobias." In *Homophobia: How We All Pay the Price*, edited by Warren J. Blumenfeld, 39–56. Boston: Beacon.

Pérez, Emma. 2003. "Queering the Borderlands: The Challenges of Excavating the Invisible and the Unheard." *Frontiers: A Journal of Women's Studies* 24 (2–3): 122–31.

Pharr, Suzanne. 1997. *Homophobia: A Weapon of Sexism*. Berkeley, CA: Chardon Press.

Pierre-Louis, Francois. 2011. "Earthquakes, Nongovernmental Organizations, and Governance in Haiti." *Journal of Black Studies* 42 (2): 186–202.

Pierre-Pierre, Gary. 2010. "Haitian Earthquake Unleashes Animosity against Voodoo." *Haitian Times-MSNBC*, March 3, 2010. http://thegrio.com/2010/03/03/haitian-earthquake-unleashed-animosity-against-voodooists/.

Plummer, Brenda Gayle. 1982. "The Afro-American Response to the Occupation of Haiti, 1915–1934." *Phylon* (1960–) 43 (2): 125–43. https://doi.org/10.2307/274462.

Polyné, Millery. 2010. *From Douglass to Duvalier: U.S. African Americans, Haiti, and Pan Americanism, 1870–1964*. Gainesville: University Press of Florida.

Puar, Jasbir K. 2007. *Terrorist Assemblages: Homonationalism in Queer Times*. Durham, NC: Duke University Press.

Ramsey, Kate. 1995. "Vodou and Nationalism: The Staging of Folklore in Mid-Twentieth Century Haiti." *Women and Performance: A Journal of Feminist Theory* 7 (2): 187–218.

———. 2011. *The Spirits and the Law: Vodou and Power in Haiti*. Chicago: University of Chicago Press.

Redfield, Peter. 2005. "Doctors, Borders, and Life in Crisis." *Cultural Anthropology* 20 (3): 328–61.

Renda, Mary A. 2001. *Taking Haiti: Military Occupation and the Culture of U.S. Imperialism, 1915–1940*. Chapel Hill: University of North Carolina Press.

Rey, Terry. 2004. "Marketing the Goods of Salvation: Bourdieu on Religion." *Religion* 34 (4): 331–43.

Robertson, Pat. 2010. *The 700 Club*. Christian Broadcasting Network. Broadcast January 13, 2010. www.cbn.com/tv/1424261392001.

Robinson, Cedric J. 1983. *Black Marxism: The Making of the Black Radical Tradition*. Chapel Hill: University of North Carolina Press.

Romain, Charles-Poisset. 1986. *Le Protestantisme dans la societe Haitienne*. Port-au-Prince: Imprimerie Henri Deschamps.

Rowell, Charles H. 1992. "Interview with Frankétienne." *Callaloo* 15 (2): 385–92.

Rubin, David A. 2015. "Provincializing Intersex: US Intersex Activism, Human Rights, and Transnational Body Politics." *Frontiers: A Journal of Women Studies* 36 (3): 51–83.

Rubin, Gayle. 1984. "Thinking Sex: Notes for a Radical Theory of the Politics of Sexuality." In *Pleasure and Danger: Exploring Female Sexuality*, edited by Carole S. Vance, 267–319. New York: Routledge.

Said, Edward W. 1979. *Orientalism*. New York: Vintage.

Saint, Assotto. 1996. *Spells of a Voodoo Doll*. New York: Masquerade Books.

Salih, Sara. 2007. "'Our People Know the Difference, Black Is a Race, Jew Is a Religion, F*g**tism Is a Sin': Towards a Queer Postcolonial Hermeneutics." *Wasafiri* 22 (2): 1–5.

Schuller, Mark. 2010. "Fault Lines: Haiti's Earthquake and Reconstruction, through the Eyes of Many." *Huffington Post*, March 3, 2010. www.huffingtonpost.com.

———. 2012. *Killing with Kindness: Haiti, International Aid, and NGOs*. New Brunswick, NJ: Rutgers University Press.

Seabrook, William. 1929. *The Magic Island*. New York: Harcourt, Brace.

Sedgwick, Eve Kosofsky. 1985. *Between Men: English Literature and Male Homosocial Desire*. New York: Columbia University Press.

———. 1990. *Epistemology of the Closet*. Berkeley: University of California Press.

Shah, Nayan. 2005. "Policing Privacy, Migrants, and the Limits of Freedom." *Social Text* 23 (3–4): 275–84.

Sheller, Mimi. 2003. *Consuming the Caribbean: From Arawaks to Zombies*. New York: Routledge.

Snyder, Mark. 2017. "UN SEA: Sexual Exploitation and Abuse at the Hands of the United Nation's Stabilization Mission in Haiti." CEPR, January. https://cepr.net/images/documents/UNSEA_11JAN17_FINAL.pdf.

Somerville, Siobhan. 2000. *Queering the Color Line: Race and the Invention of Homosexuality in American Culture*. Durham, NC: Duke University Press.

Spivak, Gayatri Chakravorty. 1999. *A Critique of Postcolonial Reason: Toward a History of the Vanishing Present*. Cambridge, MA: Harvard University Press.

Stallings, L. H. 2015. *Funk the Erotic: Transaesthetics and Black Sexual Cultures*. Urbana: University of Illinois Press.

St. John, Sir Spenser. 1884. *Hayti: Or, The Black Republic*. Edinburgh and London: Smith, Elder, & Company.

Strings, Sabina. 2019. *Fearing the Black Body: The Racial Origins of Fat Phobia*. New York: New York University Press.

Strongman, Roberto. 2002. "Syncretic Religion and Dissident Sexualities." In *Queer Globalizations: Citizenship and the Afterlife of Colonialism*, edited by Arnaldo Cruz-Malavé and Martin F. Manalansan IV, 176–92. New York: New York University Press.

———. 2008. "Transcorporeality in Vodou." *Journal of Haitian Studies* 14 (2): 4–29.

———. 2019. *Queering Black Atlantic Religions: Transcorporeality in Candomblé, Santería, and Vodou*. Durham, NC: Duke University Press.

Sudbury, Julia, and Margo Okazawa-Rey, eds. 2015. *Activist Scholarship: Antiracism, Feminism, and Social Change*. New York: Routledge.

Taylor, Diana. 2003. *The Archive and the Repertoire: Performing Cultural Memory in the Americas*. Durham, NC: Duke University Press.

Thomas, Deborah A. 2011. *Exceptional Violence: Embodied Citizenship in Transnational Jamaica*. Durham, NC: Duke University Press.

Thomsen, Carly. 2021. *Visibility Interrupted: Rural Queer Life and the Politics of Unbecoming*. Minneapolis: University of Minnesota Press.

Thoreson, Ryan Richard. 2014. *Transnational LGBT Activism*. Minneapolis: University of Minnesota Press.

Tift, Kristyl D. 2018. "Embodying Intersections: The Performance Poetry of Staceyann Chin and Lenelle Moïse." *New England Theatre Journal* 29 (1): 73–92.

Tinsley, Omise'eke Natasha. 2008. "Black Atlantic, Queer Atlantic: Queer Imaginings of the Middle Passage." *GLQ: A Journal of Lesbian and Gay Studies* 14 (2): 191–215.

———. 2010. *Thiefing Sugar: Eroticism between Women in Caribbean Literature*. Durham, NC: Duke University Press.

———. 2011. "Songs for Ezili: Vodou Epistemologies of (Trans)Gender." *Feminist Studies* 37 (2): 417–36.

———. 2018. *Ezili's Mirrors: Imagining Black Queer Genders*. Durham, NC: Duke University Press.

Trouillot, Michel-Rolph. 1990a. *Haiti-State against Nation: Origins and Legacy of Duvalierism*. New York: Monthly Review Press.

———. 1990b. "The Odd and the Ordinary: Haiti, the Caribbean, and the World." *Vibrant: Virtual Brazilian Anthropology* 17. Accessed at www.scielo.br/j/vb/a/CdG s6BGmKfrWCpm4p7kq9Mp/?lang=en.

———. 1995. *Silencing the Past: Power and the Production of History*. Boston: Beacon.

———. 2003. *Global Transformations: Anthropology and the Modern World*. New York: Palgrave Macmillan.

Ulysse, Gina Athena. 2015. *Why Haiti Needs New Narratives: A Post-Quake Chronicle*. Translated by Nadève Ménard and Évelyne Trouillot. Middletown, CT: Wesleyan University Press.

"UN Police in Haiti Accused of Sexual Abuse." 2012. BBC News, January 23, 2012. www.bbc.com/news/world-latin-america-16693441.

Valdman, Albert, Iskra Iskrova, and Benjamin Hebblethwaite. 2007. *Haitian Creole-English Bilingual Dictionary*. Bloomington: Indiana University, Creole Institute.

Valentine, David. 2007. *Imagining Transgender: An Ethnography of a Category*. Durham, NC: Duke University Press.

Vance, Carole S., ed. 1984. *Pleasure and Danger: Exploring Female Sexuality*. New York: Routledge.

Vimalassery, Manu, Juliana Hu Pegues, and Alyosha Goldstein. 2016. "Introduction: On Colonial Unknowing." *Theory and Event* 19 (4). https://muse.jhu.edu/article/633283.

Wagner, Laura Rose. 2014. "Haiti Is a Sliding Land: Displacement, Community, and Humanitarianism in Post-Earthquake Port-Au-Prince." PhD diss., University of North Carolina. Proquest.

Wahab, Amar. 2012. "Homophobia as the State of Reason: The Case of Postcolonial Trinidad and Tobago." *GLQ: A Journal of Lesbian and Gay Studies* 18 (4): 481–505.

———. 2020. "'The Darker the Fruit'? Homonationalism, Racialized Homophobia, and Neoliberal Tourism in the St Lucian–US Contact Zone." *International Feminist Journal of Politics* 23 (1): 80–101.

Walcott, Rinaldo. 2016. *Queer Returns: Essays on Multiculturalism, Diaspora, and Black Studies.* London, ON: Insomniac Press.

Walters, Christian. 2013. "Haitian Anti-Gay Marriage Protesters Kill Two Men, Threaten to Burn Down Parliament." Towleroad.com, July 22, 2013. www.towleroad.com/2013/07/haitian-anti-gay-marriage-protesters-kill-two-men-threaten-to-burn-down-parliament-video.

Warner, Michael. 1993. *Fear of a Queer Planet: Queer Politics and Social Theory.* Minneapolis: University of Minnesota Press.

Weaver, Karol K. 2006. *Medical Revolutionaries: The Enslaved Healers of Eighteenth-Century Saint Domingue.* Urbana: University of Illinois Press.

Weinberg, George H. 1972. *Society and the Healthy Homosexual.* New York: Anchor Press/Doubleday.

Weisbrot, Mark. 2011. "Is This Minustah's 'Abu Ghraib Moment' in Haiti?" *Guardian,* September 3, 2011. www.theguardian.com.

Weiss, Meredith L., and Michael J. Bosia, eds. 2013. *Global Homophobia: States, Movements, and the Politics of Oppression.* Urbana: University of Illinois Press.

Wekker, Gloria. 2006. *The Politics of Passion: Women's Sexual Culture in the Afro-Surinamese Diaspora.* New York: Columbia University Press.

Wenger, Tisa. 2017. *Religious Freedom: The Contested History of an American Ideal.* Chapel Hill: University of North Carolina Press.

Williams, Robert A., Jr. 1990. *The American Indian in Western Legal Thought: The Discourses of Conquest.* New York: Oxford University Press.

Williamson, Terrion L. 2017. "Why Did They Die? On Combahee and the Serialization of Black Death." *Souls: A Critical Journal of Black Politics, Culture, and Society* 19 (3): 328–41.

Zanotti, Laura. 2010. "Cacophonies of Aid, Failed State Building and NGOs in Haiti: Setting the Stage for Disaster, Envisioning the Future." *Third World Quarterly* 31 (5): 755–71.

INDEX

Page numbers in *italics* refer to figures.

abortion, 175
abuse, 78, 81, 146, 153, 165, 187
Acker, Kathy, 106
activism, 2, 4, 12, 39–41, 49, 74, 93, 95, 159, 172, 176, 191; Black Lives Matter and, 21, 188–90; Haitian, 5, 15, 20, 186, 198n10; of Kouraj, 160–61, 167, 170, 182; queer, 14, 118. *See also* anti-imperialism; social movements
Africa, 3, 10, 54, 88, 101, 114, 118, 138, 179; global LGBTQI and, 162, 178; Haiti and, 7–8, 30–32, 40, 50, 53, 121; voodoo/vaudoux and, 6, 37–38, 55, 59, 62; West, 28–29, 34, 195n10; zonbi and, 26–29
African American Policy Forum: *Say Her Name*, 188–89
African American studies, 28
Africanisms, 195n10
African-ness, 116
African diaspora, 13, 55
Afro-centrism, 13
Agamben, Giorgio, 132
ageism, 98
AIDS Coalition to Unleash Power (ACT UP), 17
AIDS industrial complex, 134. *See also* HIV/AIDS
Alexander, M. Jacqui, 11, 95–96
Alexander VI (pope), 27

Alison, 140, 144–45
allegory, 25–26, 119–21
Allen, Jafari S., 179
Alphonse, Maïlé, 199n12
American Foundation for AIDS Research (amfAR), 139
American Red Cross, 155, 200n24
American studies, 12
Americas, 3, 26–29, 33, 50, 53, 95, 116, 194n6
amnesia, 28–29
Amnesty International, xxi, 128–29, 190
anal sex, 37
ancestors, 33, 71, 116
animality, 37, 172
animal sacrifice, 42, 48. *See also* voodoo/vaudoux (concept)
Anri, 113–14
anthropological imaginary, 199n20
anthropology, 3, 13–16, 44, 50, 54, 179, 199n20; anthropologists, 9, 17, 28–29, 33, 45, 47, 63, 69, 102, 131
anti-Blackness, 8, 24–25, 45, 50, 60–61, 179, 187–90, 192, 193n1
anticolonialism, 10, 13
anti-dependency, 58
antidiscrimination, 116, 140–41
anti-gay protests, 170–81, 190
antiheros, 120
antihomophobia, 9, 14, 21, 74, 93, 105, 115, 150, 152, 159, 161–62
anti-immigration discourse, 9

anti-imperialism, 13, 41, 48, 82, 116; Lakou and, 122, 125–26, 160, 186; zonbi and, 18, 20, 24–25, 105–6, 118–19

antiracism, 189

Antoine, Régis, 120

Anzaldùa, Gloria E., 106

apartheid, 10, 88

Appolon, Jean, 80

Aristide, Jean-Bertrand, 122–23

art, xxi–xxii, *43*, 106–7, 110, 113, 118, 141–42, 199n15; graffiti, xxiii, 5, 124, 192; murals, 5, 6, 68. *See also* FOSAJ arts center; literature; performance studies

artists, dedications to, xix–xxiii

Asia, 50, 122

assaults, 20, 83, 92, 175, 177, 189

Assembly of God, 76

association (anthropological model), 13

Astraea Lesbian Foundation for Justice, 131, 137, 140–45, 155, 178, 185, 199n15, 199n17, 200n24

atheism, 69

Atis Rezistans, xxi, 106–7, 196n1

autoeroticism, 37

autonomy, 8, 10, 185

Avadra, xix–xx, xxii–xxiii, 82, 116–17, 198n6; homophobic violence and, 100–101, 152, 190; Lakou and, 102, 113–16, 160

Ayiti, 27

Baartman, Sara/Sarah (Hottentot Venus), 37

Bahamas, 11, 95

balance, 13, 72, 116, 163

bands, Kanaval, 115

Baptists, 39, 55, 57, 61, 63, 68, 76–77, 81–82, 148–51

Barbados, 11, 58

barbarism, 34–36, 38

bare life, 145–46

Bawon Samedi, 66, 107

Beaumont, Charles, 44

Bellegarde-Smith, Patrick, 62

Belvins, Thurman, 187

Berlant, Lauren, 117, 184

betiz (innuendo), 115

Bible, 170, 173; Genesis, 117

biennales, xxi, 20, 103, 105–26

Bigaud, Wilson, 108–9, *110*

biopolitics, 10, 24, 129, 139–40, 145, 154

bisexual Haitians, 14, 48, 75, 78, 90, 113, 117, 142–43, 165, 198n6; global LGBTQI and,

1, 9, 130, 133, 168; SEROvie and, 134–36, 138, 183

Black death, 21, 187–90, 192

Black feminism, 21, 32, 71, 188–90, 192, 193n1

Black freedom, 32–33, 40, 50

Black homophobia, 179–80

Black liberation, 32, 40, 50, 195n2. *See also* Haitian Revolution (1791–1804)

Black Lives Matter, 21, 32, 187–90, 192

black pigs (domestic animal), 32, 122

Black republic, 23, 33–38, 153, 179; US imperialism and, 8, 19, 46, 54–55, 61, 63, 118, 185; voodoo/vaudoux and, 6–7, 18, 24, 49–51, 105, 125

Black studies, 12, 67

blan (foreigners), 14, 16, 133, 161, 169, 181, 198n9

Bland, Sandra, 187, 189

blood, 5, 32, 102, 177; voodoo/vaudoux and, 25, 37, 47–48, 57, 61, 149, 195n2

bocors, 62

bonboch (rowdy party), 112

Bosia, Michael J., 9

Boston, 15, 80, 92, 189, 192

Boukman, Dutty, 32

British colonialism, 9, 34–35, 37, 95, 180

Brooks, David, 54–56, 58–60, 195n3

Brown, Karen McCarthy, 102

Brown, Michael, 187

Busy, xxi, 102, 107

Butler, Judith, 10, 101, 196n1

Bwa Kayiman, 32–33, 57, 195n2

Cacos, 39

call and response, 170–72

Cameroon, 178

Canada, 15, 107, 133, 141, 163, 177, 195n5

cannibalism, 33–35, 37–38, 42, 50, 53, 61–62, 79

capacity, 1, 7, 35, 60, 132, 137, 145, 153–54

capitalism, 39–40, 54, 118, 184, 186, 190, 198n10; modern, 25, 29; racial, ix, 3, 12, 26, 37, 50

Caribbean, xx, 37, 47–48, 63, 116, 118, 121–22, 139, 146, 195n10; heteropatriarchy and, 95, 194n3; homophobia and, 7, 11–12, 51, 178–79

Caribbean studies, 3, 13, 135, 194n8

cartography, 116–17

Cassandre, 150–51

Castile, Philando, 187

Cathédrale de Sainte Trinité, 68

Cathédrale Saint-Jacques et Saint-Philippe, 67

Catholicism, xvii, 1, 27, 54–55, 65, 67–68, 94, 117, 150; homophobia and, 7, 19, 55–56, 69–70, 72–79, 83, 100, 129–30, 148; Lakou and, 122, 124; LGBT Haitians and, 15, 73–74, 79–80, 82; Pierre-Louis controversy and, 91, 96, 98, 103; Protestantism and, 55–56, 59–62, 64; same-sex marriage and, 174, 176; Vodou and, 19, 35, 61–62, 72–73

Center for Gender and Refugee Studies, 200n6

chantè (singer), 108, 124

Chapman, Dasha A., 13–14, 194n7, 196n8

Charles, 100, 150

Charles, Carolle, 4

Chidester, David, 53–54

child sacrifice, 34–35, 37–38, 50, 62

cholera, 154

chorus, 111–12, 124–25. *See also* "Zonbi, Zonbi" (performance)

Christian Broadcasting Network (CBN), 57

Christianity, evangelical. *See* Protestantism (evangelical Christianity)

Christophe, Henri, 32

chrononormativity, 171

Church Growth Movement, 195n2

Church of Jesus Christ of Latter-day Saints, 64, 81, 176

CIA, 123

Ciné Institute, xxii

civilizational discourse, 34–35, 38, 41–42, 46, 59–60, 63, 176–77

civil society, 63, 87, 97–98

Clark, Jamar, 187

class, xxiii, 3–4, 39, 89, 117, 144–45, 190; homophobia and, 74–75, 78; LGBT Haitians and, 106–7, 142, 147, 181, 183

Clinton, Bill, 89, 97

Clorox hunger, 89

closet, concept of, 36, 75

Coalition Haïtienne des organisations religieuses et morales (CHO), 173–74, 178

Coalition of African Lesbians, 162

coalition politics, 14, 25, 159, 174–75

Cohen, Cathy, 25, 50, 118

Cold War, 121

Cole, Eli, 41

Collins, Patricia Hill, 37

Columbus, Christopher, 27, 194n6

Combahee River Collective (CRC), 32, 189–90, 192, 196n1

community, discourse of, 2, 133, 136–37

Congrès National de la Population LGBT, 2, 162–66

consumption, 11, 30, 37, 39, 42, 115, 197n4

conversion, 1, 64–65, 72, 79–82, 94

corvée (statute labor system), 39–41, 46

counter-plantation systems, 33

coups d'état, 123

Craven, Wes, 47

Crenshaw, Kimberlé Williams, 188, 201n1

creolization, 14, 133

criminal intimacies, 118, 125, 186

criminalization, 2, 9–11, 34, 79, 81, 83, 142–43, 163, 179, 187–88

critical ethnic studies, 12

crossdressing, 51, 115

cruel optimism, 184

Cuba, 39, 60, 179

Cullors, Patrisse, 187

cultural capital, xxiii, 144–45, 152, 183–84

cultural studies, 47

culture wars, 8

Currier, Ashley, 10

dance, xx, 15, 91, 171, 196n8; Vodou and, 66–67, 80, 161; in "Zonbi, Zonbi," 109, 112–13, 115; zonbi and, 26. *See also* Lakou

dance hall scene, 179

Daniel, xxii–xxiii, 69–70, 74, 78, 183–84, 191

Dash, J. Michael, 17, 42, 47, 121

Daut, Marlene, 188

Davis, Madeline, 69

Davis, Wade, 46–47

Dayan, Colin, 26, 33, 38

death threats, 190–91

de Bruijn, Wilfred de, 177

Decena, Carlos Ulises, 74

dechoukaj, 122

decoloniality, 13, 23, 95, 183

dedications, xvii–xxiii, 193n1

"Deklarasyon Masisi" (Kouraj), 167, 200–201n8

demilitarization, 154–55. *See also* militarization

demonic influence, 24, 57–59, 62, 64, 149, 195n2, 199n21

Denis, Maksaens: *Voodoo Divas*, 16

deportation, xviii, 142

Deren, Maya, 25

de Saint-Méry, Médéric Louis Moreau, 35
desire, 24–25, 44, 48, 51, 69, 124–25, 184;
  same-sex, 3–4, 13, 23, 49, 55, 117, 194n8;
  Vodou and, 70, 72, 80–81. *See also* LGBT
  Haitians
Dessalines, Jean-Jacques, 32–33, 107, 167
development, 62–64, 87–89, 117, 136, 160,
  168, 171–72, 185; US occupation and, 19,
  55; voodoo/vaudoux and, 7, 41, 58–59, 69
Dézafi (Frankétienne), 106, 119–25, 197n8
dictatorship, 23, 58, 62, 119, 121
discretion, 69, 73–76, 79, 83, 196n11; Kouraj
  and, 181, 200–201n8; Pierre-Louis controversy and, 91, 96, 98, 100, 102–3
disidentification, 25, 169
disownment, 49, 78
dispossession, 27, 38, 116, 118, 122
diversity, 141–42, 168
divine retribution, 56, 151–52, 199n21. *See
  also* earthquake of 2010
Dole Amendment (1995), 63, 132
domination, 30, 37, 94, 96, 103, 137; imperialism and, 20, 34, 40, 105, 124–25
Dominican Republic, 15, 57–58, 61, 74–75,
  101, 113, 135, 177–79, 198n8; colonialism
  and, 3, 27; US imperialism and, 39, 82
Domond, Destin, 107
Dorme, 100
Dougé-Prosper, Mamyrah A., 194n7
Douglass, Frederick, 34–36
drums, 26, 36, 80, 107–9, 112, 116
Dubois, Laurent, 30, 114, 153, 194n4
Dupont, Reginald, 136, 147
Duvalier, François "Papa Doc," 23, 62, 119,
  121
Duvalier, Jean-Claude "Baby Doc," 23, 63,
  79, 119, 121–22

earthquake of 2010, xvii, 60, 67, 153–54, 161,
  170, 180–81, 192, 195n5, 198n8, 199n18;
  global LGBTQI and, 130–55, 159–60, 162,
  167, 185, 198n6, 198n10; homophobia and,
  1–2, 7, 18, 20, 83, 129–30, 148–52, 164–65,
  179; Lakou and, 103, 126; religious/im-
  perial discourse of, 54, 56–60, 152, 173,
  199–200nn21–22
economic homosexuality, 48–49
economic mobility, xxiii, 142, 183–84. *See
  also* class
Édouard-Alexis, Jacques, 89

Elton John Foundation, 165
embargo, 123, 132
embeddedness, queer, 11
encomienda system, 27
Enlightenment, 59
enunciation/denunciation, 19, 56, 76–77, 79,
  91, 102. *See also* Protestantism (evangelical Christianity)
Episcopal Church, 60, 64, 68
eroticism, 25, 37, 44, 54
Esther, 81–82
ethnography, 3, 12, 44–46, 54, 65, 74–75, 152,
  195n10; methodology of book and, 13,
  15–16, 55, 131; *Of Men and Gods*, 16–17,
  165–66, 194n8; patchwork, 15–16
ethnology, 29, 46, 121, 197n7
Eugène, 107
Europe, 29, 34, 37, 59, 179
European colonialism, 17–18, 23–24, 39, 50,
  53–54, 94, 105, 185, 194n6; Black republic
  and, 34–38; British, 9, 34–35, 37, 95, 180;
  French, 2–4, 11, 28–32, 34–35, 54, 57, 72,
  124, 174; Haitian Revolution and, 30–33;
  homophobia and, 7–9, 12, 51, 129, 192;
  Spanish, 3, 27–28, 116, 179
evangelical Christianity. *See* Protestantism
  (evangelical Christianity)
Evans, Lewis Ton, 39–40, 55, 60–61
exceptionalism, 7–9, 11, 60, 130, 178–79. *See
  also* state of exception
expansionism, 29, 33, 36, 39
extramarital relationships, 4, 63
Ezili, 118. See also *lwa* (spirits)
Ezili Dantò, 32, 70–71
Ezili Freda, 70

family, xviii, 30, 41, 87, 98, 114–15, 142, 147,
  150; anti-gay protests and, 170–71, 173–76;
  methodology of book and, xix, 15–16, 67–
  68; religious homophobia and, 70, 73–81,
  83, 92–93, 100–101, 103, 113, 191; Vodou
  and, 70–72, 118. *See also* kinship
Fanmi Lavalas, 122
Farmer, Paul, 48–49, 154
Fatiman, Cécile, 32
feminism, 4, 10, 37, 81, 97–98, 197n10; activism and, 15; Black, 21, 32, 71, 189–90, 192,
  193n1; Black Lives Matter and, 188–90;
  Chicana, 106; Haitian, 19, 90, 92–94, 96,
  140; feminist studies/theory, 13, 54, 93–95,

131–32; Indigenous, 188; lesbian, 106, 140; lesbian of color, 196n1; transnational, 12–13, 131–32; women of color, 188

Femme en Action Contre la Stigmatisation el la Discrimination Sexuelle (FACSDIS), 136, 162–63, 165, 182, 185

Ferdinand (king), 27

Ferreyra, Marcelo Ernesto, 146

Fèt Gede, 65–66, 113

fetishism, 29, 34–35, 50, 53–54. *See also* voodoo/vaudoux (concept)

Figge Art Museum, 110

Fischer, M. Nigel, 163

five-to-ten stories method, 69

Flore, 99

Floyd, George, 187

focus groups, 16, 78, 146–47, 182

fòklò, 118, 197n7

Fon (language), 3

Fondasyon Konsesans ak Libète/Knowledge and Liberty Foundation (FOKAL), 88–89

Fondasyon SEROvie. *See* SEROvie

food crisis (2008), 89, 97

foreign intervention, 58, 89–90, 105, 122–26, 132, 162; global LGBTQI and, 5–6, 20, 140, 169, 184; US, in Haiti, 8, 24, 36, 39, 47, 54–55, 63, 94, 192

Forge, Gérard, 173

FOSAJ arts center, xxi–xxii, 65–66, 105–7, 112–14, 118, 137, 197n4, 198–99n10, 199n18; Astraea and, 140–45, 185, 199n15

Foucault, Michel, 10, 17, 96, 184, 196n1, 197n6

Fox, Samara D., 146–47

France, xxiii, 3–4, 15, 28, 34, 75, 123, 141, 173–77, 195n5

Franck, xix, xxiii, 82, 100–101, 113–14, 152, 190

Francophone literature, 119–20

Frankétienne, 106, 119–22, 197nn8–9, 197n9

French Code Noir, 4, 30, 54, 63, 124

French colonialism, 2–4, 11, 28–32, 34–35, 54, 57, 72, 124, 174. *See also* European colonialism

Froude, James Anthony, 34–35, 37

funding, 136, 139–46, 155, 160, 163, 165–66, 196n3, 198–99n10, 199n12. *See also* grants

funerals, 68

futurity, 19, 21, 30, 38, 44, 54, 106, 169, 171, 191–92

Garner, Eric, 187

Garner, Margaret, 38

Garza, Alicia, 187

Gay International, 9, 130. *See also* global LGBTQI

gay men, 48–49, 51, 73–75, 77–82, 92, 95, 118, 150, 172, 190; FOSAJ and, 142–44; global LGBTQI and, 1–2, 9, 130, 133–35, 138, 148, 165, 178; HIV/AIDS and, 47–49; Pierre-Louis controversy and, 100–101; SEROvie and, 138, 166, 168, 183; terminology, 4, 14; Vodou and, 116, 166

gede, 66, 107

gender, 3, 12–13, 16–17, 93, 95, 115–17, 119, 124, 174, 197n10; anti-Black racism and, 188–89; colonialism and, 10, 18, 167; global LGBTQI and, 2, 7, 9, 130, 132, 142–43, 146, 164, 183; Kouraj and, 168–70; and queer, meaning of, 14, 25; Vodou and, 70–71, 82, 118, 166

gender-creative Haitians. *See* LGBT Haitians

genealogies, xvii, 27, 200–201n8. *See also* lineages

genocide, 3, 27

Germany, 107, 177

Ghetto Biennale, xxi, 20, 103, 105–7, 109, 112, 118, 126

Gill, Lyndon K., 11, 195n10

Gilles, Jean-Élie, xxi–xxii, 3, 76–79; *Sur les pas de Diogène*, 16, 74–75

Glissant, Édouard, 122

globalization, 8–10, 50

global LGBTQI, 1–2, 5, 14, 20–21, 126, 129–33, 152, 197n1, 198n6, 200n24; Haitian community impact, 132–37; harms of, 145–55, 184–85; imperialism and, 6–7, 9–10, 178–79; social movements and, 70, 137–45, 182–84, 199n15

Glover, Kaiama L., 119–20, 122, 197n9

Gordon, Leah, 197n11

gossip, 45, 72, 90–91, 103, 114

graffiti, xxiii, 5, 124, 192

Gran Lakou, 126, 141, 160. *See also* Lakou

grants, 136, 139–45, 155, 160, 163, 165, 196n3, 198–99n10, 199n12. *See also* funding

Grasadis, 134

Great Britain, 9, 34–35, 37, 95, 180, 185

Guam, 39

Guedé (spirit), 45–46

Gumbs, Alexis Pauline, 193n1

Haitian Coalition of Religious and Moral Organizations (CHO), 173–74, 178
Haitian Creole. *See* Kreyòl/Haitian Creole (language)
Haitian Creole Language and Culture Summer Institute, xix, 67, 92
Haitian Gays and Lesbians Alliance, xvii, 133
Haitian Independence, 8, 18, 23, 33, 35, 59–61, 114, 167; imperialism and, 39, 50, 54–55, 153
Haitian National Police, 124, 178
Haitian Rasta community, 142, 199n13
Haitian Revolution (1791–1804), 18, 23, 50, 54, 57, 70, 153, 167, 188, 195n2; history of, 30–34; Lakou and, 20, 124, 186; zonbi and, 26, 122, 125
Haitian studies, 13, 24, 49, 67, 94, 132, 168, 194nn7–8, 199n22
Haitian Studies Association, 13, 194n7
"Haiti's Scapegoats" (video), 179–81
Halperin, Victor, 42, 44–45
Harney, Stefano, 125, 184
Harrison, Benjamin, 36
Harrison, Lawrence E., 58
Hart, Lynda S., 95
Hartman, Saidiya, 28–29, 54
Hastings to Haiti Partnership (HHP), 165, 200n6
hate crimes, 5, 178
hate speech, 101
hermaphrodite people, 197n1, 197n5. *See also* intersex people
Herskovits, Frances, 28, 195n10
Herskovits, Melville Jean, 28, 44–45, 195n10
heterocentrism, 45
heteronormativity, 14, 117–18, 124. *See also* normativity
heteropatriarchy, 11, 19, 32, 81, 92–96, 118, 192, 194n3, 194n6
heterosexism, 95, 190
heterosexuality, 6, 50, 57, 74, 81–82, 113, 116–17, 134, 163, 197n6; anti-gay protests and, 174–76; colonialism/imperialism and, 3–4, 37; HIV/AIDS and, 48, 195n11; Kouraj and, 167–68; Lakou performance and, 124–25; marriage and, 37, 62–63, 75, 171; Pierre-Louis controversy and, 93–98, 103; voodoo/vaudoux and, 42, 44–45. *See also* heteropatriarchy
Hispaniola, 27–32, 57, 61, 82

HIV/AIDS, 1, 81, 142, 151, 167; activism, 12, 15, 17, 162–63; epidemic, 18, 23, 46–50, 196n1; prevention, xxiii, 132, 134–36, 138–39, 161, 198n4
Hollande, François, 174
Hollingsworth v. Perry, 175
Holly, James Theodore Augustus, 60–61
homelessness, 150, 160
Des hommes et dieux (Lescot and Magloire), 16–17, 165–66, 194n8
homoeroticism, 44
homophobia: anti-gay protests and, 170–78; earthquake of 2010 and, 129–30, 137, 148–52; FOSAJ and, 141; global LGBTQI and, 131–33, 145–48, 154–55, 184; in Haiti, 1–2, 7–8, 18–20, 192; Jamaica and, 179; Lakou and, 105, 112–13, 115–16, 123–26; MINUS-TAH and, 5–6; neoliberalism and, 129; Pierre-Louis controversy and, 19–20, 90–96, 99–103; public health and, 49; queer studies and, 8–10; social movements against, 20–21, 161–64, 166–70; as state of reason, 51; Vodou and, 71; world-mapping and, 117. *See also* religious homophobia
homo-protectionism, 2, 8
homosexuality, xvii, 5–6, 47–49, 113, 192, 195n10, 196n1, 197n6, 200n3; anti-gay protests and, 170, 173–74, 176–77; Catholicism and, 19, 69–70, 72–76, 79–82; colonialism/imperialism and, 2–4, 50–51; earthquake of 2010 and, 1, 18, 83, 130, 137, 148–52, 199n21; Lakou and, 115, 125–26; Pierre-Louis controversy and, 19, 90–92, 96–100, 103; Protestantism and, 19, 69–70, 76–79; and queer, meaning of, 14, 17, 117; social movements and, 133–34, 144, 162–64, 167–68, 178–83, 200n3; Vodou and, 19, 65, 70–72, 79–82, 153, 165–66; voodoo/vaudoux and, 7, 24, 36–38, 44–46, 53, 62
hooks, bell, 47
Hôtel Montana, 162, 165
Hottentot Venus (Sara/Sarah Baartman), 37
housing, 74, 78, 140, 142, 147, 149, 160, 186
Housing Works Inc., 162–63, 165, 168, 178, 200n5, 201n9
Howard, John, 193n2
Hughes, Langston, 40
humanitarianism, 3, 13, 57, 64, 131–32, 139, 146, 154, 163, 192. *See also* global LGBTQI
human rights, 9, 13–14, 70, 87, 129–30, 168, 177, 182, 190–91, 200n6; earthquake of

2010 and, 129–31, 153–54; global LGBTQI and, 1–2, 6–8, 21, 126, 138–40, 146, 161–63, 165–66, 178, 193n4
Huntington, Samuel P., 195n3
Hurbon, Laënnec, 30
Hurston, Zora Neale, 45–46
hypersexuality, 24, 35, 37, 45, 51, 62

identity politics, 2–4, 9–10, 14, 105, 152–53, 167, 169, 172, 181–84; global LGBTQI and, 20, 130–31, 133, 143, 145, 152
ignorance, 41, 49, 113, 117, 150, 167
immigration, 9, 74, 129, 179
immorality, 7, 34, 37, 59, 151–52, 170–71
imperialism. See US imperialism
imports, 2–4, 14, 27–28, 30, 48, 89, 96, 124, 167–68, 181
inclusivity, 126, 148, 154, 160, 185, 188
Indigenous Peoples, 3, 27, 53–54, 188
Indigenous studies, 3
innuendo, 103, 115. See also betiz (innuendo)
Institute for Justice and Democracy in Haiti, 200n6
Inter-American Commission on Human Rights (IACHR), 154, 201n4
Inter caetera, 27
interdisciplinarity, 8, 11–14, 17, 201n1
intergovernmental organizations (IGOs), 5, 133, 146, 154–55
internally displaced persons (IDP), 149
International Day Against Homophobia (IDAHO), 2, 20, 159–66, 200n5, 201n9
International Gay and Lesbian Human Rights Commission (IGLHRC), 2, 130–33, 137, 200n6, 200n24; imperialism and, 5–6, 145–49, 152–55, 178, 184–85; SEROvie and, 138–41, 160, 165
International Lesbian Gay Bisexual Trans and Intersex Association (ILGA), 162
International Women's Human Rights Clinic, 200n6
intersectionality, 12, 188, 190, 201n1
intersex people, 1, 9, 14, 130, 143, 162, 197n1, 197n5
interviews, 16, 121, 131, 134–36, 146–47, 150, 196n10, 197n9; with Avadra, 101, 198n6; and homophobia, 69, 78, 90–91, 152, 170, 177, 180; Kouraj and, 169, 173, 182
Isabella (queen), 27
Isla Española, 27
Islam, 130, 195n4
Islamophobia, 9

Jacmel, xviii, xix–xxiii, 74, 91, 133, 140, 144, 173, 176, 198n6; earthquake of 2010 and, 126, 148–50; Lakou and, 103, 105, 113, 115, 160; methodology of book and, 15, 60, 131, 142; religious homophobia in, 76–78, 82, 99–100, 102, 151; Vodou in, 67, 71–72, 80, 199–200n22
Jakobsen, Janet R., 59
Jamaica, 32, 35, 60–61, 107, 177–80
James, Erica Caple, 131, 145
Jan, Jean-Marie, 61–62
Jensen, Jane S., 93
Jeudy, Charlot, 163, 168–69, 172–73, 180–81, 191, 201n9
Johanne, 77
Johnson, Cary Alan, 137–39, 146, 198n9
Johnson, James Weldon, 40–41
Joseph, 78
Joseph, Miranda, 136–37, 198n10
Juni, 80
Junior, 77–78, 80, 151–52

kachè (hidden), 75
Kanaval, 73, 115
Kaoma, Kapya H., 11
Kathy Goes to Haiti (film), xxi, 106
Kay Famn (Women's House), 93
Keating, Cricket, 2
Kelly, xxii
Kempadoo, Kamala, 95, 194n3, 195n10
Kennedy, Elizabeth Lapovsky, 69
kidnapping, 5, 24, 38, 53, 79, 132
King, Alexander, 42, 43
King, Rosamond S., 11
kinship, 30, 114–15, 117, 125, 190. See also family
knowledge production, 20, 132–33, 146, 178
Kominote M, 161, 167–70, 172, 182
KOSANBA, 199–200n22
Kouraj, 5, 21, 160–70, 172–73, 180–83, 185, 190–91, 200–201n8, 201nn9–10
Kraft, Charles, 195n2
Kreyòl/Haitian Creole (language), 3–4, 64, 68, 75, 90, 119, 141–42, 170–71, 197n8; Haitian Creole Language and Culture Summer Institute, xix, 67, 92; LGBT Haitians and, 131, 133, 144, 164, 167–69, 181–83, 199n15; zonbi and, 29, 121
Kuser, J. Dryden, 41–42

labor, 27, 31, 40–41, 66–67, 114, 173, 184; zonbi and, 25–26, 28–30, 38–39, 119–20

Lady, 100
Laguerre, Michel S., 60
Laguerre, Steve, 135–36, 138, 147
laïcité, 176
Lakou, 67, 102–3, 113, 148, 152, 159–60, 181–
82, 199n11, 200–201n8; global LGBTQI
and, 140–41, 143–45, 154, 185–86, 198–
99n10; Vodou and, 114–16, 118; "Zonbi,
Zonbi," 20, 25, 105–12, 118–19, 122–26, 137
lakou system, 114
LaMothe, Mario, 13–14
Lara, Ana-Maurine, 169
Lasirenn (the mermaid), 3
Latin America, 56, 146, 179, 195n5
Latin American studies, 12
Latter-day Saints, 81
Lawrence v. Texas, 9
laws and legislation, 11–12, 30–31, 40–41,
95, 124, 161, 187, 189; global LGBTQI
and, 5, 7, 166; homophobia and, 9–10, 83,
164–65, 179–80; marriage and, 4, 53, 63,
159, 172–75
Leach, Edmund, 54
Le Baron, Ronald D., 48
Legba, 113–14, 148–49, 160
Lele, 80–81
lesbian baiting, 93–95. See also sexism
lesbians/lesbianism, 16, 32, 95, 106–7, 118,
168, 183, 196n1; FOSAJ and, 140, 142, 144;
global LGBTQI and, 1–2, 9, 14, 130–31,
133–37, 143, 162, 165; homophobia and,
76–78, 92–94, 115, 150; Pierre-Louis controversy and, 19–20, 83, 90–91, 96–99,
101–3; Vodou and, 45–46, 70–72, 80–81,
116
Levi Strauss Foundation, 163, 165
Leyburn, James Graham, 63
LGBT community, concept of, 2, 5, 131, 133–
38, 146, 182, 184, 197n1, 200n24
LGBT Haitians, 2–5, 7, 14–15, 48–49, 76–79,
190–92; anti-gay protests and, 172–74,
177–78; Catholicism and, 73–76, 79–82;
earthquake of 2010 and, 1–2, 20, 137,
148–52; global LGBTQI and, 131, 133–55,
184–85, 199n15, 200n24; Lakou and, 105,
115–16, 125; Pierre-Louis controversy and,
19–20, 90–92, 96, 99–103; postcolonial
homophobia and, 8, 10–11, 21, 180, 188;
religious homophobia and, 19, 56, 68–70,
82–83; social movements of, 20–21, 159–

70, 180–86; Vodou and, 70–72, 79–82, 118,
153, 165–66
LGBTI film festival (2016), 18, 83, 191
liberalism, 8, 10, 56, 130, 133, 155, 167, 176. See
also global LGBTQI
liberation, 9–10, 59, 75, 129, 167, 196n1;
Black, 32, 40, 50, 195n2; zonbi and, 20,
120, 125
liberation theology, 122
life/death binary, 18, 24, 28. See also zonbi
(zombies)
lineages, 71, 118, 175, 201n9. See also geneaol-
ogies; kinship
literature, xxi–xxii, 9, 11–13, 25–26, 48, 119–
20, 199n22
living dead, 25, 29–30, 33, 42. See also zonbi
(zombies)
Locke, Amir, 187
Lorde, Audre, 71
Louco, 107
Louis XIII (king), 28
L'Ouverture, Toussaint, 32, 64
Lovely, 78
Lowenthal, Ira P., 33
Lugosi, Bela, 44
lwa (spirits), 32–34, 45, 66–67, 70–72, 80,
108, 118, 122, 166
lynching, 188

Madeline, 92–93
madivin, 4, 14, 70–72, 134, 137, 140–44, 183,
197n5, 198n6; homophobia and, 76–77,
79, 100, 148, 151, 171–72, 178; Kouraj and,
161, 167–69, 181; Lakou and, 113, 115–16;
Pierre-Louis controversy and, 90, 92, 97,
99, 101–2
MADRE, 153–54, 200n6
Magic Island (Seabrook), 42, 43, 45
Magnum Band, 108
majority poor, Haitian, 68, 89, 106, 121,
142, 181, 184; homophobia and, 49, 74,
99–102, 117, 172, 191; imperialism and, 63,
123; Lakou and, 105, 113, 115; Vodou and,
116, 118
Makandal, François, 31–33
makomer, 14, 161, 167–69, 181
Malinowski, Bronisław, 13
Maman Brijit, 66
mamisis, 3–4. See also masisi
Mami Wata, 3

manbo (priestesses), 32, 66–67, 71–72
Manbo M, 72
La Manif Pour Tous, 174–77
March for Marriage, 175–76
maroons, 27, 31–32
marriage, 44, 66, 71, 75, 77, 81–83, 98; colonialism and, 37, 53, 62–63; same-sex, 4, 18, 21, 83, 159–60, 170–80
Martelly, Michel "Sweet Micky," 98, 170
Martin, Trayvon, 187
Martus Project, 165
Marx, Karl, 27
masisi, 3–5, 14, 16, 137, 141–44, 182–83, 197n5, 198n6; global LGBTQI and, 133–34, 140, 165–66; homophobia and, 73, 76–79, 81, 148–52, 171–72, 178, 192; Kouraj and, 161, 167–69, 181; Lakou and, 112–13, 115–16; Pierre-Louis controversy and, 92, 99–102; Vodou and, 70–72, 81–82, 165–66, 200–201n8
Massad, Joseph A., 9, 130
Massimadi, 18, 83, 191
masters, 4, 30, 34, 41, 153; zonbi and, 26, 39, 42, 44, 108–9, 111–12, 119–21, 123–25
masturbation, 37
Mbembe, Achille, 181
McAlister, Elizabeth, 102, 115, 195n2, 197n5, 199n13; on Vodou, 57, 71, 199–200nn21–22; on zonbi, 25–26
McCormick, Medill, 61–62
McCune, Jeffrey Q., Jr., 196n11
McGarrell, Flores "Flo," xix, xxii–xxiii, 106, 113–14, 140–44, 197n4, 199n12
M community, 161, 167–70, 172, 182
Medline, 99, 103
memory, 12, 20, 28–29, 38–39, 79, 120–23
mennen, 171
men who have sex with men (MSM), xxii, 4, 14–15, 48, 70, 82, 200n2; SEROvie and, 134–35, 138–40, 160–61, 198n4
mestizáje, 179
methodology of book, 11–17, 23–24, 65–69, 131–32. *See also* ethnography; focus groups; interviews; participant observation
Métraux, Alfred, 29
metronormativity, 15
Mexico, 17, 107
Miami, 15, 89, 178
Michel, 73–74

Michel, Claudine, 199–200nn21–22
Middle East, 7, 9, 178
Middle Passage, 27, 29
miks, 14, 161, 167–69, 181
militarization, 121–23, 126, 180, 187, 192; global LGBTQI and, 5, 133, 153–55, 184–85; imperialism and, 8, 10, 12, 18, 36, 39–41, 60, 95, 195n5. *See also* demilitarization
Mintz, Sidney, 29
Mirabo, xx, 72, 113–15, 149, 160
miscegenation, 63, 179
missionaries, 1–2, 17, 24–25, 37, 68, 80, 123, 125, 192, 195n2; global LGBTQI and, 9, 20, 130, 132, 134, 138, 155, 178; Protestantism and, 4, 7, 19, 51, 54–65, 79, 82, 92, 129, 180; US occupation and, 38–39, 44, 46, 60–62
modernity, 7–8, 50, 60, 64, 75, 119, 125, 133, 166, 184–85; modern capitalism, 25, 29. *See also* premodernity
Môle-Saint-Nicolas, 36, 194n6
monogamy, xxi, 4, 37, 62–63, 171
Montréal, Canada, 15
Moore, Alexander, 48
morality, 11, 27, 58–59, 151–52, 170–71, 173; Black republic and, 7, 24, 34, 37–38, 61; Pierre-Louis controversy and, 19, 87, 90, 96–98
moral panics, 38
Morrison, Toni, 195n9
Moten, Fred, 125, 184
mothers, 28–29, 38, 53, 98, 102, 108, 143, 189; homophobia and, 73, 77, 82, 100, 150, 174–75; Vodou and, 32, 70–71, 118
mounting, 45, 70, 166. *See also* Vodou (religion)
Muñoz, José Esteban, 103, 169
murals, 5, 6, 68
murder, 21, 24, 35, 38, 178, 180, 187–92
Murray, David A. B., 9, 11

Namibia, 10
Napoleon I, 33
National Association for the Advancement of Colored People (NAACP), 40, 188
National Conference of the LGBT Population, 2
nationalism, 10, 13, 18, 121, 169, 174
National Organization for Marriage (NOM), 175
necropolitics, 13, 184

neo-imperialism, 11, 125

neoliberalism, 9, 63, 88–89, 122, 129, 132–33, 155

Netherlands, 177

New York, xvii, 15–16, 80, 88, 106, 133, 140, 146, 163, 188

New York Times, 55, 58–60

Nixon, Angelique V., 135

Noir, Femme, 72, 115–16

noirisme, 121

nongovernmental organizations (NGOs), xviii, 13, 59, 135, 154–55, 168, 183–84, 186, 192; funding, 198n10; LGBT support and, 133, 146; U.S.-led, 63, 132

nonnormativity, 11–12, 19–20, 25, 50, 55, 115, 117–18, 143, 150

nonprofits, 12, 140, 175, 198n10. *See also* nongovernmental organizations (NGOs)

Norh, 76–77, 100, 102–3

normativity, 9, 12–14, 17, 23, 105, 117–18, 124

North America, 48, 62

Obama, Barack, 59–60, 187

Of Men and Gods (Lescot and Magloire), 16–17, 165–66, 194n8

omofobi, 20, 65, 69, 162–63, 166, 200n3. *See also* homophobia

Open Society Foundations (OSF), 88

Operation Secure Tomorrow, 123

Operation Unified Response, 60, 195n5

Operation Uphold Democracy, 123

oral sex, 37

Orientalism, 9, 17, 130

ostracism, 74, 142

ougan (priests), 66, 72

oungan Ginè, 67, 116

Outright Action International, 2, 130–31

Oxfam, 168

Panama Canal, 36

Papa Legba, 107. See also *lwa* (spirits)

Paris, 15, 174, 177

Parisio, Anne, 197n11

participant observation, 16, 65–69, 91–93, 106–16, 143–45, 182

Pascal-Trouillot, Ertha, 93

patchwork ethnography, 15–16

paternalism, 27, 39, 41, 58

patriarchy, xviii, 32, 73, 81, 92–96, 98, 107, 118. *See also* heteropatriarchy

Patterson, Orlando, 30

Peace House (Jacmel), 78, 160

peasants, 38–39, 41, 45, 87, 109, 120, 122. *See also* majority poor, Haitian

pedagogy, 139, 182–84

pederas, 81, 151, 171

pedophilia, 5, 167

Pellegrini, Ann, 59, 95, 196n1

Pentecostalism, 63, 68, 76, 173, 199n21

Pérez, Emma, 17, 23

performance studies, 12, 95, 123

perversity/perversion, 7, 18–19, 23–51, 118, 130, 185

Pétion, Alexandre, 32, 60

Pétion-Ville, xvii, 71, 162

phallic agency, 10

phallocentrism, 37

Pharr, Suzanne, 93–95, 196n1

Philippines, 39

Pierre-Louis, Michèle Duvivier: controversy, 19–20, 83, 87–103, 105, 113, 159, 180, 192; plantations, 29, 31–33, 44, 114, 119, 124, 186

plasaj (nonlegal unions), 4, 63

Plummer, Brenda Gayle, 61

plural matings, 44

police, 35, 101, 124, 175, 187–91

political homophobia, 9–10

politics of verticality, 172, 181

polyamory, 4

polygamy, 7, 53, 71

pornography, 37

Port-au-Prince, xvii, xxi–xxii, 39, 69, 102, 126, 148, 152, 160–62, 181, 199nn21–22; anti-gay protests in, 159, 170, 173, 176–77; art in, 5, 6, 20, 68, 89, 106; Delmas neighborhood, 73; Leanne neighborhood, 106–7; MINUSTAH in, 123; missionaries and, 60, 64; organizations in, 15; queerness in, 74, 77–78, 80, 115, 131–33, 135, 164

postcolonial effect, 8

postcolonial homophobia, definition, 10

postcolonial studies, 3, 12–13, 17, 132

poverty, 49, 57–58, 77, 87, 89, 134, 184. *See also* majority poor, Haitian

premarital relationships, 63

premodernity, 20, 105, 119, 125, 166; Haiti and discourse of, 6, 8, 19–20, 23–24, 34, 38, 46–51, 53–56, 59–60, 65, 92, 185

Presbyterianism, 63

Préval, René, 87–88, 90, 92, 96–98
primitive accumulation, 27. *See also* slavery
prisons, ix, 9, 39–40, 101, 116, 189
private volunteer organizations (POVs), 154–55
Promoteurs Objectif Zéro SIDS (POZ), 137, 162
Proposition 8 (CA), 175
Protestantism (evangelical Christianity), 19, 21, 65, 68–71, 76–82, 117, 161–62, 167, 176, 199–200nn21–22; anti-gay protests and, 159, 170–74, 180; earthquake of 2010 and, 1–2, 18, 56–59, 137, 148–52; imperialism and, 4, 6–8, 11–12, 27, 37, 51, 53–56, 60–65, 82–83, 129–30; Lakou and, 116, 124; Pierre-Louis controversy and, 87, 90–103. *See also individual denominations*
Protestant Reformation, 59
protests, 41, 141, 170–81, 191–92. *See also* activism
Puar, Jasbir, K., 9, 129
public health, xxiii, 2, 16, 47, 49, 161, 165
Puerto Rico, 39, 60
Pulse Nightclub (Orlando), 191
pwen (points), 102

queer, terminology of, 14–15, 25, 51, 143, 168, 199n15
queer Haitian studies, 13–15, 168, 194n7
queer of color critique, 13, 17, 50
queer politics, 20, 23, 25, 36–37, 50, 117–18
queer studies, 8–15, 38, 59, 75, 132, 194nn5–6
queer theory, 2, 9, 14, 17–18, 44, 93, 95–96, 101, 116–18, 169, 184, 196n1

race, 3, 17, 27, 44, 129, 177, 179, 193n3; Haiti and, 60, 185; imperialism and, 8, 42, 196n6; interracial sexuality, 4; post-racial discourse, 187; sexuality and, 12, 17–18, 24, 47, 49–51, 53–54, 63, 126, 130, 194n3; U.S. and, 35. See also *mestizáje*
racial capitalism, ix, 3, 12, 25–26, 37, 50
racism, 9, 34, 40, 47, 58, 181, 193n1; anti-Black, 8, 24–25, 35, 42, 45, 50, 60–61, 179, 187–90, 192
radios, 1, 64, 148, 164, 172, 180; Pierre-Louis controversy and, 20, 87–90, 92, 96–97, 99, 102
Rainbow Relief-Houston, 200n24
Rainbow World Fund, 200n24

Ramsey, Kate, 32, 34, 41, 197n7
rape, 5–6, 78, 154, 190
Rara (festival), 115, 197n5
Rebecca, 140
recolonization, 11, 18, 24, 36, 50, 95–96
relationality, 3–4, 17, 125, 186
religious homophobia, 7, 19, 51, 53–55, 70, 79, 126, 129–30, 170, 173–74. *See also* Catholicism; Protestantism (evangelical Christianity)
religious studies, 12, 25, 57, 67, 71–72
relocation, 27, 149–50, 170, 191
Renda, Mary A., 39–42, 46
repertoire, 123
reproduction, 37–38, 94, 98, 103, 117, 174–75
reproductive heterosexuality, 94–95, 98, 103, 117
rescue, 13, 20, 129–55
resistance, xxi, 18, 23, 80, 141, 175, 186; anti-imperial, 30–33, 39, 41, 44, 119, 169; Black, 12–13, 114, 169, 201n9; Kouraj and, 167, 169, 201n9; Lakou and, 20, 25, 114–15, 118–19, 124, 126; "progress-resistant" Haiti discourse, 7, 56, 58, 62; queer, 18, 20, 23, 25, 92, 94, 118, 143
respectability politics, 25, 49, 98, 105, 125, 181–82
rèstavèk (indentured child labor), 173
"revenge lesbianism," 16
Rey, Terry, 72–73
Rice, Tamir, 187
Robertson, Pat, 54–60, 149, 195n2
Roosevelt, Theodore, 39, 61
Rosa, 140
Rosenthal, Judy, 3
Rubin, David, 197n1

safe-sex education, 160
Said, Edward, 17
Saint Domingue, 3, 26, 28–32, 35, 46, 54, 169
salt, 119–20, 124, 126
same-sex desiring Haitians. See LGBT Haitians
same-sex marriage, 4, 18, 21, 83, 159–60, 170–80
same-sex sexuality. See homosexuality; LGBT Haitians
Santo Domingo, 15, 29, 40, 61, 140, 198n8, 199n11. *See also* Dominican Republic
satanism, 2, 58, 62

savage slot, 50, 53
Schuller, Mark, 63, 132
Scott, Dread, 188
Scott, Walter, 188
se (sister), 101
Seabrook, William, 42, 45–46
secularism, 7, 54–56, 58–59, 125, 176, 195n4
Sedgwick, Eve Kosofsky, 9, 44, 116–17, 196n1, 197n6
selective recognition, 131, 145
self-consumption, 37. *See also* cannibalism
self-determination, 10
self-representation, 182–84
Senatus, Jean Renal, 170
SEROvie, 21, 132, 134–36, 144, 159, 162, 198n4, 198nn7–8; anti-gay protests and, 172; Gran Lakou and, 160; homophobic violence and, 191; IDAHO and, 163–66, 200n5; IGLHRC and, 137–40, 146–47, 154, 160; Kouraj and, 165–68, 180–83, 185; overview, 160
The 700 Club (show), 54, 57–59
Seventh-day Adventists, 63, 68, 76, 81, 151
sexism, 92–95, 174, 190. *See also* lesbian baiting
sex tourism, 48
sexual dimorphism, 3, 167
sex wars, 196n1
sex work, 15, 48, 135, 142, 151, 165, 167, 173
Sheller, Mimi, 37–39, 47
Shirley, 78
slavery, 3–4, 34, 36, 38–41, 50, 58, 81; Haitian Revolution and, 18, 23, 30–33, 54, 57, 153; Lakou and, 114, 124–25; zonbi and, 20, 25–29, 42, 46, 119, 122, 125
social death, 30
Socialist Party (France), 174
social movements, 2, 6, 8, 12–13, 155, 171–79, 185–86, 192; of LGBT Haitians, 20–21, 159–64, 166–70, 180–84. *See also* activism; feminism; Black Lives Matter; Lakou
Sodom and Gomorrah, 1, 173
sodomy, 9, 95, 180
Solidarite Fanm Ayisyèn (Haitian Women's Solidarity), 93
Somerville, Siobhan, 51
Soros, George, 88, 97
sortilèges, 36
South Africa, 37, 88
Spanish-American War, 39

Spanish colonialism, 3, 27–28, 116, 179. *See also* European colonialism
spells, 36
spiralism, 24, 26, 119–20, 122, 124, 197n9
spirit possession, 24, 33, 45, 62, 66, 70. *See also lwa* (spirits); mounting; Vodou (religion)
Spiritual Mapping, 195n2
Star, 77
Starline, 91, 100
state of exception, 132. *See also* exceptionalism
state recognition, 2, 4
St. John, Spenser, 33–38
strategic universalisms, 169
Strongman, Roberto, 3
sugar industry, 28–30, 44
superstition, 6, 19, 34–35, 38, 42, 55, 58
swine flu, 122, 197n11
syncretic religions, 1, 3, 24, 29, 36, 72

tacit subjects, 74
Taft, William Howard, 39, 61
Taíno nations, 27
Taylor, Breonna, 187, 189
Taylor, Diana, 123
terminology, 14–15, 25, 51, 181–84
terrorism, 9
Third Wave, 195n2
Thomas, Deborah A., 179
ti koko anba grenn, 197n1, 197n5
ti masisi/ti madivin, 101–2, 113, 116, 144, 172, 181. *See also* majority poor, Haitian
Tinsley, Omise'eke Natasha, 118
Tometi, Opal, 187
Tonton Macoutes. *See* Volontaires de la Sécurité Nationale (Tonton Mocoutes)
totalitarianism, 121–22, 126
tourism, 11, 48, 62, 95, 197n7
tout moun se moun, 70
transactional sex, 48–49
transgender embodiments, xxii, 14, 17, 65, 70–71, 78, 168, 198n8; global LGBTQI and, 1, 9, 130–31, 133, 143, 165; SEROvie and, 134–36, 138, 183
transnational queer studies, 12–13
transnational turn, 8
transphobia, 130–31, 137, 145, 147–48, 162, 184, 200n5, 201n4
Treaty of Ryswick (1697), 28

trennen, 171–72
Tres Gatas, 140, 199n11
triage interventions, 145
triangulated desire, 44
Trinidad (island), 195n10
Trinidad and Tobago, 51
Trouillot, Michel-Rolph, 31, 49–50
twice-told stories, xviii, 193n2

Uganda, 2, 11
undercommons, 103, 125, 141
United Nations (UN), 7, 124, 133, 146–47, 155, 162, 182; Human Rights Committee, 154, 165; International Covenant on Civil and Political Rights (ICCPR), 165; Mission in Haiti (UNMIH), 123; Stabilization Mission in Haiti (MINUSTAH), 3, 5–6, 6, 123, 154, 163, 185
US Agency for International Development (USAID), 63, 122, 132, 160, 185
USA PATRIOT Act, 9
US Centers for Disease Control, 47, 49
US Civil War, 35
US imperialism, 17–18, 94–96, 119–23; Black republic and, 23–24, 40–41, 46, 48–53; global LGBTQI and, 131–33, 153–55, 168–69, 178–79, 184–86; homophobia and, 2–3, 5–8, 11–13, 155, 167, 173–74, 180, 184, 192; Lakou and, 20, 25, 103, 105, 116, 118–19, 122, 124–26; Protestantism and, 19, 27, 60–65, 82, 129–30, 148–49, 161
US occupation of Haiti (1915–1934), 4, 23, 63, 116, 121, 153; corvée and, 40–41, 46; history of, 18–19, 38–46; methodology of book and, 17; Protestantism and, 55, 60–62, 82, 130, 149, 180; Tourism and, 48; voodoo/vaudoux and, 7, 19, 24, 36, 41, 44–46, 50, 92; zonbi and, 18, 24, 38–39, 42, 44–46, 122
US Senate Inquiry into the Occupation and Administration of Haiti and Santo Domingo, 40–41, 61–62
US Supreme Court, 9, 173, 175–76

vakabon, 171
Valentine, David, 14, 199n20
vèvè, 107
victimization, 131, 145, 190
visibility, 47, 89, 103, 111, 126, 146, 161, 180–81
Vodou (religion), 3, 44, 87, 106, 142, 161; Ca-

tholicism and, 72–73, 76, 79, 94; Duvalier (Papa Doc) and, 62, 121–22; earthquake of 2010 and, 1, 152, 199–200nn21–22; Haitian Revolution and, 32–34; Lakou and, 20, 103, 107–8, 114–16, 118, 125–26, 200n8; methodology of book and, 15–16, 65–68; Pierre-Louis controversy and, 97, 102; prohibitions against, 34, 36, 41; Protestantism and, 79–80, 94, 170, 199–200nn21–22; queerness and, 19–20, 49, 55–56, 65, 70–73, 79–82, 103, 118, 150–53, 165–66; resistance and, 169, 186; voodoo/vadoux and, 6, 24–25, 32, 34, 36, 57; zonbi and, 20, 25–26, 29, 31, 33, 47, 103, 107–8, 119, 125–26
Volontaires de la Sécurité Nationale (Tonton Mocoutes), 121, 124, 197n10
voodoo/vaudoux (concept), 41–46, 92, 125,185; HIV/AIDS and, 47–50, 167; imperial discourses of, 6–7, 18–19, 24–25, 33–38, 50–51, 53–54, 105, 130; Protestantism and, 55–62, 64–65, 167; Vodou (religion) and, 6, 24–25, 32, 34, 36, 57; zonbi and, 18, 20, 41–48, 126
vulnerability, 89, 147, 163, 187–89

Wagner, C. Peter, 195n2
Wahab, Amar, 51
Warner, Michael, 18, 23, 25, 117–18, 143
Watts, Kristi, 57
Weinberg, George H., 167
Weiss, Meredith L., 9
Werleigh, Claudette, 93
West Africa, 28–29, 34, 195n10
West Indies, 10, 34–35, 37
white man's burden, 39
white supremacy, 118, 153, 187
Williamson, Terrion L., 189–90, 192
Wilson, Woodrow, 39, 61
women's liberation movement (US), 196n1
women's studies, 13
women who love women, 32
World Congress of LGBT Jews, 162
World Health Organization, 163
world-mapping, 116–17
World's Fair (1893), 34, 194n6

Yanvalou, 161, 181
Yèle Haiti, 141
yon fi ki prefere fi, 14, 134

Zaka (FOSAJ assistant director), xxi–xxii, 107

zonbi (zombies), 28, 35, 41, 43, 48, 51, 62, 120–21; anti-imperialism and, 18, 20, 24–25, 105–6, 118–19; imperialism and, 18, 24, 27, 38–39, 42, 44–46, 122; Lakou per-formance and, 20, 25, 103, 105–12, 118–19, 123–26, 137; Vodou and, 20, 25–26, 29, 31, 33, 47, 103, 107–8, 119, 125–26

Zonbi, Jean, 33

"Zonbi, Zonbi" (performance), 20, 25, 103, 105–12, 118–19, 123–26, 137

ERIN L. DURBAN is an assistant professor of anthropology at the University of Minnesota–Twin Cities.

NATIONAL WOMEN'S STUDIES ASSOCIATION /
UNIVERSITY OF ILLINOIS PRESS FIRST BOOK PRIZE

Sex Tourism in Bahia: Ambiguous Entanglements   *Erica Lorraine Williams*
Ecological Borderlands: Body, Nature, and Spirit in Chicana Feminism
    Christina Holmes
Women's Political Activism in Palestine: Peacebuilding, Resistance, and Survival
    Sophie Richter-Devroe
The Sexual Politics of Empire: Postcolonial Homophobia in Haiti   *Erin L. Durban*

The University of Illinois Press
is a founding member of the
Association of University Presses.

Composed in 10.5/13 Minion Pro
with Penumbra San Std display
by Lisa Connery
at the University of Illinois Press
Manufactured by Sheridan Books, Inc.

University of Illinois Press
1325 South Oak Street
Champaign, IL 61820-6903
www.press.uillinois.edu